FOR BEGINNER COOKS

A LIFETIME IN THE KITCHEN

Volume One

Other books by Fanny Cradock

Fiction
The Lormes of Castle Rising
Shadows over Castle Rising
War Comes to Castle Rising
Wind of Change at Castle Rising
Uneasy Peace at Castle Rising
Thunder over Castle Rising
Gathering Clouds at Castle Rising
Fateful Years at Castle Rising
The Defence of Castle Rising
Scorpion's Suicide
My Seed Thy Harvest
The Rags of Time
O Daughter of Babylon
The Echo in the Cup
Gateway to Remembrance
The Eternal Echo
The Land is in Good Heart
Women Must Wait
Dark Reflection
Shadow of Heaven

Children's Books
When Michael Was Three
When Michael Was Six
Always
The Dryad and The Toad
The Story of Joseph and Pharaoh
Naughty Red Lion
Naughty Red Lion Beware
Fish Knight – Sea Maiden
The Gooseyplums of Duckpond in The Dip
Brigadier Gooseyplum Goes To War
The Gooseyplums By The Sea

Cookery and Travel. By Fanny and Johnnie Cradock
A Cook's Essential Alphabet
The Daily Telegraph Cook's Book
Fanny and Johnnie's Freezer Book
The Sherlock Holmes Cookbook
The Practical Cook
The Ambitious Cook
The Daily Express Cookery Book
Bon Voyage
Bon Viveur in London

Around Britain with Bon Viveur
Bon Viveur's London and The British Isles
Bon Viveur in The Austrian Tyrol
Bon Viveur in Barcelona and The Balearics
Bon Viveur in Belgium
Bon Viveur in Denmark
Bon Viveur in Holland
Holiday on The French Riviera
Bon Viveur in Sweden
Holiday in The Touraine
Bon Viveur's Guide to Holidays in Europe
Cooking with Bon Viveur
Bon Viveur Request Cookery Book
Wining and Dining in France with Bon Viveur
Beginning to Cook with Fanny and Johnnie
Children's Outdoor Cookery with Fanny and
    Johnnie
The Young Chef with Fanny and Johnnie
Children's Party Cookery by Fanny and
    Johnnie
Veg and Vim
Cabbages and Things
The Daily Mail Cookery Book
The Cook's Book
The Sociable Cook's Book
The Cook Hostess's Book
Common Market Cookery – France
Common Market Cookery – Italy
Three Hundred and Sixty-Five Puddings
Three Hundred and Sixty-Five Soups and Their
    Accompaniments
Home Cooking
Problem Cooking
Giving a Dinner Party
Colourful Cookery
Fanny Cradock Invites
Eight Special Menus
Modest but Delicious
Time to Remember

A Lifetime In The Kitchen
Volume One: For Beginner Cooks
Volume Two: Family Cookery
Volume Three: The Ambitious Cook

FOR BEGINNER COOKS

A LIFETIME IN THE KITCHEN

Volume One

Fanny and Johnnie Cradock

W.H. ALLEN · LONDON
1985

Copyright © Fanny and Johnnie Cradock, 1985

Typeset by Phoenix Photosetting Ltd, Chatham
Printed and bound in Great Britain by
Mackays of Chatham Ltd, Kent
for the Publishers, W.H. Allen & Co. PLC
44 Hill Street, London W1X 8LB

ISBN 0 491 03460 1

Contents

Introduction   7

Part One   11

Part Two   119

Index   333

We have received no additional remuneration for brand-naming various products which we have used with the greatest success for many years.

Nothing has caused so much controversy as specifying the number of persons for whom a recipe is adequate. We are either accused of being extremely frugal or excessively lavish. The recipes in Part 1 of Volume One are primarily intended for one person, while those in Part 2 are for two people.

All references to flour imply self-raising, which we always use for everything – from transparently thin pancakes to hugely risen soufflés.

Fanny and Johnnie Cradock's
Gastronomic Honours

Chevalier et Grande Dame des Chevaliers du Tastevin
Commandant et Grande Dame de la Chaîne des Rôtisseurs
Compagnons du Beaujolais
Membres du Club Prosper Montagné *en raison de leur haute connaissance gastronomique et culinaire*
Officier et Grande Dame de l'Ordre de St Fortunat
Membres Honoraires du Club des Becs de Cannes
Honorary Members of the Worshipful Company of Meadmakers
(only 2 others: Sir Winston Churchill and HRH Prince Philip)
Honorary Members of the Order of King Christian IV of Denmark
Diplôme de Médaille Vermeil de la Societé des Arts, Science et Lettres (Fanny)
Chevalier de l'Ordre de la Courtoisie Française (Johnnie)
Grand Mousquetaire d'Armagnac (Johnnie)
Chevalier et Grande Dame de la Tripière d'Or
Chevalier et Grande Dame de la Gastronomie Normande
Membres de la Jurade de St Emilion
Compagnons du Bon Temps du Médoc

Introduction

Many years ago, Henry Caldwell of BBC *Café Continental* fame was a guest at one of our regular dinner parties in our London home. Behind screens in our dining-room, as in all our other reception rooms, a cooker lurked so that Fanny could make special dishes *in situ*. Fanny made a soufflé that was served after the main course. She rose, in her white chiffon evening dress, the screens were folded back and she went to work. While the soufflé was handed round, Henry Caldwell pronounced, 'Do that on television and you'll make a bomb. What's more, I'll produce you for nothing.'

'What, the pair of us?' Johnnie exclaimed.

'Of course,' Henry retorted. 'What a splendid thought, old boy.' Johnnie said. 'There's only one small snag. I cannot fry an egg.'

'Then learn,' Henry advised him. 'I'll be back in four weeks to taste the result. The pair of you are always laying down the law about how anyone can cook a decent meal, provided the recipe is sufficiently accurate and explicit. Now's your chance to prove it.'

Johnnie did, and one way and another we have been at it ever since. Neither of us has ever had a cookery lesson in our lives, yet together we have managed to collect more gastronomic and vinous honours than any other couple in the world – at least, that is what our agent once told us.

We can say after all these years, *we do test recipes*. *'Nothing is*

7

published which has not been tested prior to publication.' We would hold ourselves in contempt if we did otherwise.

Of course television is the perfect medium for teaching cookery, always provided that programmes are backed by supporting books. Our audience was vast, despite all the domestic science teachers who protested to Auntie BBC about what we taught. They were incensed by the not wholly unmalicious remarks of their pupils: 'Please, Miss, my mum says we should do it the Cradocks' way. Mum says it's much better and we like it.' Blessings on dear 'Auntie', she supported us – and gave us more series after these protests.

After we began doing huge stage cookery performances for the Gas Council and *The Daily Telegraph* we became even more aware of our responsibilities. We gave two performances a day of two and a half hours' duration to well over a thousand people. The audiences queued for hours and then sat on hard seats without even an interval to stretch their legs. We start every stage show with these words: *We have set out to try and cut the corners on time, labour and expenditure, provided we do so without taking anything from the finished quality of any dish. Anyone can hash up nasties at speed, but only the best is good enough for you, and indeed for us.*

Here we must digress for a moment to tell you the story of a woman called Agnes Bertha Marshall, who ran a splendid school of cookery and also cooked in public, winning the highest commendation from the national newspapers of the day. She was beautiful, brilliant and probably the best cook who ever lived in England. At the height of her fame she was painted by Watts, and was a friend of the then Princess of Wales, although in those days daughters of East End cabinet makers did not normally become intimate with royalty. Only a woman of her genius and determination could have overcome so many obstacles to rank among the greatest culinary experts of her time, both at home and abroad. Yet Agnes Bertha Marshall died as obscurely as she was born. We are determined to restore her works to the limelight, thus putting paid to the spurious career of another woman who became famous through publicity, not merit. We refer, of course, to Mrs Beeton.

The only evidence in existence that Mrs Beeton ever cooked anything comes from her younger sister, who at the age of eight wrote: 'Dear Bella ran about the kitchen in a very pretty dress. She made a cake, which turned out more of a biscuit and was a sad failure.'

In later years, 'Dear Bella' slaved away at journalism with considerably more success, and edited *Mrs Beeton's Original Book of Household*

Management and the less well known *Gardening Encyclopaedia*, although she knew nothing at all about either subject. She and her husband Sam ran a threepenny magazine called *The Gentlewoman*, and it was the subscribers who provided the hodge-podge of recipes in the *Household Management* book. The Beetons got over a million recipes from the British public – good, bad and indifferent. All they paid for this assortment was thirty-five shillings – a pound for first prize, ten shillings for second and five shillings for third. Johnnie worked out that if 'dear Bella' had cooked for thirty-two hours per day every day from the time she was two-and-a-half to the day she died, she could only just have tested those recipes once! Everyone who knows anything about cookery knows that sometimes half a dozen tests must be made in order to arrive at the best solution.

Conversely, ABM, as she was known affectionately to her thousands of pupils, wrote superb cookery books, which we are currently adapting to contemporary requirements. Mrs Marshall died at the height of her fame quite suddenly of a carcinoma – which is indistinguishable from arsenic poisoning. We believe she was murdered. We also believe that the suppression thereafter of her name and works was, and still is, deliberate.

We have cooked a great many of the recipes in this book before hundreds of thousands on stage and television, and cook/tested all herein. Many have been gleaned by cooking with the great chefs of France whom we are proud to call our friends.

You can imagine with what trepidation we embarked upon the writing of *A Lifetime in the Kitchen*. We faced the grim fact that all big cookery books follow much the same pattern, lumping all the egg dishes, all the puddings and all the sauces *et al* into single chapters. Thus cooks searching frantically for 'how to poach an egg' must wade through mountains of totally irrelevant egg recipes in order to find what they need.

Volume One of *A Lifetime in the Kitchen* is mostly an assembly of quick snacks and beverages, eminently suited to the young self-catering on grants at universities or colleges, as well as more mature live-aloners. In fact, the recipes are there ready to be dipped into by the rest of us should we, at any age, find ourselves needing something filling and quickly made for those occasions when we are intent upon going to bed with a book and a tray. Our quickly-made soups and snack foods also save the purse-pinched from the fate of what are euphemistically called 'convenience foods', whose only convenience that we can see is in lining the pockets of the manufacturers. The second part of Volume One is primarily for those

9

setting setting up house, flat or flatlet for the first time. The recipes provided for evening meals take no more than half an hour at most to prepare and get to table. We provide suggestions for modest week-end entertaining, such as Saturday night supper or Sunday brunch.

Volume Two is for the home cook, the family cook, Mum in fact, whose work is never done. She has to cope with such huge and varied demands upon her time that the rest of us should really take off our hats to her. Not forgetting the age-old drag, 'Mum, what can I eat, I'm starving?', there are all the additional chores like baking for school or church bazaars, preparing birthday parties, putting up things for bring-and-buys or coffee mornings or to take to school. Then there is getting ready for Christmas, New Years, Bank Holidays, annual holidays and little extras like Hallowe'en and all the other demanding family jazz which is taken for granted.

There are recipes to suit the requirements of all these, including ones for when Mum and Dad entertain on their own account. For the occasion when they want something grander, they can turn to Volume Three.

Volume Three is for the ambitious cook-hostess who has the time, the means and the opportunity to do more elaborate things. Here are some of our very special treasure recipes: dishes we have tasted or made with chefs abroad, or found in ancient receipt books. We owe the opportunities for accumulating these to our good fortune in being on television for so long. Through this work have come the invitations to visit other countries, to meet great chefs and indeed to work with them as well.

We are bound to be in the dog house with some of you for leaving out something you had hoped to find because somehow you have lost the original cutting. Forgive us. This is only a cross section of all the things we have cooked and tested throughout our cooking lives.

We just hope that some of the recipes will give you, your family and friends pleasure at the table.

Fanny and Johnnie

Part 1

Contents

Improvise and Make Do   12
Notes for Beginner Cooks   17
Basics   21
No Cooking   25
Soups   33
Fish   37
Eggs and Cheese   41
Meat & Poultry   59
Vegetables   65
Starches   71
Drinks   75
Sweet Things   81
With a Grill   87
With an Oven   95

Improvise and Make Do

However simply you are compelled to live in a bed-sitting room or an area allocated for communal self-catering, there are a few things you really must have if you are going to cook at all but in many instances the name of the game is improvisation.

If you drink tea, you will need a pan for boiling water but you can even dispense with a teapot if you buy a billy-can, which costs far less.

Should you be a coffee addict, your only requirements to make the best real coffee in the world are an ordinary enamel jug, a small strainer and a scrap of foil. Alternatively, if you are prepared to settle for 'Instant', quite the best that we have found is Brooke Bond's Brazilian. An 8 inch (20 cm) diameter, fairly steep-sided saucepan can serve both as a water boiler and a fat fryer for making super chips.

If you can possibly run to a steamer with a lid, then you can cook scrubbed potatoes in it and peel the skins off after cooking – or you can use a thick fold of Alcan Foil as a divider and steam two or even three vegetables simultaneously. The steamer base should have three grooves so that it will sit securely over different sizes of saucepans. You can also use the inverted lid to keep, for example, some

12

potatoes – wrapped in Alcan Foil – hot while a portion of fish steams.

To make the excavation of pudding basins easy, fold Alcan Foil over and over into a strong 2 inch (5 cm) wide strip, long enough to go across the steamer base and come right up both sides. Sit the basin on this and when wanting to take it out, just tow up by the two ends of the strip.

To take fried or poached eggs out of their pan if lacking a metal slice, use the removed lid from a tin, but remember to bend one edge up to give you a good grip without the risk of dipping an incautious finger into either the hot fat or hot water.

Eggs are easily poached in your only frying pan if you break each one into a saucer first and then slide into improvised poaching rings. To make these remove the base as well as the top of any small emptied tins 3 inch (7.5 cm) in diameter and a bare 2 inch (5 cm) in depth.

Scour the junk shops for an old, pre-stainless steel table knife. If cleaned up and brazenly sharpened against a stone kerbside, it will serve as a kitchen cutting knife until you can raise the wind for a set of professional ones by Sabatier, and a carborundum for sharpening these very costly ones properly.

If you are lucky enough to possess a small, sharp, pointed knife, do try to keep a cork pushed onto its slender tip for protection.

The least costly metal slices have handles which tend to get burned. Wrap a piece of insulating tape around yours to protect it and double its useful life.

Be sure to buy one ordinary, round sieve with a no-scorch metal handle. This makes straining vegetables very easy, enables you to rub through even lumpy first attempts at sauces and is essential for straining tea residues when cooking dried fruits in the oven.

Never waste money on a pastry board when you are unlikely to make much pastry anyway; but you may well use packs of Jus-rol puff paste which is excellent. Buy a laminated plastic offcut from a DIY shop. These are cold, smooth and ideal for your modest needs.

When you do set up house, invest in a solid boxwood rolling pin without any silly handles sticking out at the ends to make you put more weight on them rather than the actual pin; but in the meantime make do with a wine bottle filled with very cold water and securely corked.

13

Squeezing the juice from lemons and oranges can be done without a lemon squeezer. Just halve each fruit centrally. Drive a small fork into the cut side, hold fruit firmly in one hand and squeeze/press while turning the fork prongs. Out comes the juice and if you are careful, up come the pips as well, enabling you to flick these off and thus dispose of the need to strain the juice.

Meat batters, made in metal and used by professional chefs, are dipped into cold water and used to flatten out pieces of meat thinly, on the dip, bang down, dip and repeat routine. Scrounge any old flat iron from a dump or family attic. Rub down with coarse sandpaper and use in the same way, thus enabling you to flatten slices of beef for beef olives, pieces of costly veal for veal escalopes or thick rashers of bacon.

You can also use it with any icing sugar which has become lumpy. Slip a little at a time into a fold of brown paper. Bang down with the flat iron, then the sugar runs easily through a sieve. Only ignoramuses throw those lumps away.

If you do not have an electric hand whisk – the kind which, on a long flex, can be carried straight to pan on cooker or gas ring – then buy a balloon whisk (diagram) or a rotary whisk, the one you wind round by its small handle. Remember that it always takes longer to use either the balloon or rotary to achieve stiffly whipped egg whites.

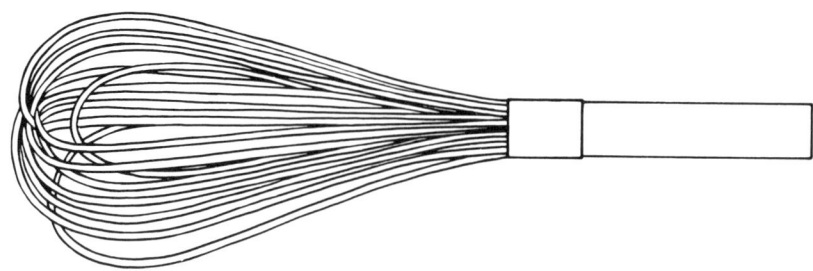

Try to invest in a plate rack and stand it on a tray if you have not got a sink from which to work. Then things dry themselves without the need of tea towels. Choose plastic bowls: they will not break when dropped.

A HOME MADE TOASTING FORK FOR
BED-SITTING ROOM TOAST

You will need a pair of pliers, a scrap of insulating tape and 3 wire coathangers.

Please follow the diagram exactly.

Unwind the coathangers. Straighten out the wires with the pliers. Cut into the three given lengths. Twist the two 21 inch (52.5 cm) wires onto the central stem wire. When all are twisted and bent as shown, plait the two side prong wires to the main one which forms the handle. Nip the ends together as neatly as possible, then bind the tip with insulating tape to ensure no-one jabs a hand with the exposed wire tip.

Now go ahead and make toast comfortably in front of either a gas or electric fire.

MAKE YOURSELF A MEASURING JUG

Use an ordinary glass jug of any shape. Pour in 2 tablespoons (2 × 15 ml spoons) of water, mark the level on the outside with nail varnish, and so proceed to 20 fluid oz or 1 pint (600 ml). If you do not possess such a jug, use a clear plastic ½ pint (300 ml) beaker and settle for 1 fluid oz (30 ml) to 10 fluid oz (300 ml). It saves time and money to be accurate.

MAKE YOURSELF A MEASURING BOX
Follow the diagram below:-

Cut out your box in any thick typing paper. Pinch firmly along the dotted lines. Stick together by the little tabs using either Uhu or very narrow Sellotape. Filled level with the top with dry goods items, the weights will be as follows:-

Flour 4 oz (100 g) Caster Sugar 4 oz (100 g) Soft Brown Sugar 4½ oz (115 g) Drinking Chocolate Powder 3½ oz (85 g) Sultanas, Currants and Diced Citron Peel 4 oz (100 g) Coffee Beans 3 oz (75 g) Atora Suet 3½ oz (85 g) Desiccated Coconut 2½ oz (60 g).

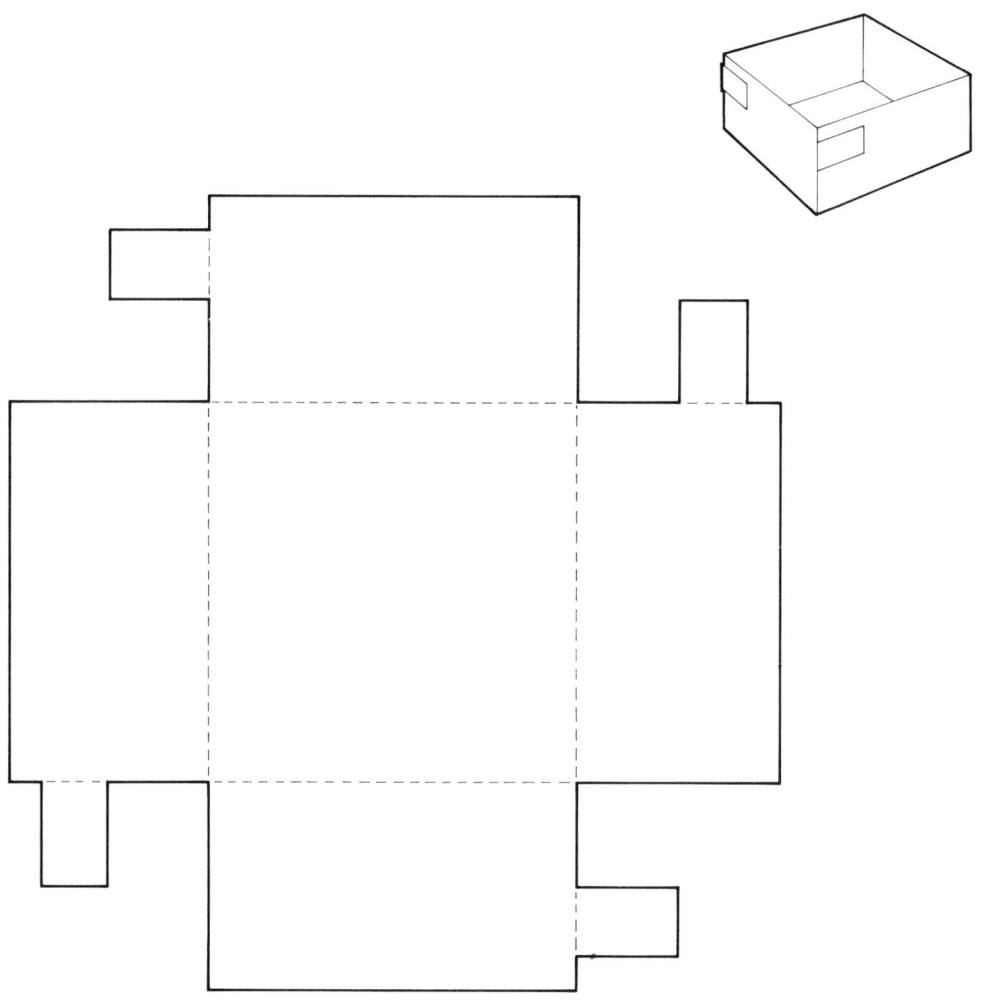

Notes for Beginner Cooks

Please read any recipe right through before beginning to cook to make sure you have all the ingredients.

It is easy to avoid that scorched layer on the base of a milk pan. Just skim the base of the pan with water, boil up for a moment and then add the milk. Alternatively, if you can get your hands on a real old-fashioned marble, slip that into the milk and boil as usual.

For whipped cream use either double cream or whipping cream, which is less costly and has a much lower butter-fat content. Single or coffee cream does not whip up stiffly. For substitute whipping cream remove wrapping from a large tin of Ideal unsweetened milk and stand in a pan of water to cover. Boil for 20 minutes. Refrigerate when cold for a minimum 24 hours. Then open tin. The contents will whip up stiffly but will not remain so for long, so do the whipping just before using. *Forget if you have no refrigerator.*

Peeled onions must always be covered immediately with cold water, and then fished out and wiped just before using. Onions which remain uncovered after peeling absorb all the impurities in the air.

No food should be left in tins after opening. Please turn into some small non-tin container and be safe from tummy ache or worse.

17

The amount of made English mustard which was thrown away enabled mustard producers to become very rich! We ensure it keeps perfectly by running a very thin skin of oil over any remainder. Cover the little container with a scrap of foil and use it up when it suits you.

We have failed to find any bacon, even the most costly, which is not too salty for our taste these days. This also applies to those bargain bags of bacon pieces frequently offered for sale. Separate the rashers – or tumble the pieces – into a roomy pan or bowl. Pour boiling water over them. Leave 5 minutes, drain, wipe and dry. The salt will have parted company with the bacon, turning the water briny instead.

Never buy limp vegetables or saladings. Test them first. If they are firm and crisp, they are fresh, but if limp, they are probably old and useless.

There are four kinds of mushrooms sold by English greengrocers: very large flat ones which are usually field mushrooms and very flavoursome tiny round ones called 'buttons'; larger half opened ones called 'cups' and bigger ones which are fully opened called 'flats'.

Cucumbers do not cause indigestion, or make Auntie moan about their 'repeating' on her *if* the skins are left on. Just remove any blemished parts, then slice thinly, grate or dice.

A garlic clove is one of the very small pieces which cluster together to make a garlic head. Crushing garlic is best done by first chopping a clove (after skinning) roughly and then using a small table knife with a rounded end. Put your thumb over the tip and press down onto the chopped bits to crush them down easily. To complete the pulp, work the knife tip over as if working water into a small quantity of sand and cement. This ensures no threads remain to get into anyone's teeth.

The flavour in parsley is all in the stems and cleaned roots. This is why these are used in so many stockpots, and for soups, sauces and casseroles. Parsley heads are used for colour and decoration. They are either milled in a little Mouli Parsmint which is marvellous, or else chopped finely.

Grapefruit can be very bitter. This inherent bitterness is made totally unpalatable if they are not cut properly. The inner segments of skin which enclose each section must not be cut through all round the inside of each half, as is done in shoddy hotels and restaurants. Once cut in halves, and whether working with a proper serrated-edged curved grapefruit cutter or just a small sharp, pointed-tipped knife, what you must do is work *round* each segment leaving the holding skin uncut. Always begin at the centre. Remove the central core. Then insert the chosen cutter and go round inside each segment loosening the flesh and ignoring the skin. Only thus is the maximum good flavour obtained. Remember that pink grapefruit have the fullest and best flavour, their skins are detectable from the common ones.

Jam which crystallises is due to beet sugar instead of cane sugar having been used. The only manufacturers we know who produce pure cane sugar now are Messrs Tate and Lyle. Pass the information on when a Mum or Aunt gives you a pot which crystallises. Then just tip the jam into a small pan and set over a mere thread of heat. Allow it to heat through very gradually and all the crystals will vanish making the jam edible once more. Rest assured though the crystallisation will return if the jam is not eaten up straight away.

It is really worth while investing in a single Victoria sponge tin in order to butter toast, crumpets, muffins or scones properly. In cold weather, and even if it has been in a refrigerator, butter is very hard to spread gently and evenly. We never bother since Fanny's Mum invented the way of spreading which never tears the surface of hot toast or anything else.

Just melt, in a Victoria sponge tin and over the lowest possible heat, a lump of butter, Gold or, occasionally, dripping when wanting dripping toast. When the first slice of toast is done, just slap it down into the chosen melted fat and lift it out. It will be smoothly coated and underneath the toast will be crisp and not soggy.

If you happen to be someone who hates crisp crusts, give them the quick softening treatment before dunking. Hold the blade of an ordinary table knife and then just bang the handle tip along the crust edge, which softens instantly.

Dunk crumpets in exactly the same way as for toast but split muffins before toasting, then dunk and clap together again. Do the same with toasted scones. We always treat the toast for scrambled eggs this way too. It tastes far nicer.

Dripping is one of the most insanitary items in many homes. The ubiquitous 'dripping jar' stands beside the cooker and receives layer after layer, added over sometimes as much as three or four months. Thus nosy flies or bluebottles fall in and stay there if the last layer of dripping is not completely set.

Cleaning it is very simple. Scrape your hoard into a roomy bowl or pan. Cover liberally with absolutely boiling water. Stir until dripping has dissolved completely. Put the bowl in the coldest available place and leave until firmly set. Cut wedges in it. Turn them over and you will find all the impurities clinging to the underside of each removed wedge. Scrape off and return cleaned dripping to its chosen jar. Try to keep this covered with a piece of wetted transparent cling wrap.

Flour can be misleading. We use only self-raising flour which in our experience doesn't have enough raising agent to raise a hair on a pussy's tail. We make with equal success, hugely risen featherweight soufflés and flat pancakes thin enough to read newsprint through them with self-raising flour.

Cooked beetroot tastes much nicer if it is cut into slim chips (the French way) than it does when sliced into rounds (the English way).

Jerusalem artichokes – the inexpensive ones which are so easily grown – taste like Brazil nuts when peeled, washed, sliced and used in winter salads.

If from your flatlet or bed-sitting room you can see some healthy looking dandelions flourishing below, cover them with a flower pot to blanch the leaves. Then use and enjoy in your salads.

Kippers should never be boiled. Either grill them on the inside only or lay out dry on baking sheets and bake at Gas Mark 4 (approx 350°F, 180°C) for 10–15 minutes, depending upon their size. They yield their own oil and need no further lubrication.

Basics

French dressing
Real basic mayonnaise
Simple white sauce
Simple cheese sauce
Garlic butter (inc Parsley butter)

FRENCH DRESSING

This is a classic plain French dressing (Sauce Vinaigrée).

2 flat teasps (2 × 5 ml spoons) salt
1 flat teasp (1 × ml spoon) freshly milled black pepper
1 scant level teasp (1 × 5 ml spoon) French mustard
½ pint (300 ml) best possible oil
1½ fluid oz (45 ml) wine vinegar

Work the salt, pepper, mustard and a drip of oil with a wooden spoon to form a thick paste. Work down very gradually with more oil, cut with a drop of vinegar, add more oil and so continue until all ingredients are absorbed. Store in a screw-topped bottle on shelf. Never refrigerate. Shake vigorously before using.

Note
Wine vinegar can be replaced by strained lemons or orange juice when considered more suitable.

REAL BASIC MAYONNAISE

½ pint (300 ml) oil
2 separated No 4 egg yolks
1 small flat teasp (1 × 5 ml spoon) salt
1 small flat teasp (1 × 5 ml spoon) dry English mustard
2 generous pinches of black pepper
1 generous teasp (1 × 5 ml spoon) lemon or orange juice or wine vinegar

Put yolks into a bowl with salt, pepper and mustard. Whip relentlessly with a rotary or loop whisk (or ideally in an electric mixer) until the mixture forms a very thick batter. Now begin dripping in very small quantities of the oil. Try cutting a Vee in the side of a cork, placing oil in bottle, returning the cork and then pouring in a very thin trickle down the side of the container until the oil bites on the batter and it shows clear signs of becoming much thicker. Go on like this until you have incorporated half the oil. Then add the lemon or orange juice, or wine vinegar, just to cut the mixture. Resume your oil pouring, only a bit faster now, but continue whipping

22

throughout. Without an electric mixer you should get a friend to do the pouring while you whip as fast as you can.

Turn this basic mayonnaise into a bowl. Level off top surface. Run a piece of grease-proof under a cold tap and slap it down on top to avoid any crusting during waiting time, which can be anything up to a month in refrigeration but only about one week otherwise.

The dilutions and variations from here are endless. To make Spanish-type mayonnaise, whip up the separated egg whites and fold into the basic mayonnaise until absolutely smooth. This uses up the whites, makes the mayonnaise go further and renders it less indigestible. For a few other examples, you can add concentrated tomato purée to achieve Tomato Mayonnaise, a very modest few drops of real curry paste for Curry Mayonnaise, or onion juice and cream to taste for Onion Mayonnaise . . . and so on.

SIMPLE WHITE SAUCE

½ pint (300 ml) milk
1 oz (25 g) butter, dripping or
    rendered down pork or
    chicken fat
Salt
Black pepper
1 oz (25 g) flour

Melt chosen fat in a small pan. Stir in flour and continue stirring over a low heat for 3 minutes to cook out the taste of flour. The mixture should form a soft ball in the pan. Add half the given milk, ease the soft ball off the base of pan and allow milk to boil before first stirring and then beating to an absolutely smooth paste. Add remaining milk with a generous pinch of salt and a small pinch of pepper. Repeat the boiling, then stirring and final beating.

SIMPLE CHEESE SAUCE

Add 3 oz (75 g) grated hard cheese with the remaining milk in the above recipe.

GARLIC BUTTER

1 oz (25 g) butter or Gold
1 small pinch salt
1 peeled, crushed garlic clove
1 flat dessertsp (1 × 10 ml spoon)
    finely chopped parsley heads

Chop the garlic. Lay the blade of a table knife above and just press down very hard to crush the little pieces. Then work crushed garlic to a paste, add remaining ingredients and blend in with the knife. Wrap tightly in a scrap of Alcan Foil to insulate the pong!

To make Parsley Butter, omit garlic and increase given quantity of parsley to 1 rounded tablespoon (1 × 15 ml spoon).

Use either butter on any meat, poultry portions or fish steaks or fillets before grilling.

24

No Cooking

Swedish birds' nest
Vegetables to eat raw
Bacon and watercress salad
Potato and bacon salad
Grapefruit and cream cheese salad
Potato salad
New England salad
Corned beef salad
Japanese salad
More salad suggestions:
Cabbage and apple salad,
Cabbage and celery salad,
Cauliflower salad,
Sour cream dressing
The giant sandwich
American club sandwich
Jewish salt beef sandwiches
Orange, nut and cream cheese open sandwiches
Cinnamon toast

SWEDISH BIRDS' NEST

If you like Steak Tartare you will like these and they cost far less.

3–4 oz (75–100g) cold, cooked, diced potatoes

1 tbsp (1 × 15 ml spoon) finely scissored chives

1 tbsp (1 × 15 ml spoon) finely chopped parsley heads

1 very small peeled, finely chopped onion or shallot

1 dessertsp (1 × 10 ml spoon) finely chopped and drained capers

4 finely chopped anchovy fillets

2 No 3 or 4 eggs

Salt

Black pepper

Shape potatoes into two rings side by side on a large plate. Border these with chopped anchovies, then with raw onion, then with a very fine line of capers and finally make an outer ring of chives and parsley, separately or mixed together. Break a raw egg into the centre of each completed ring. Season lightly with salt and pepper.

Traditionally these are accompanied by slices of black bread or Pumpernickel spread liberally with butter or Gold.

VEGETABLES TO EAT RAW

The French call these generically *Les Crudités* and experts in professional kitchens cut a great variety of them with a costly piece of kitchen equipment called a *mandoline*. You can achieve very good results either by grating your cleaned raw vegetables on the coarsest side of an ordinary tin grater or by using a small, sharp knife.

The modest way of enjoying these excellent and nourishing mixtures is to arrange them on a plate and pour on French dressing (*Vinaigrée*). A great advantage here for the average bed-sitting room or flatlet dweller is that this sauce does not deteriorate over several weeks of storage *out of refrigeration*; indeed it is very foolish to put it in a fridge – ever.

For coarse grating

Peeled Jerusalem artichokes (so treated they taste like Brazil nuts); peeled or scraped carrots; peeled, finely grated onions; carefully trimmed Brussel sprouts; raw peeled beetroot (keep away from any others as their 'blood' dyes everything it touches); very young, peeled turnips; unskinned cucumbers.

For slicing thinly

Tomatoes; radishes; spring onions; unskinned cucumbers; carefully washed leeks; red and white cabbage; chicory; celery; mushrooms.

First put mushrooms (unstalked) into a sieve or colander. Pour on boiling water to scald and remove any impurities. Never skin them.

The best of the flavour would thus be discarded. Having scalded just remove the stalks, chop finely and also slice the mushrooms thinly.

Cut into matchsticks

Topped, tailed French beans; topped, tailed and strung runner beans; peeled or scraped carrots; celery; celeriac.

Additions to a raw vegetable assembly

All forms of green salading from watercress through all the lettuce family, plus endives, young blanched dandelion leaves, small young nasturtium leaves which *must* be torn apart. Never let a knife come near any of these. When cut with a knife, they weep their goodness away.

Note 1

When preparing a mixture for a number of hungry young people, accumulate your choice from the above suggestions and pile them into bowls or dishes. Put a bowl of French dressing in front of them and let everyone help themselves. Serve an assortment of different breads, not forgetting diet biscuits like Primula Extra Thins and Hovis Wheat Germ Enriched for those who are slimming. Also serve butter or Gold.

Note 2

Hard-boiled eggs served whole are sometimes included in these assemblies with washed but unskinned button mushrooms.

BACON AND WATERCRESS SALAD

1 small bunch very fresh, green
  watercress ·
French dressing
Either 2 rashers of de-rinded
  streaky bacon or the
  equivalent taken from a bag of
  bacon pieces
1 very thinly sliced bread crust
1 cut garlic clove

Place bacon in a dry frying pan over a low heat and allow to cook through slowly so that the fat runs. Dice bacon and return to pan. Pick all brown leaves from watercress, chop off half stalks from the end of the bunch and wash and drain the remainder very thoroughly. Rub the very thin crust vigorously with the cut garlic until it is thoroughly impregnated. Cut crust into very thin matchsticks. Pick watercress into small neat sprigs. Mix with bacon dice and all drawn pan juices. Toss well and hand dressing separately.

POTATO AND BACON SALAD

1 large cup steamed, peeled diced potatoes
2 rashers of fatty bacon (or use economical bacon pieces)
2 tbsps (2 × 15 ml spoons) finely chopped or scissored chives
A few unblemished outer cabbage or cos lettuce leaves
1 tbsp (1 × 15 ml spoon) French dressing

Fry bacon in a dry pan over a low heat until the fat runs freely and the bacon is too crisp for ordinary use. Dice or crumble this and mix with potatoes. Stir/turn quickly to blend in bacon and bacon fat. Add chives and turn into a salad bowl. Work up mixture with well-shaken French dressing.

GRAPEFRUIT AND CREAM CHEESE SALAD

This makes an excellent quick lunch or supper dish in winter.

2–3 oz (50–75 g) cream cheese
1 very small bunch of watercress or a small lettuce heart
1 very small grapefruit
½ oz (15 g) unsalted peanuts
Paprika (optional)

Peel the grapefruit with a very sharp knife. Divide into segments and remove all enclosing skins. Chop segments in halves and fold into cream cheese. Rub skins from peanuts, chop fairly finely and work into the cheese mixture. Wash watercress, pick off all browned leaves and discard the stems. Spread over a small plate.

Note
Cottage cheese can be used instead of cream cheese.

Mound cheese mixture in the centre and optionally scatter powdered paprika on top.

POTATO SALAD

You cannot make a real one without a stock pot so this is a bed-sitting room substitute.

Steam 1 lb (500 g) scrubbed old or new potatoes, cool a little and then peel off the skins. Cut into fairly large dice and tumble into a bowl. Rub a very thin bread crust vigorously with the cut side of a garlic clove. Then rub the salad bowl (or substitute) with the garlic. Put 2 tablespoons (2 × 15 ml spoons) mayonnaise and 2 tablespoons (2 × 15 ml spoons) French dressing together in a very small pan and heat them through fast. Cut the garlicky crust into slender matchsticks, turn in with the potatoes and tumble the hot mixture overall. Turn and stir until well blended.

You can add tiny sprigs of endive, a chopped up cold 'banger', matchsticks of any charcuterie meats to this, also a few left over peas, chopped French beans or even a finely chopped hard-boiled egg.

NEW ENGLAND SALAD

2 oz (50 g) diced corned beef
2 oz (50 g) diced cooked potatoes
2 oz (50 g) chopped celery
1 tbsp (1 × 15 ml spoon) raw
    grated onion and its juice
1 hard-boiled No 3 egg
Tomato mayonnaise (Basics,
    p. 22) or French dressing

Rough chop the egg and mix well with all remaining ingredients. Mound on a bed of any chosen green salad for serving.

CORNED BEEF SALAD

4 oz (100 g) corned beef
1 medium tomato
1 hard-boiled egg
A handful of any available green
    salad
A few very thin slices of
    unskinned cucumber
2 radishes, topped, tailed
    washed and sliced thinly
French dressing

Dice the corned beef and pile into a central mound on a plate or dish covered with chosen green salad. Slice tomato in halves centrally, cut each half into slim crescents and arrange around corned beef. Border with cucumber, then radishes. Moisten with well-stirred or shaken-in-a-stored-bottle French dressing.

JAPANESE SALAD

1 breakfastcupful cooked Patna
    rice
1 flat tbsp (1 × 15 ml spoon) raw
    grated onion
3 tbsps (3 × 15 ml spoons) well
    shaken French dressing
1 tbsp (1 × 15 ml spoon) wine
    vinegar
2 sardines
2 oz (50 g) shrimps
Half a small lettuce
1 hard-boiled egg
1 small gherkin chopped finely
1 teasp (1 × 5 ml spoon) capers
1 teasp (1 × 5 ml spoon) bottled
    chilli sauce

Mix together rice, onion and half the given French dressing. Steep sardines and shrimps in wine vinegar for 10 minutes. Mix remaining dressing with chilli sauce and capers. Heap rice mixture into a mound on a small dish or plate covered with a bed of torn lettuce. Split sardines lengthwise, remove spine bones and tails. Arrange around rice in small pieces. Then make an outer ring of shrimps. Add vinegar to French dressing and shake/drip over rice mound.

29

MORE SALAD SUGGESTIONS
Cabbage and apple salad
Grate on coarse side of grater 3 oz (75 g) tight white cabbage, 2 oz (50 g) scraped or peeled raw grated carrot and 1 peeled sweet apple. Work up in a bowl with a pinch of salt and a little French dressing.

If liked a rounded teaspoon (1 × 5 ml spoon) chutney may be added. Blend this into a tablespoon (1 × 15 ml spoon) of well-shaken French dressing.

Cabbage and Celery Salad
Coarse grate 3 oz (75 g) red cabbage and mix with 2 oz (50 g) finely chopped celery and 1 tablespoon (1 × 15 ml spoon) coarse-grated onion. Blend with Sour Cream Dressing.

Cauliflower Salad
Blend 3 oz (75 g) coarse grated raw cauliflower sprigs or florets with 1 small green pimento, which must be halved and all white pith and pips removed before cutting into very fine strips. Blend in 2 tablespoons (2 × 15 ml spoons) mayonnaise with 2 teaspoons (2 × 5 ml spoons) chutney and 1 tablespoon (1 × 15 ml spoon) Del Monte's unsweetened pure orange and pineapple juice.

All the above mixtures should be set on small plates on a bed of any chosen green salads.

Sour Cream dressing
Mix together 3 tablespoons (3 × 15 ml spoons) red wine vinegar, a generous pinch of salt, a generous pinch of paprika powder and 2½ fluid oz (75 ml) soured cream.

THE GIANT SANDWICH
This is more a description than a recipe.
Cut a minimum of 10 inches (25 cm) from a long French *flute* of bread. Split across centre down its length, just leaving sufficient crust on one side to act as a hinge. Fold back the top half, spread with butter or Gold and proceed with filling. Cover buttered base with torn lettuce leaves. Put in folded, very thin slices of any charcuterie meats. Intersperse with lengthwise quartered crescents of hard-boiled egg. Tuck in trimmed, cleaned, sliced radishes, here and there, alternating with cucumber slices, tomato crescents and tufts of cleaned spring onion. Spread mayonnaise over the lot. Press the upper half down very firmly.

When taking on picnics, watching rugger matches, or indulging in spectating at any other sports, wrap the sandwich up tightly in Alcan Foil. Of course the above fillings are only suggestions intended to stimulate your own inventiveness.

AMERICAN CLUB SANDWICH

3 slices buttered toast
Crisp heart-of-lettuce
Cold cooked chicken or any other meat cut into thin slices
Mayonnaise
Crisply fried bacon rashers or cold thinly sliced gammon
Extremely thinly sliced onion rings and tomato

Cover first slice of buttered toast with crisp lettuce leaves and allow their edges to overhang. Cover with chosen sliced meat. Spread with mayonnaise and cover with second slice of toast. Spread mayonnaise over buttered surface, cover with several cut pieces of bacon or gammon, lay over a few onion rings and then some tomato slices, spread with mayonnaise. Cover with third slice of toast. Press firmly together. Cut into triangles. Arrange on a plate with a flattened lettuce leaf base and optionally garnish with a couple of well-washed sprigs of watercress and a few black and green olives.

JEWISH SALT BEEF SANDWICHES

If you want to know how good these are, and how satisfying, go to Bloom's in London's Aldgate and just try one.

Not too thinly sliced Kosher salt beef
Ordinary English made mustard
Rye bread with whole grains in it

Cut two large ½ inch (1 cm) thick slices of rye bread for one sandwich. Spread each slice lightly with runny mustard. Lay salt beef on one such slice making sure that a little of the very special fat is included. Press on the covering slice, quarter and eat with at least one fat, pickled gherkin.

31

ORANGE, NUT AND CREAM CHEESE OPEN SANDWICHES

1 small thin-skinned orange
3 oz (75 g) cream cheese
2 oz (50 g) chopped or milled
  hazel nuts
1 small chopped gherkin
1 teasp (1 × 5 ml spoon)
  powdered paprika
Salt and pepper
2 × ½ inch (1 cm) slices brown or
  white bread
Butter or Gold

Spread both bread slices with chosen fat. Mix cheese with nuts, gherkin and a pinch of both salt and pepper. Divide equally between the two slices of bread. Spread over thickly and evenly. Cover with thin slices of orange. To do this cut peel from orange with a sharp knife so as to remove all outer white pith as well as skin. After slicing jerk out all pips. Dust powdered paprika on top with a pinch of salt and a larger pinch of pepper. Serve on a base of any chosen, torn green salad.

Note
Cottage cheese can be used as an alternative to cream cheese.

CINNAMON TOAST

This was a fashionable item at tea time during the Victorian/Edwardian era.

4 slices of ½ inch (1 cm) thick
  bread
2 oz (50 g) butter or Gold
1 level teasp (1 × 5 ml spoon)
  sifted icing sugar
1 flat eggsp (1 × 2.5 ml spoon)
  cinnamon

Prepare cinnamon butter by working the cinnamon with butter or Gold and sifted icing sugar. Make toast and cut off crusts. Spread cinnamon butter thickly over hot toast. Sprinkle very lightly on top with extra cinnamon, cut into fingers and criss-cross these on a heated plate for service.

32

Soups

Vegetable soup from a tin
A packet of dehydrated mushroom soup
Beetroot soup
Lightning mushroom soup
A mini vegetable soup
Fresh pea soup

When making soup from a tin or packet at speed and without the aid of stock, use the following instead of water to 'lift' the flavour:

1 concentrated meat cube to ½ pint (300 ml) water with 1 dessertspoon (2 × 5 ml spoons) soy sauce.

½ pint (300 ml) simple white sauce (Basics, p. 24) thinned down to soup consistency with extra milk or milk and water.

VEGETABLE SOUP FROM A TIN

Serves one very hungry or two ordinary people.
Empty contents of tin into a saucepan. Fill tin with milk. Stir into soup. Heat over a medium heat while grating 2 rounded dessertspoons (1 × 15 ml spoon) of cheese ends. When soup boils, turn into one or two heated bowls and scatter cheese over top.

A PACKET OF DEHYDRATED MUSHROOM SOUP

Use half contents of one pack for one serving. Empty this into a bowl. Stir in sufficient cold milk or water to make a smooth paste. Boil ½ pint (300 ml) of milk with, whenever available, 1 rounded tablespoon (1 × 15 ml spoon) of mushroom stalks. Stir milk mixture into bowl paste. Turn back into pan and stir over a very low heat (to avoid base scorching) and just until mixture thickens. Leave, giving an occasional stir, for 20 minutes. This helps to develop the flavour.

BEETROOT SOUP

Imitation Bortsch.

1 medium cooked peeled
  beetroot
1 small onion or shallot
¾ pint (450 ml) boiling water
1 crumbled chicken bouillon
  cube
1 teasp (1 × 5 ml spoon) soy
  sauce
Salt and black pepper to taste
1 tbsp (1 × 15 ml spoon) soured
  cream (optional)

Grate beetroot and onion on finer side of grater. Put in a pan with crumbled chicken cube, water and soy sauce. Simmer gently for 15 minutes. Season to taste. Drink like this, or turn into a heated bowl and trickle a spoonful of soured cream on top.

LIGHTNING MUSHROOM SOUP

4 oz (100 g) fresh mushrooms
  and their stalks
Boiling water
9 fluid oz (270 ml) milk
Pinch of salt
Pinch of black pepper
1 No 3 egg

Put unpeeled, unstalked mushrooms into a small sieve. Pour boiling water over to kill bacteria. Slice up both cups and stalks, put into a pan, pour on milk and raise very slowly to boiling. Turn into a sieve with a bowl underneath. Press down gently to express all moisture. Now that milk has had time to come off the boil, break the egg into it, whip up until slightly thickened and rather creamy. Season with salt and pepper to taste. Use the remaining mushrooms fried.

A MINI VEGETABLE SOUP

1 × 6 oz (175 g) old potato
4 oz (100 g) peeled onion
4 oz (100 g) peeled or scraped
  carrots
1½ pints (900 ml) water
1 flat teasp (1 × 5 ml spoon)
  mixed dried herbs
2 hoarded bacon rinds (before
  soaking see Notes for
  Beginner Cooks, p. 17)
2 meat or chicken cubes
A few drops of Lea and Perrins
  real Worcestershire Sauce
Salt and pepper if needed

Grate all the vegetables. Crumble the cubes into the water, put all in a saucepan and raise to boiling. Steady off at a gentle simmer and maintain for at least 1 hour, or until everything is really tender. Correct seasoning and serve. Scatter grated cheese on top when possible.

Note
If you have both a suitably sized casserole and an oven, cover casserole pot with either a lid or a piece of double duty Alcan Foil and leave on floor of oven at Gas Mark ¼ (240°F, 110°C) overnight, or during working hours of the day.

FRESH PEA SOUP

3 oz (75 g) well mashed, cooked peas (fresh or frozen)

A tip of mint nipped from a sprig and chopped finely

½ pint (300 ml) simple white sauce (Basics, p. 24)

3 fluid oz (90 ml) milk or water (extra)

2 bacon rinds

Stir mashed peas into sauce, stir in extra milk or water. Add mint, then immerse bacon rinds. Cook over a very low heat giving an occasional stir and allowing rinds long enough (10–15 minutes) to infuse soup with their flavour. When using shop bacon add no more salt, except possibly at table.

Note

Hunter's Pot – see With an Oven, p. 97. Meal-in-itself Soup – see With a Grill p. 90.

Fish

Herring roes on fried bread
Anchovy and egg snacks
Fisherman's platter
Fried fish

HERRING ROES ON FRIED BREAD

10 oz (275 g) soft herring roes
White pepper
1 fluid oz (30 ml) oil
Salt
2 × ½ inch (1 cm) thick slices of
   brown or white bread
2 oz (50 g) dripping
3 fluid oz (90 ml) milk in a
   shallow container
1 large tbsp (1 × 15 ml spoon)
   flour in a saucer

Make the fried bread croûtons first. Draw each slice of bread through the milk just as soon as the dripping is 'singing' hot in a frying pan. Fry briskly until richly browned. Drain, set on a plate and tent with foil to keep warm while frying the roes. Pour oil into frying pan, then draw the roes, singly, through the flour and lay in the pan set over a medium heat. They will almost immediately curl up a little. Cooking time is only 1½ minutes for each side. Lift them out, set them on the fried breads and season lightly with salt and pepper.

Note
Never leave bread in milk or it will collapse when lifted out for frying.

ANCHOVY AND EGG SNACKS

1 smallest tin of anchovy fillets
   in oil
4 slices of white or brown bread
   ½ inch (1 cm) thick
2 No 3 hard-boiled eggs
2 tbsps (2 × 15 ml spoons) oil
2 tbsps (2 × 15 ml spoons) butter
   or substitute
Pepper

Halve eggs lengthwise. First chop the eggs and then mash with a fork. Stir in two chopped anchovies, setting aside the rest for garnishing. Heat the oil with chosen fat in a frying pan and when piping hot, fry slices of bread on both sides until crisp and lightly browned. Drain and spread with the egg/anchovy paste. Season with black pepper and criss cross remaining anchovies, or halved ones if preferred, over the top.

FISHERMAN'S PLATTER

8 oz (225 g) whiting fillet
1 small peeled, crushed garlic
   clove (see Notes for Beginner
   Cooks, p. 17)
2 fluid oz (80 ml) oil
1 peeled, diced tomato
Salt
Black pepper
A generous squeeze of lemon
   juice

Put oil into a small frying pan and soft fry the crushed garlic for 1 minute. Add the tomato and stir until well blended, working over a medium strength heat. Lay in the fish, season lightly with salt and pepper, give a generous squeeze of lemon juice and cook for 5 minutes. Turn over, season again and repeat lemon juice. Cook for further 5 minutes. Serve with mashed potatoes.

FRIED FISH

(Without winding sheets of batter)
This does not imply you cannot use batter provided it is puffy and crunchy and not a whole lot of flab to give a mean bit of fish its bulk.

1 small separated, not too fresh
   egg white
2 heaped tbsps (2 × 15 ml
   spoons) flour
Tap water

Put flour into a bowl and take to the nearest tap. Adjust to give you a very mean trickle of water and work up first to a stiff paste and then to only a fairly loose paste, making absolutely certain you have worked out every vestige of lumps. If possible try to use a wooden spoon and work the lumpiness down against the side of the bowl with the back of it. Once smoothness is achieved, thin down again until batter just flops from a lifted spoon. Leave until actually frying.

  First set heat under your chosen container for oil frying. Then whip up that solitary egg white until really stiff. If your room is fuggy, open the windows and whip in a draught

39

to catch air particles. Then fold into your batter.

Draw your chosen fish through a little extra flour on both sides of each piece. Tap off the surplus and bury the piece in your batter. Hold it up over the bowl to let the surplus flop off.

When the oil is heated properly to 390°–400°F (195°–200°C) – or, as you are unlikely to have a thermometer, until the top throws off a very faint haze of heat – slide in your fish. Let it puff up and turn golden brown. Turn over carefully and repeat on the underside, but for flat fillets of fish like plaice, turn off the heat after 3 minutes and cook over the slowly diminishing heat. With fish steaks, like cod, hake, halibut, monkfish, conger or ling, allow 5 minutes before turning off the heat. When cooked drain on absorbent kitchen tissue, or if necessary, newspaper, to absorb any remaining grease.

Serve with proper crisp chips (Vegetables, p. 66) and if you must have vinegar, just for once scorn that malt stuff which isn't vinegar at all really because it is made with malt and not soured wine (*vin-aigre*). Use red wine vinegar, and see if a splash or two of that isn't much nicer. Try for Dufrais, it is far and away the best.

Note
The given amount of batter is sufficient to cook two 5 oz (135 g) plaice or sole fillets, or two small hake steaks.
For other recipes, see With a Grill, p. 87, and With an Oven, p. 95.

40

Eggs and Cheese

How to boil an egg
How to fry eggs
How to poach eggs
How to scramble eggs
Kramer eggs
Curate's eye
Omelettes: herb, bread, potato
Savoury omelette fillings
Sweet omelette fillings
A filling savoury omelette
The flat peasant omelette
Belgian soufflé omelette
Belgian eggs
Scotch eggs
Egg sausages
Waffles
Tunisian brics
Tunisian egg dish
Oeufs sur le plat
Egg nog
Cheese fritters
Egg and cheese fritters
Croque M'sieu
Croque Madame

HOW TO BOIL AN EGG

Make sure the water in the pan is absolutely boiling and deep enough to immerse the eggs completely. Lower the eggs in gently on a spoon. Do not bang them down and possibly cause cracks through which the egg white leaks and the water sneaks in.

For a soft-boiled egg, allow 3½ minutes in fully bubbling water.

For yolk-set boiled eggs into which you cannot dunk 'sojers' successfully, allow 4½–5 minutes.

For hard-boiled eggs, allow 8 minutes. Then hold pan against side of sink and thus expel the boiling water. Fill up with cold water. Leave until cold if possible because the eggs have a tendency to blacken when shelled hot. Tap each egg gently against the side of the sink. Nick out a scrap of the shell. Turn on cold tap to thinnest possible trickle. Hold egg underneath and water will force itself through the shell and outer skin enabling you to rip these off in seconds without defacing the white surface.

Note
Never eat boiled duck eggs. These can prove dangerous if used for any form of cookery in which they are cooked for less than 7 minutes.

HOW TO FRY EGGS

It is assumed that no one really likes fried eggs which have a browned and bubbling pie frill around their edges, due to their having been fried *fast*. Here's how to do them properly.

Melt just enough oil, butter or clean dripping in a frying pan so that the base is just covered when the chosen fat liquefies. Break the egg by tapping it against a thin sharp edge – a tumbler is excellent or the rim of an emptied tin – and slide onto a saucer. Hold the saucer over the fat-coated pan, tip it up and slide in the egg. Keep heat on low. Leave until the white begins to set. Take a large spoon and – gently please – flick the hot fat over each egg *working away from you at all times*. Thus a film of white forms over the yolks too. Each egg is cooked when the outer rim of egg white is just set. Lift out carefully and slide onto toast or a plate.

Remember that an egg goes on cooking even on a warmed plate so always cook eggs last and serve immediately.

HOW TO POACH EGGS

Break each egg into a saucer and slide into an improvised ring (Improvise and Make Do, p. 12) set in a frying pan filled with just-heaving water, to which a spoonful or two of wine vinegar has been added. As soon as they are set remove the improvised rings and lift eggs out on a slice.

HOW TO SCRAMBLE EGGS

There are three ways of scrambling eggs successfully. The first is the easiest. Break your chosen number of eggs into a bowl and add an equal number of tablespoons of milk. Season lightly with salt and freshly milled black peppercorns. Dissolve 1½ oz (40 g) butter (to every 3 eggs) in a thick saucepan. Whisk eggs until they are well blended. Turn into the pan over a low heat and exert patience in stirring steadily until the mixture forms flakes against the spoon. Tap these off and repeat until the mixture is only just moist, because scrambled eggs go on cooking in the pan or even on a plate and if really set, will be very disagreeable.

The second method uses eggs whipped with salt and pepper and with ½ oz (10 g) melted butter to every egg dissolved over a low heat as before, but this time you turn the gas up to give you a medium to strong heat and work the mixture swiftly with a loop whisk until creamily flaked.

The third method is pure enhancement. Allow 1 dessertspoon (1 × 10 ml spoon) of thick, fresh cream to every whipped, seasoned egg and stir away as for the second method.

Please remember very few people cook scrambled eggs really well so do be prepared to take some pains over yours.

Suitable additions

Add a flat teaspoon (1 × 5 ml spoon) of finely scissored chives or milled fresh parsley heads to every whipped egg; or ½ oz (10 g) of coarsely chopped shrimps; or ½ oz (10 g) of any chosen, diced charcuterie meat and pile the finished mixture onto ½ inch (1 cm) thick slices of hot, buttered toast. Ideally provide a second slice of toast cut into quarters and set on the edge of the plate.

KRAMER EGGS

We watched that enchanting small boy and his father making one of these in the film Kramer versus Kramer, *rushed home to make some and have been eating them ever since.*

1 No 3 egg	Cut crusts from bread. Break egg
2 tbsps (2 × 15 ml spoons) milk	into a small bowl, add milk, a
Salt and pepper	generous pinch of salt and
1 × ½ inch (1 cm) thick slice of	pepper optionally. Whip up
white bread	mixture with a fork. Now be
1 oz (25 g) butter, oil or dripping	careful! Slide bread into mixture

but do not leave it in so long that it disintegrates when lifted out. It must just soak through, so have fat hot in a little frying pan when ready to lift soaked bread out. Then trickle remaining fluid over bread as it fries over quite a brisk heat. When the under-side is lightly browned turn over, repeat and eat.

CURATE'S EYE

1 × ½ inch (1 cm) thick slice from a sandwich loaf, either white or brown
Salt and pepper
A little oil to fry
1 No 2, 3 or 4 egg

Cut a 2 inch (5 cm) diameter hole in the centre of the bread slice. Heat just enough oil to skim the base of the frying pan, or you can use clean dripping. When the chosen fat sizzles, lay in the bread slice and immediately break the egg into the central hole. Fry until the base is just set. Lift up on a slice to have a peek underneath. When bread is browned, turn over and fry fast for a minute on the reverse side. Sprinkle lightly with salt and pepper.

We used to slide Curate's Eyes onto small plates and then munch them at the wander; but if preferred they can be eaten with a knife and fork.

OMELETTES

Fundamentally these mean classic French omelettes but there are useful variants from other countries. The classic original was brought to England by the Normans who called it an 'amulet' and made it with eggs, herbs and breadcrumbs whipped up with a bunch of goose feathers.

The prime thing to remember is that the classic one as we know it today must always be very moist inside (Fr *baveuse*). If any French omelette is cooked right through, it ceases to be a French omelette.

The Making

This consists of beating up eggs *very lightly* with a fork with chosen sweet or savoury seasonings and sometimes herbs.

The Omelette Pan

This should be a solid iron one with steep sides. It is never washed but merely wiped thoroughly with a very slightly damp cloth after using and then stored with a disc of oiled greaseproof paper laid over the base to protect it from dust. A classic one is never used for anything else and lasts more than the average lifetime.

The Substitute

Many years ago we were asked by the then Egg Marketing Board to find a solution to making perfect omelettes in any old pans. We collected a number with dented bases and wobbly handles from a nearby tip. We then scoured them outside and in and tried to make classic French omelettes in them. They stuck like glue to the pans – of course. We tried, well, almost everything including Saindoux (With an Oven, p. 118) without success.

Finally after researching for a long time we found the answer. Go and ask any pork butcher for a 4 inch (10 cm) square of raw, unsalted pork fat on the rind. Set any old cheap, dented, handle-wobbly but clean pan over a very low heat. When it is really viciously hot, use the bit of pork fat as a pad to burnish the base and sides really vigorously. Then proceed as usual for classic omelette making – but remember to put that piece of pork fat into a cool place or refrigerator and cherish it, for if you have a dicey frying pan, or use your only one for lots of different things, you will need to heat it dry and then burnish with the pork fat each time you make an omelette.

Method of Cooking Classic French Omelettes

Set pan over lowest possible heat and leave to heat up dry while you prepare your chosen mixture. When pan smokes slightly, toss in a generous nut of butter (or Gold) and immediately turn up heat to fullest. Only when fat melts and browns at the edges do you pour in the prepared egg mixture. Then with pan handle in one hand and table fork in the other, go to work *fast* using only the *flat* of the fork, passing it across the base of the pan and catching up the frills as they form around the edge, all the time shaking the pan handle with the other hand. It is just like rubbing your tummy with one hand and tapping your head with the other, so it is a good plan to practise first in mime!

As soon as the base of the mixture is set and the upper part only is glistening with moisture, either turn heat to a mere thread while putting in a sweet or savoury filling or fold instantly. Do this by running a metal spatula (or a knife) under the edge nearest to you. Flip this over to centre, and turn off the heat. Now take a warmed plate or dish in one hand and tip both pan and plate or dish at very sharp angles to each other, which causes the omelette to fall onto the plate, making a second fold in so doing.

HERB OMELETTE

2 eggs No 3 or 4
1 oz (25 g) butter or Gold
2 generous pinches of salt
1 fat pinch of black pepper
1 flat eggsp (1 × 2.5 ml spoon) of
  finely chopped parsley and
  the same of scissored chives,
  of chervil and of tarragon

Beat eggs, herbs and seasoning lightly with a fork. Proceed thereafter as already explained.

BREAD OMELETTE

This is the one which makes the plain omelette go further.

1 thin slice from a sandwich loaf
1 oz (25 g) dripping or 1 fluid oz
  (25 ml) oil
2 No 3 or 4 eggs
1 oz (25 g) butter or Gold
1 fat pinch black pepper
2 fat pinches salt

Melt and heat dripping or oil in a small frying pan. Cut up bread into small dice. Heat fat until it smokes slightly. Toss in bread dice and turn and fry until these croûtons are crisp and browned. Drain and set aside.

Wipe pan, re-heat and rub with raw pork fat square. Step up heat to fullest and toss in butter. Let it melt and turn brown at the edge. Having beaten eggs, salt and pepper lightly together, draw in the prepared croûtons and make as explained.

POTATO OMELETTE

2 No 3 or 4 eggs
2 oz (50 g) cold, cooked, diced
  potatoes
½ oz (10 g) rendered down pork
  fat or bacon fat
2 fat pinches salt
1 fat pinch black pepper
1 teasp (1 × 5 ml spoon) fresh
  chopped parsley or scissored
  chives (optional)

Melt and heat the bacon or pork fat in a small frying pan, over a moderate heat. Slide in the potato dice and turn and fry until well crisped on their outsides and nicely browned. Drain and turn into lightly beaten eggs with salt and pepper, and parsley or chives when available. Proceed as already explained.

SAVOURY OMELETTE FILLINGS

1. On the economical level these should depend upon small bits of cooked left-overs like a tablespoon (1 × 15 ml spoon) of spinach purée mixed with a flat dessertspoon (2 × 5 ml spoons) of grated hard cheese ends, and a tablespoon (1 × 15 ml spoon) of top-of-the-milk. Put these into a tiny pan over low heat to become piping hot, stirring occasionally. When omelette in pan reaches the *baveuse* or wet-in-the-centre stages, spread hot filling over surface and flip over and tip out as already explained.

2. Mix together a few croûtons, odd remnants of cooked vegetables and a dessertspoonful (1 × 10 ml spoon) or so of stale grated cheese ends. Just moisten with top-of-milk or just milk to enable you to heat mixture through and use as explained for No 1 Savoury filling.

3. Slice a medium onion very thinly. Melt 1 oz (15 g) dripping in a small pan and fry onion gently until it is soft and yellow but not brown and crisp. Beat up 2 No 3 or 4 eggs, add two pinches of salt and two of pepper, then turn in the onion mixture and flip round with the fork. Make omelette as already explained.

SWEET OMELETTE FILLINGS

Make omelette as already described, then run a thin line of jam down the centre to within ½ inch (1 cm) of the edges. Flip over and when folded onto a plate, dust the top with sifted icing sugar. Any jam, jelly or honey can be used in this way.

A FILLING SAVOURY OMELETTE

For filling bed-sitter suppers.

1½ oz (60 g) unsalted pork fat,
    dripping or butter
2 No 4 eggs
1 tbsp (1 × 15 ml spoon) cream
    or top-of-milk
1 flat teasp (1 × 5 ml spoon)
    curry paste
1½ oz (60 g) cold, cooked rice
1 large finely chopped shallot or
    very small onion
1 diced ½ inch (1 cm) thick slice
    cut from a sandwich loaf

Melt half the chosen fat in a shallow pan. Toss in bread dice and fry very briskly until browned all over and quite crisp. Drain and set aside. Add remaining given fat to pan residue and reduce heat to low. Fry finely chopped onion or shallot until soft and yellow but never browned. Beat up eggs lightly with a fork, beat in milk or cream, then rice, croûtons and the curry paste or powder. Step up pan heat again to fullest, turn in mixture and proceed as already explained.

Hand cheese, salt and pepper separately and serve fast.

THE FLAT PEASANT OMELETTE

2 No 3 eggs
½ a slice from a sandwich loaf
    diced small (crust and crumb)
1 small cold, cooked potato
    (diced small)
1 cold cooked sausage halved
    lengthwise then sliced thinly
A few dabs from a tube of
    concentrated tomato purée
1 small, skinned tomato sliced
    thinly and then halved across
    the slices
1 fluid oz (25 ml) oil
1 oz (25 g) butter
Salt and pepper

Put half given oil and butter together in a frying pan. Allow to melt and heat through together. When sizzling, toss in bread dice, fry to golden brown, drain and set aside. Leave pan with residue over a mere thread of heat.

Beat eggs lightly with a fork, season with a pinch of both salt and pepper. Add potato dice to egg mixture, step up heat to full under pan, flick bread dice into egg mixture and also tomato pieces. Turn into the pan. Work the flat of a fork fast across pan base and around edges while keeping the pan moving with opposing hand. Continue just until mixture is about half set.

Lower heat, scatter on sausage pieces and dab a few bits of tomato purée here and there. Remove pan from heat, give a good shake, then slide omelette *flat* onto plate.

There is a more professional way. For this place a large plate over pan and invert completely; but be careful to see omelette has absorbed all the fat or you could burn your hand with drops of oil and very probably even drop the lot.

BELGIAN SOUFFLE OMELETTE

Very easy, very economical, and excellent as a basis for either sweet or savoury fillings.

1 No 4 Egg
1 tbsp (1 × 15 ml spoon) cold
  water
½ oz (10 g) butter

Separate the egg, putting yolk in a very small bowl and white in a slightly larger one. Whip white until as stiff as possible. Add water to yolk and blend with a fork, beating only lightly. Scrape onto stiff white and fold in with a fork, gently but thoroughly. Melt butter in a small frying pan. Turn in golden foam over a low heat and shake pan to settle mixture evenly. Leave until bubbles begin to break on upper surface. Spread in chosen filling. Ease a metal spatula underneath and turn over to make a double fold. Slide from pan to plate and eat immediately.

Suggested Fillings

2 tablespoons (2 × 15 ml spoons) Corned Beef Hash (With an Oven, p. 104) or 2 tablespoons (2 × 15 ml spoon) thick cheese sauce with a few left-over cooked, chopped vegetables folded in, or use 2 tablespoons (2 × 15 ml spoons) of jam or jelly for a sweet omelette.

BELGIAN EGGS

2 × 3 inch (7.5 cm) diameter circles stamped out from a sandwich loaf
2 oz (50 g) mashed potato
Salt and pepper
2 thin 3 inch (7.5 cm) diameter slices of liver sausage or any cooked meat
1 No 3 egg
A scrap of butter or Gold
Oil to fry in a pan or fryer

Spread both bread circles with chosen fat. Lay a slice of chosen meat on both. Work up mashed potato with the separated egg yolk and a pinch of both salt and pepper. Spread over meat. Whip egg white very stiffly indeed and dome equally over the two assembled circles, using a small knife to mould until these resemble miniature bee-skeps. Lay each in turn on an ordinary metal slice. Lower into slightly-hazed-with-heat-oil until the bread base is immersed – just. Then, holding a tablespoon in one hand and keeping the slice and its contents perfectly level, flip oil over the top until the dome becomes a good golden brown. By this time the bread will be crisply fried underneath.

Note
Always flip fat over *away* from you, never towards you.

SCOTCH EGGS

These are easy, provided you remember to have a bit of raw egg white handy. This seals so securely that the sausage-meat never gawps apart during the frying.

8 oz (225 g) pork sausage-meat
A little flour
A 2 inch (5 cm) depth of hot oil in a saucepan or deep fryer if you are lucky enough to have one
3 hard-boiled No 2 eggs
A little raw egg white

Scatter flour over a working surface or a board. Remember to flour your real or improvised rolling pin too. Roll out sausage-meat into a fairly thin strip. Cut into three equal pieces. Put an egg on each one and moisten the edges of the sausage-meat all round with raw

50

egg white. Then wrap up each egg, pinching edges together to enclose completely. Lower carefully into fairly hot oil (360°F, 185°C) and fry/turn until richly browned all over. Drain on absorbent paper and then halve each one with a really sharp knife.

EGG SAUSAGES

½ oz (10 g) butter or Gold
1 dessertsp (1 × 10 ml spoon) flour
3 fluid oz (75 ml) milk
2 hard-boiled No 3 eggs
Salt
Black pepper
1 oz (25 g) grated hard Cheddar cheese or similar
1 very small egg
1 beaker of breadcrumbs
2 oz (50 g) clean dripping
1 teasp (1 × 5 ml spoon) scissored chives
1 teasp (1 × 5 ml spoon) milled or chopped parsley heads

Melt the chosen fat in a small pan over a low heat. Stir in the flour and cook for 3 minutes. Add the milk gradually, beating between each addition to obtain a smooth thick white sauce. Add the chives and parsley. Chop the eggs finely and work in. Then work in the grated cheese. Season to taste with salt and black pepper. Turn all onto a plate and leave until quite cold.

Divide into 8 equal pieces and shape into little sausages. Beat up the little egg with a fork and turn the breadcrumbs into a soup plate. Draw the sausages through the beaten egg, shake off the drips and bury them in the crumbs, one at a time. Pat crumbs in and tap off surplus. Heat dripping in frying pan until it 'sings'. Fry the little sausages until well browned and then drain.

Serve with either a little melted butter or with tomato sauce.

51

WAFFLES

If you can raise the wind for a round waffle iron, you can do some splendid snacks at speed. The batter, which is very easy, will keep in

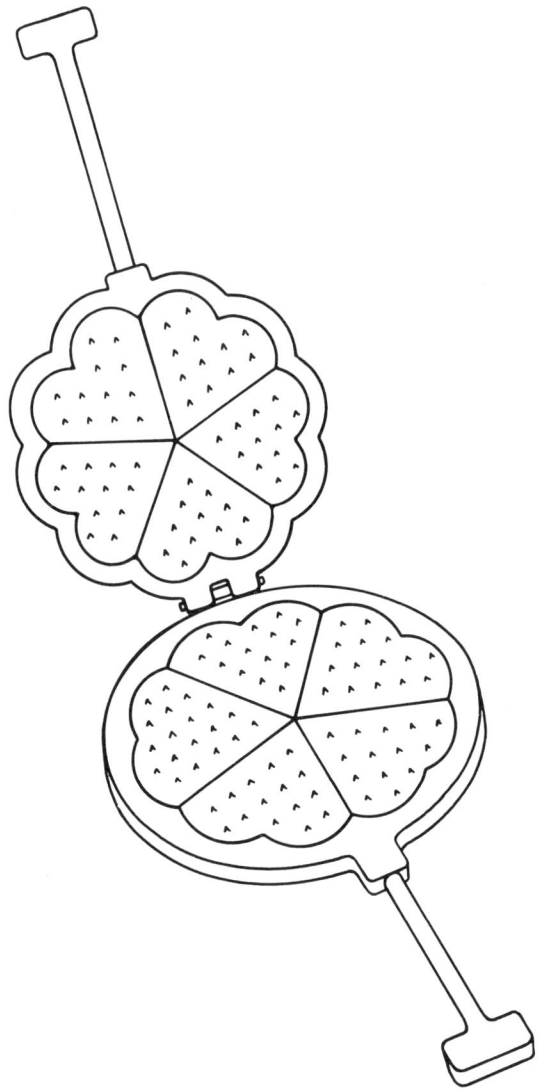

a cool place – ideally a refrigerator of course – for several days, and, apart from any other vital consideration, these waffles cost a fraction of the price for bought frozen ones. They also taste deliciously different.

11 oz (325 g) self-raising flour
1 level teasp (1 × 5 ml spoon)
    soda bicarbonate
1 level teasp (1 × 5 ml spoon)
    baking powder
2 No 3 eggs
Approx ½ pint (300 ml) milk
4 oz (100 g) softened butter or
    Gold

Sieve the flour, baking powder and soda together into a roomy bowl. Scoop out a hole centrally. Drop in the eggs and about half the milk, then stir rather than beat to a thick springy dough. Stir in the remaining milk but please avoid beating. Lastly, just soften your chosen fat in a warm place and stir in until it vanishes.

The Waffle Iron

Place this, closed, over a low heat. Leave until it begins to throw off a faint haze of smoke. Brush fast all over with melted lard or, if you are an ambitious bed-sit-dweller, use the professional mixture called *saindoux* (With an Oven, p. 118).

Cooking Waffles

Adjust burner to medium strength. Drop 2 fat tablespoons (2 × 15 ml spoons) of waffle batter onto the smoking base of the iron, then instantly use the spoon to spread mixture to within 1 inch (2.5 cm) of the edge all round. Brush the upper iron as explained and press this down onto the batter. This forces the mixture to the edge all round. Leave for a slow count of 60, then turn iron right over and lift upper half to see if waffle is crisp and golden. If so, cook the other side for a further minute until the waffle comes cleanly away from the iron.

Savoury Waffles

1. De-rind 2 thinly cut bacon rashers, then snip them up small with scissors (it's the easy way). Fry dry with removed rinds in a frying pan until wavy and slightly crisp over a low heat to obtain maximum bacon fat. Make waffle, drain bacon and scatter over. Peel core and slice a cooking apple (preferably Bramley because these are the best) fairly thickly. Fry in remaining bacon fat in pan. Lay over bacon bits and pour any remaining fat over the top.

Note

Do invest in a bag of bacon bits as sold, for example, by Sainsbury's. These are usually very fatty but melt down to yield bacon fat which keeps for weeks in a cool place and makes super fried bread for many savoury uses!

2. Put a rounded dessertspoon (1 × 10 ml spoon) of butter or Gold

into a small pan with 2–3 rounded dessertspoons (2–3 × 10 ml spoons) of grated Emmenthal cheese (the melting one). Set over lowest possible heat, stir well until mixture forms a paste and spread over a circular waffle.

3. Pile scrambled eggs on top of a waffle instead of toast.
4. Make a Waffle Sandwich with a freshly made, halved waffle. Dab a few flakes of butter or Gold onto one half. Cover with one very thin slice of cooked ham or other charcuterie. Cover with thin slices of tomato and a spread of mayonnaise.

TUNISIAN BRICS

Adored by young Tunisians who walk around eating them. They never spill a drop of egg on themselves.

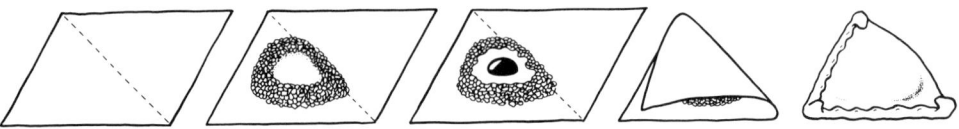

4 oz (100 g) frozen puff-paste (Jus-rol)
2 oz (50 g) grated, stale cheese or moist cooked mince, or finely chopped cooked mixed carrots and peas, or cooked flaked fish
2 No 2 or No 3 eggs
1 extra very small, well-beaten egg
Salt
2 dessertsps (1 × 15 ml spoon) cream
Black pepper
Hot frying oil in a saucepan or small deep-fryer
A little flour
1 rounded tbsp (1 × 15 ml spoon) finely chopped parsley heads

Lay thawed puff-paste on floured working surface and roll out as thinly as you can to cut two 10 inch (25 cm) squares. Make a little crease, very lightly, to mark the diagonal as shown in the diagram. Put half the chosen filling inside one of these triangles, making a little crescent shaped wall 2 inch (5 cm) in from the edges with either the cheese, the fish, the mince or the vegetables. Very carefully, break an egg *inside* this wall, sprinkle lightly with salt and pepper and liberally with half the parsley over each and drip on half the given cream (or top-of-the-milk). Wet the bare paste edges very generously with beaten egg. Lift

54

the bare triangle up and over the filled one until the edges meet. Then *nip very firmly* together. Repeat.

Lower each *bric* into oil which must be at just below the stage when it is slightly hazed with heat. Have a tablespoon (15 ml spoon) to hand and with it flick oil over the *bric* as it begins to puff up. Please be careful to do this away from yourself. As soon as the triangle is golden brown underneath, turn over to repeat on reverse side then lift out to drain on paper for a moment. Hand each in a folded paper table napkin and munch away.

TUNISIAN EGG DISH (*Chaehouka*)

8 oz (225 g) skinned, sliced, ripe tomatoes
4 oz (100 g) very thinly sliced pimentos (after removing white pith and seeds)
1 No 4 egg
1 tbsp (1 × 15 ml spoon) top-of-the-milk or single cream
1 very finely crumbled dried basil leaf
1½ oz (40 g) butter
1½ fluid oz (45 ml) oil
Triangles of toast
Salt
Pepper

Heat 1 oz (25 g) of the butter and 1 fluid oz (30 ml) of the oil in a frying pan. Add the tomatoes, pimentoes and basil and simmer gently to pulp. Turn into a small container and cover to keep warm. Whip egg with milk or cream, season lightly with salt and black pepper. Heat remaining butter and oil in the frying pan and when these sizzle, pour in the egg mixture and stir with a fork over a low heat until thick and creamy. Spread down the centre of a plate. Border on each side with the tomato mixture. Set triangles of toast around outside and serve immediately.

OEUFS SUR LE PLAT

A very easy way of cooking eggs, also very easily digested and excellent when slimming.

2 No 3 eggs
Salt
Pepper
¼ oz (5 g) Gold or butter

Rub the chosen fat over a heat-resistant plate which fits over a 6, 7 or 8 inch (15, 18 or 20 cm) saucepan half filled with boiling water. Break the eggs onto the slightly buttery surface, sprinkle lightly with both salt and pepper and cover either with a piece of Alcan Foil or with an inverted bowl. Leave until the white is set with water just steaming underneath and eat from the plate.

Variations

1. Cover the plate with a slice of any chosen cooked meat. Break eggs on top and cook as before.

2. Chop up 2 heaped tablespoons (2 × 15 ml spoons) of cooked cauliflower, cabbage or Brussels sprouts. Season as before and sprinkle with ½ oz (10 g) grated hard cheese ends. Spread out on the plate and break eggs on top.

EGG NOG

For when there is no time to eat anything.

1 No 3 egg
1 teasp (1 × 5 ml spoon) sugar
½ pint (300 ml) milk
Nutmeg

Whip given ingredients, strain into a tall glass, add a generous grate of nutmeg on top and drink.

Optional alcoholic addition
When practical, complete the nog except for nutmeg, stir in 2 tablespoons (2 × 15 ml spoons) of any desired alcohol, add nutmeg and serve.

Note
For other recipes, see With an Oven, p. 95.

56

CHEESE FRITTERS

These can be made successfully with ordinary Cheddar or with the more costly Gruyère or Emmenthal cheeses.

2 oz (50 g) sifted flour
1 small flat eggsp (1 × 2.5 ml spoon) baking powder
1 tbsp (1 × 15 ml spoon) beer
6 oz (175 g) chosen cheese
1 pinch of salt
1 teasp (1 × 5 ml spoon) oil
2–2½ fluid oz (60–75 ml) cold water
Oil in saucepan or fryer

Sift flour with salt into a bowl. Drop oil into a central hole. Add beer first then water, both very gradually, either working up with a wooden spoon and beating thoroughly or whisking with a hand electric whisk. When thick enough to flop slowly from lifted whisk or spoon, give a further beating until top is very bubbly. Rest 1 hour before using.

Remove any rind from cheese and cut into fat fingers approximately 3 inch (7.5 cm) × ¼ inch (5 mm) thick. Heat oil in pan to slightly smoking, then mix baking powder into batter and beat once more. Draw the cheese fingers through to coat them thickly, slide into oil and fry until well browned in batches of four or five depending on size of pan. Drain and serve fast.

EGG AND CHEESE FRITTERS

2 No 3 eggs
Oil (never more than two-thirds filled) in a small saucepan for deep frying
4 slices from a cut sandwich loaf
Butter or Gold to spread on bread slices
2 slices of Kraft's Processed Cheese
A little made English mustard

Beat up eggs thoroughly. Lay cheese slices on two of the slices of buttered bread. Spread with a little mustard, cover with remaining slices and press together very firmly. Then cut into eight small squares. Pass these singly through the beaten egg and slide into the very hot oil to puff up and turn a rich golden brown. Drain, pile onto a warm plate and eat with one of the dreadful bottled sauces!

CROQUE M'SIEU

2 × ½ inch (1 cm) thick, matching crustless slices of new bread
Butter or Gold
1 matching sized 1 inch (2.5 cm) thick slice of Gruyère or Emmenthal or other melting cheese
French mustard (use made English if preferred)
1 raw, beaten, strained egg
Fine soft breadcrumbs
Oil in a pan or fryer

Butter the bread slices. Spread lightly with chosen mustard. Lay the matching cheese slice over one buttered slice. Cover with the second bread slice and press very firmly together. Cut this sandwich in halves lengthwise. Pass both through raw egg, then bury in the breadcrumbs and pat in thoroughly. Tap off any surplus before lowering into hot oil at just under the slightly smoking stage. Fry until both sides of the sandwich are richly browned. Drain and serve.

If you have egged and crumbed the sides as carefully as the tops and bases, you should bite into a delicious central goo of cheese. If not, the goo will have oozed out quite a bit during the frying.

CROQUE MADAME

Make exactly as explained for Croque M'sieu except that you slip a matching-sized slice of ham under the cheese before assembling the sandwiches for frying.

Note
For variations on the croque, see Brunches and Sandwiches (p. 305). For other recipes, see With an Oven, p. 95.

Meat and Poultry

Cornish cutlets
Sausageburgers
Pitt-y-panna
Buffins
Fried chicken portions
Savoury fried sandwiches
Danish meat patties
Hamburgers and beans

CORNISH CUTLETS

4 × ½ inch (1 cm) thick squares
    of cold cooked meat or poultry
4 × ½ inch (1 cm) thick squares
    of crustless bread
Salt
Pepper
Concentrated tomato purée
1 small strained egg
Fine soft breadcrumbs
Hot oil for frying
4 oz (100 g) cold cooked potatoes
    mashed finely
2 tbsps (2 × 15 ml spoons) milk

Spread each bread square with a little tomato purée like jam. Lay on the chosen meat or poultry, season lightly with salt and pepper. Mash potatoes with the milk, add salt and pepper and a teaspoonful of beaten egg. Work to a smooth paste and dome neatly over each 'cutlet'. Draw all through remaining egg, then bury in breadcrumbs and pat down lightly. Slide each into slightly smoking hot oil and turn off heat immediately so that the squares fry to a rich golden brown in the slowly diminishing temperature.

SAUSAGEBURGERS

If you have never even fried an egg, you can make these with ease. Just be sure that you buy a piece of pork sausage-meat. This is sold by the pound and is less costly than sausages.

4 oz (100 g) pork sausage-meat
2 plain burger buns from the
    local bakery
A little made English mustard
1 heaped tbsp (1 × 15 ml spoon)
    flour
A very little lard or dripping

Cut the sausage-meat thinly into four slices. When doing this without a refrigerator the knife is likely to press while cutting, making a funny shape. Turn in flour, then pat edges back to restore the slices to rounds and pat them down to the same size as the split buns. Spread each cut side with mustard.

Melt the dripping or lard in a small frying pan, just using enough to skim the base. Fry the sausage rounds over a low to moderate heat. Lay one over each mustard-spread bread half. Spread more mustard meanly over the fried rounds. Clap them together in pairs. Wrap in a small piece of Alcan Foil to keep their heat for a few minutes while you get yourself a plate, knife and fork.

No work with accompanying vegetables either if you use tinned peas heated in their own liquor in a small pan or just baked beans. If the latter, do remember to open just 1 inch (2.5 cm) around the rim and then stand the tin in an inch or two of hot water to heat through without making a fearful mess of the pan, which happens if you empty the contents out for heating up.

PITT-Y-PANNA

Swedish. A supper dish served even in very elegant restaurants as an after theatre dish.

1½ oz (40 g) dripping
1½ oz (40 g) crustless bread diced small
1 small rasher of de-rinded, diced, streaky bacon
1½ oz (40 g) any cooked diced meat or poultry
Salt
Pepper
2 oz (50 g) diced cooked old potatoes
1 No 3 or No 4 raw separated egg yolk in its half shell

Dissolve the dripping in a small pan. When hot toss in bread dice and fry/turn until well-browned all over. Lift out, drain and set aside. Fry bacon in remaining dripping in pan, and when slightly crisp turn in meat dice and potatoes. Turn and fry for 1 minute, add bread dice, turn/fry for a little longer. Turn all to mix well and season lightly with salt and pepper. Tip into a small bowl and inset the egg yolk in its shell at centre. The drill is to tip out the yolk over the base mixture at table, and turn over quite quickly with a fork. The hot dice then *cook* the raw egg yolk instantly and make a creamy mixture of the completed dish.

61

BUFFINS

1 medium onion
1 heaped tbsp (1 × 15 ml spoon) flour
Cold water
Made English mustard
4 oz (100 g) minced raw beef, gammon or lamb
1 teasp (1 × 5 ml spoon) finely chopped parsley heads
1 generous pinch black pepper
1 flat eggsp (1 × 2.5 ml spoon) salt
2 oz (50 g) soft brown or white breadcrumbs
1 teasp (1 × 5 ml spoon) concentrated tomato purée from a tube
Dripping or oil to fry in a small pan
2 muffins
Soy sauce
Butter or Gold

Peel and slice onion into fine rounds. Separate these carefully. Mix flour with very little water, just sufficient to make a smooth paste of the consistency of thick cream. Slide in the rings and turn to coat them completely.

Put chosen mince into a bowl with breadcrumbs, parsley, salt, pepper and tomato purée and work up together adding a few drops of soy sauce to bind. Shape into two muffin-sized discs and fry briskly in hot oil or dripping just below the temperature where the frying agent is hazed with heat.

When lacking a grill just split and toast the muffins on an old fashioned toasting fork before a gas or electric fire. Spread one half of each with butter or Gold and the other half with mustard. Clap together with the burger in between them and cover to keep warm.

Raise heat to slightly smoking stage and one by one drop in the onion rings to sizzle and turn a rich golden brown. Drain and pile on top of the buffins.

FRIED CHICKEN PORTIONS

Have ready a pan barely half filled with oil heated until it throws a faint haze, generally called the 'slightly smoking stage'. Turn the chosen chicken portion in flour, tap off surplus and slide into the oil to cover completely. Cook over a brisk heat for 1 minute, then turn off heat altogether and complete the cooking in the slowly descending temperature.

Remember to allow 1½ minutes with the heat on when deep-frying a leg/thigh portion. Also remember that no chicken should ever be fried for so long that it becomes beige and dry. Flesh should be very moist and even faintly pink at the bone.

Serve with Corn Fritters, (Vegetables, p. 69) and Fried Bananas (Sweet Things, p. 83).

SAVOURY FRIED SANDWICHES

Fanny's Mum's invention to use up caviare(!) sandwiches left over from a wedding buffet. Just keep the buttered bread (a) thin and (b) crustless and use any savoury filling from potted meat upwards.

Small square or triangular crustless savoury sandwiches which are a bit stale and curled up at the edges

1 No 2 egg

2 heaped tbsps (2 × 5 ml spoons) flour

A little milk

Oil to fry

Put flour into a small bowl and make well at centre. Break in the egg and add a splash of milk. Beat with a spoon until smooth and very thick. Dilute gradually until batter is just thick enough to coat a dropped-in sandwich and cling to the bread all over. Treat each sandwich like this. Drop a few at a time into a small saucepan of very hot oil until each one puffs up and turns a rich golden brown. The oil should be hot enough to be faintly hazed on top.

Serve with any chosen bottled or home-made sauce, like tomato or cheese.

When your batch is completed, strain the oil free of any little blobs of batter so that it is ready to use next time.

Warning
No matter what size saucepan you use, never fill it more than just under half full with oil, lard or dripping as there is a tendency for hot oil to seethe up during frying.

DANISH MEAT PATTIES (*Frikadeller*)

1 lb (450 g) minced beef
1 medium onion, chopped
   coarsely
3 oz (75 g) sifted flour
3–5 fluid oz (90–150 ml) soda
   water
1 well beaten No 4 egg
1 small teasp (1 × 5 ml spoon)
   salt
1 generous pinch black pepper
Fat to fry
2 heaped tbsps (2 × 15 ml
   spoons) finely scissored chives
A little additional flour

Place minced beef with onion in a roomy bowl, dust given flour over. Add 3 fluid oz (90 ml) of the soda water and the well beaten egg. Season with salt and pepper. Work up to see whether you need to use the remaining soda water, as this is not required when the meat is really juicy. Pack the mixture into a small, lightly floured container and refrigerate for 1 hour.

Turn out onto a cold surface and shape up using additional flour on the hands as needed. Shape into ovals measuring 4 inch × 2 inch × 1 inch (10 cm × 5 × 2.5 cm). Just cover the base of a thick roomy pan with oil or clean dripping. When thoroughly hot lay in patties side by side and fry over a moderate heat until well browned. Turn over and repeat on the reverse side. Drain on absorbent kitchen paper.

Note
The Danes serve these with scrubbed, cooked-in-their skins new potatoes. An alternative method is to put each *Frikadeller* onto a well-toasted crumpet which has been dunked in melted butter and top with crisply fried onion rings.

HAMBURGERS AND BEANS

2 hamburgers
1½ oz (40 g) dripping
1 small tin baked beans

Melt and heat dripping in a small frying pan. Lay in the hamburgers and cook over a medium heat for 3 minutes. Turn them over and repeat for 3 minutes on undersides. Drain on a piece of absorbent paper (or a bit of hoarded tissue) and set on a heated plate or dish surrounded by the heated beans.

Note
For other recipes, see With a Grill, p. 87, and With an Oven, p. 95.

Vegetables

Perfect potatoes
Mashed potatoes
Crisp chips in a saucepan
Courgette fritters
Genoese gnocchi
Delicious cabbage
Corn fritters
To string beans

PERFECT POTATOES

Whether cooking old or new potatoes the procedure is identical. By steaming you obtain all the goodness instead of doing that dreadful peeling, boiling and then straining all the goodness away down the kitchen sink. Remember that with few exceptions good vegetables are never boiled (Vegetables, p. 255).

Old or new potatoes
Salt
A little butter or Gold

Put 4 inches (10 cm) of water into the base pan on which the steamer rests. Scrub the potatoes to remove all soil and residues of sundry handlings. Place potatoes in steamer, cover with lid or Alcan Foil and cook them over sufficient heat to make the base water throw steam into the upper container. Maintain until potatoes are cooked which, of course, depends upon their size. Once cooked maintain a bead of light under the steamer. Take each potato in a thick fold of tea towel and rip off (easily) the paper-thin skin which is the only useless part. Return each potato to the steamer when done.

Note
By peeling raw new potatoes with a knife or 'peeler', you ensure the best is removed for hens or dustbin.

When all are peeled turn off the heat and sprinkle lightly with salt. Place butter or Gold on top before service.

MASHED POTATOES

4 medium, old potatoes
½ oz (10 g) butter or Gold
1 tbsp (1 × 15 ml spoon) milk
Salt
White pepper

Steam the potatoes until quite tender as described above, then skin them and mash down with the butter or Gold and a light seasoning of salt and white pepper. Add the milk and beat again until fluffy.

CRISP CHIPS IN A SAUCEPAN

All the best chips are fried twice: this takes only the same amount of time as frying completely from the raw.

Old, peeled potatoes
Oil
Salt
Pepper

Note
Uncoloured chips, after first 3½ minutes frying, can be laid on a scrap of muslin and left overnight to be fried brown when needed. Given this classic treatment they are always crisp and delicious.

Pat potatoes dry. Cut into ¼ inch (5 mm) thick slices. Slice across in ¼ inch (5 mm) chips. Heat oil gently over a low heat until when a single chip is dropped in, it draws just a few tiny bubbles up from the base of the pan. Soft fry chips for 3½ minutes or until they are cooked through *but still white*. Strain and chill them. Return oil to pan. Heat until oil throws a faint haze on its top surface (390–400°F, 195–200°C). Return chips to pan at this fierce heat and keep them moving by shaking pan very gently (not slopping, please!) while they turn fast to a rich golden brown. Lift onto a fold of absorbent kitchen paper to dispose of surplus grease, then sprinkle with salt and pepper.

COURGETTE FRITTERS

2 heaped tbsps (2 × 15 ml spoons) sifted flour
Cold water
Powdered paprika
8 oz (225 g) topped, tailed courgettes/zucchini
Oil in deep fryer at 360°F (185°C)
Cooking salt

Place flour in a small bowl, add a very thin stream of cold water and beat to a very thick batter.

Slice unpeeled courgettes into ¼ inch (5 mm) thick rounds and draw through the vegetable fritter batter. Lift out, slide into the hot oil immediately and fry to a rich golden brown. Drain on absorbent kitchen paper, dish up and sprinkle with salt and powdered paprika for service. The courgettes should be creamily soft inside the crisp and puffy batter.

GENOESE GNOCCHI

2 large potatoes, steamed and
then mashed
1 No 2 egg yolk beaten lightly
with a fork
1 flat teasp (1 × 5 ml spoon) salt
1 oz (25 g) flour
1 dessertsp (1 × 10 ml spoon)
butter
1 tbsp (1 × 15 ml spoon) grated
cheese
3½ oz (85 g) peeled tomatoes

Work mashed potatoes with egg yolk and salt. Sprinkle the flour onto a working surface and press/fold/turn this into the potato mixture until quite smooth. Shape small pieces into little balls, about half the size of ping-pong balls.

Have ready a pan half-filled with boiling water, add an extra dessertspoon of salt and drop in the little potato noodles. Cook over a medium to strong heat. As soon as the first lot floats to the top, lift out and drop in another lot. Put the cooked ones in a bowl and keep warm with a covering of foil.

As soon as all are ready, empty out the poaching water and add tomatoes just to heat through. Cut up roughly while doing this, then add cheese and butter to heated tomatoes. Turn to mix well, then tip over noodles and turn thoroughly again before eating.

DELICIOUS CABBAGE

This recipe does not even remotely resemble cabbage poultice as presented in dark green pads by canteens and inferior restaurants, which may be splendid for drawing boils but is no use whatever to the human tum.

1 large mug of finely shredded
cabbage
1 flat teasp (1 × 5 ml spoon) salt
5 fluid oz (150 ml) tap water
Small walnut of butter or Gold

If your kitchen knife is not really sharp, take it walking until you find a good hard kerbstone and sharpen it on that until you can slice a match in mid-air. Then slice the given quantity of cabbage with it into the thinnest possible shards.

Boil the water in a smallish
pan with the salt, stir in the
cabbage, cover with a piece of
foil or a lid and turn your bottom
heat to two-thirds full strength.
Let water bubble and blow for 4
minutes. Remove lid, stir round
vigorously, re-cover and
continue for 3 more minutes.
There will be scarcely any water
left but strain it anyway, stir in
the nut of butter or Gold and
that is properly cooked cabbage.
It will be brilliantly coloured too
without your having committed
the awful sin of adding a scrap of
soda!

CORN FRITTERS

Make the batter given in the recipe for Cheese Fritters (Cheese,
p. 57). Fold in a well drained 4 oz (100 g) tin of sweet corn. Stir well,
add the baking powder as instructed in batter recipe and then fry.

Heat an iron griddle or iron frying pan over a low heat. When very
hot rub base all over very vigorously with a small piece of raw
unsalted pork fat on the rind (Eggs, p. 41). Drop small tablespoons of
the mixture onto the griddle or pan keeping each well clear of its
neighbours. Lift the edges when bubbles begin to break on upper
surface. Peek to see if the fritters are a light golden brown
underneath. If so, lift with a metal slice or spatula and slap down
hard onto the reverse side. This causes the fritters to rise. When
cooked on both sides, slide the required number onto a small dish
and serve particularly successfully with fried chicken portions (Meat
and Poultry, p. 62).

TO STRING BEANS

This term, so familiar to the average home cook, must be as clear as
mud to the inexperienced. It means, quite simply, that you cut one
end from a runner or French bean leaving a fraction dangling. Pull
this down the bean. If a strand comes away with it, the bean is
stringy, in which case you either pare these 'strings' off before
cooking or else haul strands from your mouth at table!

Note For other recipes, see With a Grill, p. 87, and With an Oven,
p. 95.

Starches

Spaghetti with tomatoes and cheese
Spaghetti with cooked meat and egg
Noodles with cheese
Bread fritters
Soup croûtons

SPAGHETTI WITH TOMATOES AND CHEESE

Two-thirds fill a roomy pan with boiling water and add 1 flat dessertspoon (1 × 10 ml spoon) of salt. When water bubbles, pay in the spaghetti allowing 3 oz (75 g) per head. Do not break it up into little bits, please: just swirl it into the water which softens it immediately. Cook for 12 minutes exactly, drain and return to the saucepan after drying this out thoroughly.

Tip in the contents of an 8 oz (225 g) tin of tomatoes, add 1 fluid oz (30 ml) oil, and 2 – 3 oz (50 – 75 g) stale, grated cheese ends and stir over a low heat until all is well blended. Hand a small extra bowl of grated cheese and shake some over the top of each serving.

Note

Put the remainder into a small bowl. Sink it into the steamer with hot water underneath and thus heat up another day. This way it will not suffer by re-heating. Just remember that a crushed garlic clove considerably enhances the flavour of this simple, filling dish.

Eating spaghetti comfortably requires a spoon and a fork. Having thoroughly mixed a bowlful, drive the fork down centrally, hold the bowl of the spoon at the back and turn, turn to wind spaghetti round and thus push into the mouth with only a small suck to draw in any stray ends.

SPAGHETTI WITH COOKED MEAT AND EGG

3 oz (75 g) plain unbroken
    spaghetti, cooked and drained
1 No 3 egg
Salt
Black Pepper
1 tbsp (1 × 15 ml spoon) oil
1 tbsp (1 × 15 ml spoon) grated
    hard cheese
2 – 3 oz (50 – 75 g) of sliced
    salami, mortadella or garlic
    sausage

Skin and dice chosen charcuterie and fry gently in the oil for 3 minutes, turning and cooking over a very low heat. Beat egg and chosen cheese together. Turn onto the hot spaghetti, add dice of meat and the remaining oil, then stir all round to blend. Use black pepper to complete seasoning at table.

Ideally eat from an old-fashioned soup plate.

NOODLES AND CHEESE

5 oz (135 g) plain noodles
2 oz (50 g) cream or cottage
  cheese
1 No 3 raw, beaten egg
Powdered nutmeg (optional)
1 oz (25 g) grated hard cheese
  ends
1 oz (25 g) oil or Gold
3 pints boiling salted water

Pay unbroken noodles slowly into water when fast boiling. This takes water off the boil. Wait until it bubbles again, give a good stir and boil for 12 minutes. Then drain thoroughly and return to hot pan.

Meanwhile put both cheeses into a bowl with the raw egg. Beat up with a fork to blend well. Turn right over the hot, drained noodles and stir/turn until mixture is evenly distributed. It turns itself into a thick coating sauce by so doing. Optionally sprinkle nutmeg over for service.

BREAD FRITTERS

Use when feeling very economical
2 halved slices of ½ inch (1.25
  cm) thick crustless bread
1 crushed garlic clove
3 – 4 fluid oz (90 – 120 ml) milk
1 No 4 egg
Salt
Pepper
Oil for frying
1½ oz (40 g) grated hard cheese
  ends

Rub crushed garlic over the halved bread slices. Beat egg into milk with a pinch of both salt and pepper. Heat oil in a pan or small fryer. Draw each bread slice through the egg/milk mixture and lower into slightly smoking hot oil (390°–400°F, 195°–200°C). When a good golden brown, drain on absorbent kitchen tissue, then sprinkle thickly with grated cheese.

73

SOUP CROUTONS

Almost more than in a proper home, we think you need this simple little item. Croûtons make soups go further and taste more interesting and they take only a moment or two to do.

3 slices of thin-cut bread from a sandwich loaf
1 fluid oz (30 ml) oil and 1 oz (25 g) butter
or 2 oz (50 g) clean dripping

Leave crust on the bread. Cut into ¼ inch (5 mm) strips and cut across afterwards to obtain small dice. Either heat the oil with the melting butter in a frying pan or melt and heat the dripping. Toss in the bread dice over a fairly strong heat and turn them over and over with a slice to impregnate them fast.

This amount of bread dice absorbs the given amount of oil and butter or dripping leaving a dry pan in which you go on frying and turning over and over until the dice are crisp and richly browned. Turn them into a small bowl – no draining is necessary – and put large spoonfuls into a cup of soup.

This quantity is really sufficient for two people but we suspect you will manage to ingest the lot.

Note
For other recipes, see With a Grill, p. 87, and With an Oven, p. 95.

74

Drinks

Making perfect coffee
Tea in a jug
Iced tea
Iced Coffee
Hot blackcurrant cordial
Home-made lemonade
Simple hot chocolate
Hot honey and lemon for colds
Mulled ale
Sangria
Simple claret cup (hot)
Simple wine cup (cold)
Tomato juice cocktails

MAKING PERFECT COFFEE

If you happen to have been properly brought up by a Mum who believes that 'Instant' is simply not the same thing as that made from fresh coffee beans ground by her in a mill, a food processor, an electric mixer attachment, or by the shop which sells it, this will help. With coffee beans all anyone ever needs to make a perfect brew of coffee is an ordinary enamel jug, some muslin or a strainer and a piece of Alcan Foil just large enough to fit over the top of the jug.

Use 1 pint (600 ml) of freshly boiled water to 4 rounded table-spoons (4 × 15 ml spoons) of freshly ground coffee. Put the coffee in a jug and pour on the boiling water. Stir well, then cover with the foil very securely. Leave for 3–4 minutes. Stir again and pour through a strainer into a pot or jug with a lid.

A Point to Remember

When this little ritual has been completed in French kitchens, the jug is immersed in an outer container of water. This is never allowed to boil. We suggest using an ordinary meat baking tin two-thirds filled with hot water and set over a very low heat. The water should just shiver but never bubble. Treated like this coffee will stay piping hot for hours without any deterioration.

TEA IN A JUG (No teapot!)

If you pour boiling water into an ordinary enamel jug, such as we suggest for making excellent coffee, you can also make equally palatable tea.

First swill some hot water around in the jug. Put in the standard 1 teaspoon (1 × 5 ml spoon) of tea per head, add one for the pot and pour on the boiling water. Stir well, cover with a fold of Alcan Foil and rest for 4 minutes before pouring through a strainer into cups or mugs.

ICED TEA

To every 1 pint of strained, fairly strong freshly-made tea, allow:

6 ice cubes

4 lumps of sugar or 4 small teasps (4 × 5 ml spoons) granulated or caster

1 small lemon sliced very thinly

Whenever possible, 2 bruised heads of fresh mint

Place ice cubes in a jug with chosen sugar, lemon and the mint heads which you have crushed tightly for a moment in well-scrubbed hand. When the tea is made, pour given quantity through a strainer into the jug and stir until ice cubes are melted.

ICED COFFEE (the cheat way)

Half a vanilla ice cream brick
1 pint (600 ml) milk
1 rounded tbsp (1 × 15 ml
    spoon) instant coffee powder
1 rounded dessertsp (1 × 10 ml
    spoon) soft brown sugar
6 tbsps (6 × 15 ml spoons) water
6 ice cubes

Put water, sugar and coffee powder into a pan and stir over a low heat until they blend into a syrup. Place ice cubes in a roomy bowl. Pour on the syrup and stir until ice cubes are almost melted. Stir in the milk. Break up ice cream and add, working this down with clean fingers to blend with the rest. Serve immediately where no refrigerator is available. With a refrigerator it can be made and served over a period of three days.

Note
A 5 fluid oz (150 ml) carton of single cream enriches this brew marvellously.

HOT BLACKCURRANT CORDIAL

For sore throats or loss of voice.
1 hugely heaped tbsp (1 × 15 ml
    spoon) blackcurrant jam
    (preferably home-made)
The strained juice of 1 medium
    lemon
Boiling water
1 hazelnut-sized piece of butter

Put butter, jam and lemon juice into a tall glass and do not forget to put a spoon in or the glass may crack! Fill up with boiling water. Stir until the blackcurrants in the jam become purged and pallid. Let these settle at the bottom of the glass. Wrap the glass in a napkin for easy holding. Drink the rest slowly, when in bed.

Note
A tablespoon (15 ml spoon) of rum from a miniature bottle with either this or the honey and lemon drink can only be an improvement. Just stir in before adding water.

77

HOME-MADE LEMONADE

As this can be stored indefinitely in old lemonade bottles in refrigeration, it can be made in larger quantities than those given.

1 large thin-skinned lemon
6 oz (175 g) granulated sugar
1½ pints (900 ml) boiling water
1 rounded dessertsp (1 × 10 ml spoon) citric acid (from a chemist)

Peel the lemon and strain the juice. Put both into a jug with the citric acid and sugar. Pour on the boiling water and stir until all traces of sugar and citric acid vanish. Use a small funnel to pour into bottles, then secure the tops. When using, put a little test quantity in a glass and dilute to taste with cold water to determine the amount needed for each tumblerful.

SIMPLE HOT CHOCOLATE

2–3 teasps (2–3 × 5 ml spoons) drinking chocolate
1 cup or mug hot milk

Put drinking chocolate into chosen container. Heat milk to almost boiling point, and pour onto drinking chocolate, whisking up vigorously with a small fork.

Note
No sugar is needed with this brew, but a pinch of real vanilla powder added, when available, is strongly recommended.

HOT HONEY AND LEMON FOR COLDS

Prepare when ready for bed.

1 rounded dessertsp (1 × 10 ml spoon) thick honey
The strained juice of 1 medium lemon
Boiling water
1 generous grate of nutmeg or a generous pinch of ground nutmeg
Hazelnut-sized piece of butter

Place butter and a long spoon into a tumbler and wrap this around with a table napkin (cloth or paper). Add lemon juice, honey and nutmeg. Fill up with boiling water. Stir well.

Hop into bed and sip while still extremely hot.

MULLED ALE

Made in a saucepan and very cheering in cold weather.

2 pints (1.2 litres) old ale
1 level teasp (1 × 5 ml spoon)
   powdered cinnamon
1 level tbsp (1 × 15 ml spoon)
   brown sugar
2 bay leaves
¼ teasp 1 × 2.5 ml spoon)
   ground ginger
2 thick slices of lemon

Place all ingredients in a pan and heat up slowly. The mixture must become piping hot but should not be allowed to boil. Slip a small poker under the pan to get red-hot. When the brew is hot enough, plunge poker into it and hold vertically centre while it seethes crossly. When it subsides, pour into heated mugs or glasses. If the latter remember a spoon to stop glass from cracking.

Note
If you do not have a poker, use a short length of iron rod which you have rubbed down to free it from rust and then wiped thoroughly before using.

SANGRIA

1 bottle inexpensive claret
Sugar to taste
2 fairly thick slices of both
   unpeeled orange and lemon
Strained juice of remaining
   orange and lemon
Fat pinch of both powdered
   cinnamon and nutmeg
1 miniature bottle of brandy
1–1½ small bottles of soda water
6 ice cubes

Empty claret into a large jug or bowl, add sliced citrus fruits and strained orange and lemon juices, then stir in cinnamon, nutmeg and brandy. Leave in coldest possible place with a scrap of foil over the top until the moment of service. Add ice cubes, stir well and stir in sugar to taste. Finally stir in soda water.

SIMPLE CLARET CUP (Hot)

1 bottle low-priced claret (plonk)
4 fluid oz (120 ml) fresh orange
    juice or Libby's unsweetened
    orange juice
1 small lemon
1 eggsp (1 × 2.5 ml spoon) each
    of powdered cinnamon,
    powdered cloves, powdered
    nutmeg and ground ginger
6 sugar cubes
1 bay leaf
1 small thin-skinned orange
1 miniature bottle of ordinary
    brandy

Place wine and orange juice in a saucepan. Add the spices and the bay leaf torn in halves. Slice both lemon and orange thinly, remove all pips and discard the two end pieces on each. Add to the pan brew, add the sugar and raise very gently to boiling point but on no account allow it to boil. Stir in brandy and pour into napkin-wrapped glasses, making sure you put a teaspoon into each first.

SIMPLE WINE CUP (Cold)

1 bottle low-priced dry white
    wine (plonk)
13 fluid oz (390 ml) bottle of fizzy
    lemonade
8 thin slices of cucumber cut
    with the skin left on
6 sugar cubes
6 thin, de-pipped slices of lemon
8 ice cubes

Pour the wine into a tureen or bowl. Stir in the sugar, add cucumber and lemon slices and keep cool until required. Pour in the fizzy lemonade. Stir in the ice cubes, stir well and serve in any chosen glasses.

TOMATO JUICE COCKTAILS

1 pint (600 ml) Del Monte tomato
    juice
1 flat teasp (1 × 5 ml spoon)
    celery salt
4 ice cubes
1 large sprig mint
14 drops Lea and Perrins
    Worcestershire Sauce

Mix tomato juice, celery salt and Worcestershire sauce together in a glass jug. Add ice cubes and half-immerse the mint sprig.

Note
For a 'Bloody Mary' add a shot of vodka to 4 fluid oz (120 ml) of above.

Sweet Things

Viennese biscuit cake
Jelly cream
Fried bananas
Jellabys
Torrijas
Mum's sweet fried sandwiches
Sweet waffles
Poor knights
French pain perdu

VIENNESE BISCUIT CAKE

This is made in a small saucepan.

8 oz (225 g) coarse-crumbled
   digestive or petit beurre
   broken biscuits
2 oz (50 g) butter
2 rounded tbsps (2 × 15 ml
   spoons) golden syrup
4½ oz (115 g) chocolate chips
A few drops of oil
Half a very small cut lemon

Cut a circle of greaseproof paper to fit the base of a round Victoria sponge tin. Brush all over the interior with oil.

Put chocolate chips, butter and golden syrup into a little saucepan, set over a low heat and stir until butter and chocolate have melted and syrup has merged with both. Stir in the chosen crumbled biscuits and work up until you have a fairly firm paste. Turn this into prepared tin and press out mixture with cut side of lemon to cover base evenly and completely. Then press lemon over top surface to smooth evenly. Leave until cold. Turn out, peel off base paper and, for long-keeping, just wrap in Alcan Foil and store in a dry place. Cut into small slices because this is quite a rich mixture.

Note

The top may be dusted with sifted icing sugar if liked or decorated with a few chocolate chips alternated with either pieces of glacé cherry or halved walnuts. We serve ours plain with a spiral of whipped cream on each slice.

JELLY CREAM

Any sweet-loving bed-sit dweller can make this at speed.

1 pkt jelly
1 × 14½ oz (410 g) tin Libby's
   unsweetened milk
6 fluid oz (180 ml) water

Rough cut jelly into cubes. Place in a pan with water over a low heat and stir until just melted. Then remove from heat and

Note
Done like this the cream sets very fast and is then ready for service.

pour unsweetened milk in slowly, whipping or beating until the mixture forms a thick cream. Pour into individual bowls or into a cold-water-rinsed jelly mould and unmould when set.

FRIED BANANAS

Also ideal for serving with portions of Fried Chicken (Meat and Poultry, p. 62).

1 peeled banana
2 finely crumbled rusks or Hovis Wheatgerm-enriched Crackers
A very little milk
Hot oil in fryer or small pan

Chop the banana into three equal lengths. Dip each into milk. Roll crumbled biscuits inside a scrap of brown paper to very fine crumbs. Make sure that oil is heated to the slightly hazed stage by this time. Roll banana pieces in the crumbs and slide into oil. Fry to a rich brown by which time the banana pieces will be quite soft.

JELLABYS

These are fun to make and very appealing to anyone with a sweet tooth.

2 oz (50 g) flour
1 No 2 egg
1 dessertsp (1 × 10 ml spoon) oil and extra oil in fryer or pan
Sufficient milk to make a batter the consistency of fresh, single cream
Golden syrup in its tin

Begin by piercing five holes in the base of a clean, emptied soup tin. Make batter by putting flour in a bowl, adding egg and oil and a little milk and beating well. Then draw in more milk gradually while beating steadily. Set batter aside when the consistency of single cream. Rest it for 1 hour by which time it will have thickened a little more. Add a spoonful or two of extra milk and beat once more.

Stand golden syrup tin in an outer pan of hot water to make it runny. When oil in pan is

slightly smoking hot
(390°–400°F, 195°–200°C), clap
one hand against the base of
tin – where the holes are – and
pour in some batter.
Immediately withdraw the
covering hand and shake the tin
about over the surface of the hot
oil to make squiggles and loops.
A little practice soon makes this
very easy. Fry until swollen and
golden brown. Drain and turn
into a shallow dish.

Spoon syrup over the Jellabys
and eat normally or pick up in
your fingers. When possible use
maple syrup rather than golden
syrup.

TORRIJAS

These resemble the most delicious doughnuts but are actually made with bread.

2 or more slices of ¾ inch (1.75 cm) thick bread stamped into 2½ inch (6.25 cm) diameter circles

1 No 2 egg beaten and poured into a saucer

2 tbsps (2 × 15 ml spoons) inexpensive sherry in a second saucer

2 oz (50 g) icing sugar sifted with 1 scant teasp (1 × 5 ml spoon) powdered cinnamon put into a third saucer

Oil in pan or fryer to deep fry

Slide bread circles through the sherry. Then almost soak in the beaten egg, being careful not to leave long enough for the bread to collapse. Lower on a slice into slightly smoking hot oil and fry until well puffed and richly browned. Lift out, drain and bury thickly in icing sugar mixture.

Eat immediately.

Note

We used to blindfold members of our audiences and let them taste these. When asked what they were eating, they always replied 'Hot doughnuts!'

84

MUM'S SWEET FRIED SANDWICHES

1 banana
1 oz (25 g) grated milk chocolate
4 crustless ¼ inch (5 mm) thick
  slices of buttered bread
Sifted icing sugar
1 dessertsp (1 × 10 ml spoon)
  fresh or Del Monte orange
  juice
Oil in pan to fry
2 rounded tbsps (2 × 15 ml
  spoons) sifted flour
1 small egg white
Ordinary beer

Mash banana with a fork and mix with chocolate and orange juice. Divide equally between the two buttered bread slices. Cover with the remaining two, press together then cut into quarters. Pass the squares slowly through batter (see below). When oil reaches 385–390°F (193–195°C) slide in sandwiches, fry until puffed and richly browned then liberally drench in sifted icing sugar and serve fast.

The Batter
Place flour in a basin, make a well at centre and trickle in just sufficient ordinary beer to make a smooth paste. Always stir this paste down with a spoon but *never beat*. When the paste is the consistency of stiffly whipped cream, rest until required. When the oil in the pan or fryer is beginning to get hot, whip the egg white stiffly and stir into the batter until totally blended.

SWEET WAFFLES

1. Dab flakes of butter or Gold over the upper surface. Pour on maple syrup or golden syrup or use any jam or jelly instead.
2. Dab with flakes of butter or Gold. Slice a peeled banana thinly. Spread slices over a hot crisp waffle. Shake soft brown sugar over the top. Add a generous squeeze of lemon juice and top up with whatever cream you can afford, or just use top-of-the-milk.
3. Divide waffle down the middle. Pile hulled halved strawberries, or whole raspberries or halved loganberries or really ripe whole blackcurrants on one half. Spoon any available sugar on top and finish with blobs of yoghurt or whipped whipping cream or soured cream. Clap remaining waffle on top.

POOR KNIGHTS

1 brioche or 3 × ½ inch (1.25 cm) thick slices cut from a milk loaf
2 oz (50 g) butter
2 heaped tbsps (2 × 15 ml spoons) red currant or other jelly and an additional 2 oz (50 g) jelly
1 fluid oz (30 ml) water and sweet white wine or sweet cider

If using a brioche, cut into ½ inch (1.25 cm) thick slices. Soften and heat butter in a frying pan, then stir in the heaped 2 tablespoons of chosen jelly. Mix and then fry bread or brioche slices slowly in this until very thoroughly impregnated and only just browned at the edges. Lay fried slices on a preferably heated plate. Heat remaining jelly with chosen fluid. Pour over breads for service.

FRENCH PAIN PERDU

4 tbsps (4 × 15 ml spoons) milk
Half a currant loaf, sliced ½ inch (1.25 cm) thick
3 oz (75 g) of any jam
Oil to fry
1 No 3 egg
A little sifted icing sugar
2 tbsps (2 × 15 ml spoons) water

Beat milk with egg. Turn into a shallow dish. Heat oil in a fairly shallow pan to 380°F (190°C). Slide bread slices through egg/milk mixture. Lift on a slice or spatula and slide into hot oil. Fry to a golden brown on both sides. Drain on absorbent kitchen tissue or a bit of hoarded tissue paper. Sift icing sugar thickly over each drained slice. Stir jam with water in a small pan until bubbling and hand this separately.

Note
For other recipes, see With a Grill, p. 87, and With an Oven, p. 95.

With a Grill

How to grill successfully
Toasted sandwiches
Meal-in-itself onion soup
Trout pâté
Milk-poached mushrooms
Frankfurter kebabs
Assorted hot meat or poultry sandwiches
Corn on the cob
Croûte Landaise
Caramelised oranges

HOW TO GRILL SUCCESSFULLY

Always begin by lighting the grill in time for it to become really hot, so that the essential first job of sealing in the natural juices is done under full heat.

Never season raw meat with salt before grilling because this hardens the flesh, so remember to season *after* cooking and placing on a heated plate or dish.

Make sure that the grill rack, which is supplied with all grill pans, is placed with the little legs in the higher of the two positions, thus exposing the meat to the strongest possible heat. Seal all chops and steaks for 1 minute on each side. Then reverse the grill to the lower position and grill until cooked to your taste.

There are three cooking stages for all steaks:
No 1, called 'Rare' which means underdone
No 2, called 'Medium' which means fairly pink in the middle
No 3, called 'Well done' for which the synonym is *'Ruined'*.

When the piece of meat has been sealed on both sides and the grill rack is in the lower position, allow the following times:
Rare: 2½–3 minutes on each side
Medium: 4–4½ minutes on each side
Well done: 5 minutes on each side.

Note
There is a fourth gradation, more used in the United States and France than in England, known in the former as 'very rare' and the latter as *'bleu'*. For this stage cook for 1 minute on each side after sealing.

'Steak' is a generic and needs to be supported by some fairly specific information or the given cooking times will be inaccurate. The various 'steaks' should be cut as follows:
Sirloin (1 inch [2.5 cm] thick); rib steak (minimum 1 inch [2.5 cm] thick); fillet steak (minimum 1 inch [2.5 cm] thick); rump steak (1 inch [2.5 cm] thick); porterhouse steak (minimum 1½ inch [3.75 cm] thick); *tournedos,* or eye of the fillet, cut into a round with raw pork fat tied around (minimum 1½ inch [3.75 cm] thick).

The following cuts are also suitable for grilling:
Lamb steaks, cut from the broad end of the leg; lamb chops; lamb cutlets; pork fillet; pork loin chops; pork steaks; venison steaks.
Treat lamb steaks in the same way as beef steaks, but for the rest

we find the most successful method is to place the required number on the base of the grill pan without using the rack at all. Like this cook under a brisk grill for 3, 4 or 5 minutes, depending on whether you like lamb to be rare (bloody), medium (pink in the middle) or ruined (cooked right through). Then turn over and repeat. Remember that all pork items need to be cooked right through, whereas lamb cutlets and even chops are generally liked when just pink in the middle. Just make a half-depth tiny incision with a very sharp knife when in any doubt. With all these items pour the collected pan juices over the item which has been set on a warmed plate or dish.

Grilled Liver
This needs your careful attention too. It is rich in iron, but will never retain any of this valuable property if even slightly over-cooked. It should be given a light brushing of oil or melted butter and just cooked through on the base of the grill pan. Cut off a tiny sliver and taste-test. Slices should never exceed ½ inch (1.25 cm) in thickness.

The best liver for grilling is the most expensive calves' liver. The least costly is ox liver and the in-between one is pork liver. Both pork and ox liver can be made to taste like calves' liver by a little trick it may help you to know.

To transform pork or ox liver
Place the sliced liver in a basin and just cover with low grade milk. Leave for 24 hours. The milk will now be port-coloured and only drinkable to dogs or cats, who adore it. The liver will be tenderised by this soaking and if grilled gently and carefully, will taste like calves' liver. Try it; it's what shoddy restaurants substitute for the real thing anyway.

Gammon and bacon rashers
Scissor off the rinds on all bacon and gammon before grilling. Gammon – which should be a minimum of ¼ inch (5 mm) in thickness – should also be snipped through the rind side at 1 inch (2.5 cm) intervals down the length. This stops the rashers from rising up under the heat and curling over which makes even grilling very difficult.

Gammon rashers should be placed on the base of the grill pan, to allow for each one to be half cooked in 3 minutes. Turn over and repeat on the reverse side. If liked, have ready a half slice of ½ inch (1.25 cm) thick bread with the crust left on. Lift the gammon onto a preferably heated plate and turn the bread in the residue pan fat to coat both sides. Then grill until nicely browned on each side. Should these rashers be very lean ones with scarcely any fat, add ½–1 oz (10–25 g) of dripping or pure lard to the pan. Let this melt and start sizzling in the pan, then slide in bread and proceed as explained.

Grill thinly cut bacon rashers on the rack in the low position, but with the grill heat at full. The thinnest ones will quickly contract and become wavy down their length. That is the stage at which they are cooked for the average taste; but if liked well-done, then give them a moment or two on the reverse side. Ideally cooks use a pair of metal lifting tongs to turn them. Lacking a pair slide an ordinary table knife underneath at centre and flip over.

TOASTED SANDWICHES

Make up any sandwiches suitable for toasting in a professional electric toaster. Instead of doing so, slip these inside an Alcan Roastabag and set in the grill pan without any grill rack. Put under a full grill and toast one side to your satisfaction, then turn over and do the reverse side in the same manner.

MEAL-IN-ITSELF ONION SOUP

2 large onions
1 oz (25 g) dripping
1 flat dessertsp (2 × 5 ml spoons) flour
Salt
Black pepper
½ pint (300 ml) milk
1 slice toast
1 oz (25 g) grated stale, hard cheese ends
1 generous pinch dry English mustard

Peel and slice the onions thinly, then rough chop. Melt dripping in a saucepan, add onions and fry over a very low heat until they are soft but not browned. Stir in the flour, mustard and a little milk. Let this bubble up and then stir to make a thickish paste. Add remaining milk and stir over a strong heat until mixture boils. Reduce bottom heat to very low and let soup simmer gently for 15 minutes. Season to taste with salt and black pepper. Pour into a Pyrex soup bowl or soup plate. Lay toast on top. Sprinkle grated cheese all over toast and allow to bubble and brown by standing the container on the base of the grill area.

TROUT PATE

10 oz (275 g) trout
1 crustless, ½ inch (1.25 cm)
   thick slice of brown or white
   bread from a sandwich loaf
2 oz (50 g) mushrooms
Top-of-the-milk or single cream
6 tbsps (6 × 15 ml spoons) dry
   cider
1 teasp (1 × 5 ml spoon) oil
½ teasp (1 × 2.5 ml spoon)
   anchovy essence
Salt
Black pepper

Brush gutted and cleaned trout on both sides with the oil. Lay in a grill pan without a rack and grill under a fairly moderate heat for 3 minutes on each side. Then excavate the 'pearl' or tiny collop of white flesh which lies behind the gill on each side. Remove all skin, then bone the flesh carefully and discard head, skin, bone and tail. Break flesh up with the fingers. Poach chopped mushrooms and stalks in the cider for 4 minutes. Strain and drip fluid over prepared bread until this is soft enough to mash with the trout flesh. Add the anchovy essence and a light seasoning of salt and black pepper. Rub through a sieve and pack into a small bowl for service.

Alternatively with a Moulinex all-purpose food processor you can put in all the prepared ingredients, switch on full and maintain in 10 second bursts with 5 second pauses until a smooth creamy paste is achieved.

MILK-POACHED MUSHROOMS

4 oz (100 g) milk-poached
   mushrooms (Soups, p. 34)
1 fluid oz (30 ml) oil
1 × ½ inch (1.25 cm) thick round
   of toast
A little butter or Gold
1 slice from a pack of Kraft
   Processed Cheese Slices

Make the toast. If you dislike crusts, just reverse an ordinary table knife and bang the edges of the toast on all four sides to soften them easily. Spread with chosen fat. Pile the mushrooms on top. Lay the cheese slice over. Slip under a moderate grill to melt and turn golden brown.

FRANKFURTER KEBABS

3 oz (75 g) small cocktail
   frankfurters
Half a slice of ½ inch (1.25 cm)
   thick bread spread with Garlic
   Butter (Basics, p. 24)
Salt
Pepper
2 torn bay leaves
2 de-rinded rashers of streaky
   bacon
A little oil
French dressing (Basics, p. 32)

Remove the bread crusts and cut bread into triangles. Divide each bacon rasher into three and tear bay leaves in halves. Alternate these with the frankfurters on small skewers. Brush with oil, set on a grill rack with the legs in the low position and grill, moistening with a teaspoonful of French dressing each time you turn the skewers, which is four times in all.

When skewer-loads are cooked, set on a small bed of rice and serve with a spoonful of hot French dressing poured over.

ASSORTED HOT MEAT OR POULTRY SANDWICHES

The secret is to moisten the chosen bread slices with the natural juices of the meat or poultry after cooking.

Pairs of bread slices
Natural juices
Dripping from appropriate
   meats or poultry
Salt
Black pepper
Thin slices of chosen meat or
   poultry

Toast chosen bread slices. Spread with appropriate dripping. Season with salt and pepper. Cover with hot chosen meat or poultry slices. Moisten with natural juices. Cover with second slice of prepared dripping toast.

If a slow worker, resulting in the cooling of both toast and filling, slip completed sandwich into an Alcan Roastabag. Lay on grill rack with legs in lower position and slip under a grill for a few moments to heat up. Serve immediately.

CORN ON THE COB

Strip each head of corn down to the seed, removing all green leaves and tassel and chopping any stem off level with the first seeds on the pod. Plunge into fast-boiling, slightly-salted water, raise to boiling

92

again, then steady off at a strong simmer and maintain until the corn grains are tender. Drain well and then brush all over with melted butter or Gold. Set on an ordinary grill rack under a hot grill. Allow grains to brown lightly all round.

Pierce both ends of each head with a sliver of wood or matchstick. Rub all over with an extra knob of butter or Gold and serve piping hot to eat in your fingers.

CROUTE LANDAISE

1 × 1 inch (2.5 cm) thick, crustless slice of white or brown bread

1 × ¼ inch (5 mm) slice of any desired pâté

¼ pint (150 ml) simple cheese sauce (Basics, Part 1)

Oil in pan or deep fryer

2 small flakes of butter

1 smallest possible egg

1 tbsp (1 × 15 ml spoon) milk

Cut crumb of bread with a small very sharp knife leaving a ¼ inch (5 mm) wall all around and excavating to a ½ inch (1.25 cm) depth. Beat egg with milk, draw bread slice through and slide into slightly smoking hot fat to fry fast to a good golden brown. Set on a heat-resistant plate. Trim pâté slice to fit inside the removed crumb area. Pour cheese sauce overall, dot top with a flake or two of butter and slip under a fairly hot grill to bubble and brown.

CARAMELISED ORANGES

4 small thin-skinned sweet oranges, ideally blood oranges

A little cooking sherry

Darkest possible soft brown sugar (never use demerara for this)

Place oranges in boiling water, cover and simmer until completely soft (approx 40–60 minutes depending on their size). Cool sufficiently to handle. Halve centrally, remove all pips and pack close together in a Victoria sponge tin or similar container. Pat soft brown sugar thickly over cut surfaces. Give each a teaspoonful of sherry, then set in a grill pan without any rack and caramelise under a very moderate grill. Remember these are only correct if the caramelisation is done slowly.

93

With an Oven

A miniature hunter's pot
How to cook sprats
Whiting and tomato pie
Rock salmon pie
Cheese puffs
Sardine rolls
Cheese croissant bake
The parcel cooking of one-portion foods
Sausages which never burst
Kidneys in the manner of French butchers
Pish-pash
Corned beef hash
Ham and cheese bake
Sausage rolls
Stuffed tomatoes
Stuffed courgettes
Stuffed mushrooms
Vegetable pie
Sauté of potatoes with onions
Jacket baked potatoes
Potato bake with shrimps
Potato eggs

Potato Macaire
Spinach and cheese noodles
Cheat pizzas
Adriatic rice
Italian crostini
Baked banana
Baked apples
Dried apricots and prunes
Baked apple charlotte
Baked Viennese omelette
Fruit juice rice pudding
Yorkshire parkin
Gran's hot buns and sugar glaze
Mum's yeastless quick bread
Herby breads
Bun pudding
Saindoux

A MINIATURE HUNTER'S POT

A meal in itself.

2 buttered slices of white bread cut from a thin sliced sandwich loaf

Half a small pack of Primula processed cheese slices

4 oz (100 g) onion peeled and sliced as thinly as possible

1 pint (600 ml) boiling water

1 meat cube

Salt

Black pepper

Halve buttered slices and slap one butter side downwards, onto the base of a small ovenproof casserole. Separate the sliced onion by pushing out the rings, then scatter one-third over bread. Season lightly with salt and pepper. Halve and lay on one-third of processed cheese slices and repeat twice more, thus finishing with bread on top. Put all your weight on this to press down very strongly. Make a hole with a wooden spoon handle or similar, at centre and right through to base.

Blend water and crumbled meat cube in a jug or even a teapot. Stand on a chair and from this height direct the stream of fluid into the central hole until the pressed-down mass shifts and rises to the top. Put uncovered in the oven at Gas Mark 2 (300°F, 150°C) and leave undisturbed for at least 1 hour or until an excavated bit of onion is completely tender. Ladle into a bowl. Eat rather than drink.

HOW TO COOK SPRATS

Wash, wipe and lay these little fish, head to tail on a dry baking sheet and bake on the middle shelf at Gas Mark 4 (350°F, 180°C) for 10 minutes. They are rich in oil, and this provides sufficient lubrication without any help from you.

WHITING AND TOMATO PIE

8 oz (225 g) whiting, topped and
    tailed weight
4 oz (100 g) tinned tomatoes
1 teacupful of soft breadcrumbs
1 tbsp (1 × 15 ml spoon)
    Worcestershire sauce
Salt
Black pepper
2 oz (50 g) butter or Gold

Steam the fish for 8 minutes over boiling water and under a lid. Cool, then remove all the skin and bone and flake the fish into a bowl. Add a light seasoning of salt and black pepper and Worcestershire sauce. Mix well. Rub base of a small pie dish with a nut of chosen fat. Put in a layer of the flaked fish. Cover with chopped tomatoes and a moistening of the tin's fluid. Repeat. Then melt remaining chosen fat in a very small pan and work in the breadcrumbs. Spread over the contents of the pie dish. Bake in the oven Gas Mark 4 (350°F, 180°C) for 20 minutes and serve piping hot.

ROCK SALMON PIE

8 oz (225 g) skinned rock salmon
    (ask fishmonger to remove the
    central bone for you)
½ oz (10 g) dripping (bought or
    home-accumulated)
1 teasp (1 × 5 ml spoon)
    Worcestershire sauce
Salt
Black pepper
1 medium tomato
1 slice of bread

Rub a scrap of dripping over base and side of a very small pie dish. Season the fish with salt and pepper. Cut into 1 inch (2.5 cm) pieces. Place half in the little dish, cover with a sliced tomato and moisten with half the Worcestershire sauce. Then repeat. Melt remaining dripping in smallest pan. Stir in crumbled bread slice with crust removed. Brown very lightly, then turn over pie dish contents. Pat down and bake on middle shelf at Gas Mark 4 (350°F, 180°C) for 15 minutes to a maximum 20 minutes.

CHEESE PUFFS

Puff paste trimmings
12 × ½ inch (1.25 cm) thick 1 inch (2.5 cm) wide fingers of Gruyère, Emmenthal or just ordinary moist Cheddar cheese
A little English mustard
A little top-of-the-milk

Roll out the puff paste ¼ inch (5 mm) thick and cut out 12 rectangles measuring 2 inch (5 cm) wide and 4½ inch (11.25 cm) long. Brush the edges all round with the top-of-the-milk. Lay down a finger of chosen cheese centrally on each and spread lightly with mustard. Fold each one up like a little parcel. Lay widely spaced on a flat baking sheet, which has been rinsed under the cold tap and the surplus water just shaken off as this helps the paste to puff up. Brush each little parcel with top-of-the-milk and bake one shelf above centre at Gas Mark 5 (375°F, 190°C) until well browned and risen. Thus you give the melting cheese inside a proper chance to become deliciously gooey.

Eat while piping hot, so serve in a folded napkin, or, if wishing to serve later, under-bake slightly to reheat at a low temperature when required.

SARDINE ROLLS

These are made in exactly the same way as Cheese Puffs, using boned sardines instead of fingers of cheese.

1 small tin Marie Elisabeth sardines in oil
Jus-rol puff paste
A little wine vinegar
A little top-of-the-milk
White pepper

Prepare the sardines by slipping a small knife under the broad end of each and thus open it and lay it out flat. Remove the tail and spine bone. Moisten each little fish with a few drops of wine vinegar. Season with white pepper. Then fold each fish up again.

99

Then follow the instructions given for Cheese Puffs but make the puff paste rectangles 5 inch (12.5 cm) long. Serve piping hot.

CHEESE CROISSANT BAKE

We did this originally to use up stale croissants. Now we make real or substitute ones because of the demand for this simple dish.

2 stale croissants
A generous ½ pint (300 ml) milk
1 oz (25 g) soft, white crumbs
1½ oz (40 g) grated hard cheese
   (like mousetrap)
2 No 3 eggs
Salt and pepper
A very little butter or Gold
1 (optional) thin slice of
   processed cheese from a small
   pack

Rub the butter over the base and sides of a small heat-resistant dish which is just large enough to accommodate the croissants. Place these on buttered surface. Heat milk until just warm – no more, please. Whip the eggs up lightly with a pinch of both salt and pepper, whip in the grated cheese and pour on the milk while still whipping. Pour back and forth from pan to bowl three times, then pour slowly over the croissants. Optionally cut the cheese slice into fingers and float these on top. Bake uncovered at Gas Mark 5 (375°F, 190°C) on middle shelf for exactly 7 minutes. Reduce heat to Gas Mark 3 (325°F, 160°C) and continue baking until custard is just creamily set.

THE PARCEL COOKING OF ONE-PORTION FOODS

This method enables the live-aloner to cook a single piece of meat, fish or poultry in its own sauce or juices. The basic requirement is a roll of Alcan Foil. Also have a little bottle of oil available and any pastry brush or paint brush, providing the latter has been thoroughly sterilised in boiling water beforehand. Use to brush the central area of a 12 inch (30 cm) square of foil lightly with oil to prevent the food sticking. Place the chosen ingredients inside. Draw up foil at top and bottom. Make a tiny double fold to lock together. Fold over the ends equally securely. Bake on a flat metal surface like a baking sheet, or a

100

meat tin, and when cooked just take to table, unwrap and trundle the ready sauced item onto a heated plate.

Chicken portion
Season the chicken lightly with salt and black pepper. Set in the centre of the oiled foil. Add 1 rounded tablespoon (1 × 15 ml spoon) of sliced mushrooms and their stalks, 1 tablespoon (1 × 15 ml spoon) top-of-the-milk or single cream. Draw up foil as explained and bake for 25 minutes if a leg and thigh portion at Gas Mark 4 (350°F, 180°C) but only 20 minutes if just a wing portion.

Pork Fillet
Lay a 6 inch (15 cm) long piece of pork fillet down centrally on the oiled foil. Peel and slice 1 small sweet apple. Strew all over fillet. Scatter a single leaf of crumpled dried sage over apple. Moisten with 2 tablespoons (2 × 15 ml spoons) cider, season lightly with salt and black pepper, then fold up and bake at Gas Mark 4 (350°F, 180°C) on the middle shelf for 25 minutes if a slim piece of fillet, 30 minutes if a fat one.

Gammon Rasher
Nick the rind on a thick gammon rasher at 1 inch (2.5 cm) intervals down the length using a pair of scissors. Lay rasher on prepared foil, lay a single round of tinned (or fresh) pineapple on top. Moisten with 1 tablespoon soy sauce and 2 tablespoons cold water. Fold up and bake on the middle shelf at Gas Mark 5 (375°F, 190°C) for 20 minutes.

Liver and Bacon
Lay 5–6 oz (135–175 g) ½ inch (1.25 cm) thick slice of liver onto the oiled foil surface. Cover with one or two rashers of de-rinded streaky bacon. Cover with one thinly sliced, cold cooked potato. Season lightly with salt and pepper and flick a dessertspoon of oil overall. Fold up and bake middle shelf of oven at Gas Mark 4 (350°F, 180°C) for 15 minutes.

Cod Steak
Lay 6 oz (175 g) cod steak on oiled foil surface. Brush top of cod steak with a little oil. Season lightly with salt and pepper. Moisten with 1 tablespoon (1 × 15 ml spoon) tomato sauce mixed with 2 tablespoons (2 × 15 ml spoons) milk. Fold up and bake at Gas Mark 4 (350°F, 180°C) middle shelf for 16 minutes.
  Any fish steak of similar size may be so treated.

Monkfish Steak

Spread 6 oz (175 g) monkfish steak liberally on both sides with parsley butter (Basics, p. 24). Lay on oiled foil. Set an extra cherry-sized piece of parsley butter on top, season lightly with salt and black pepper. Fold up and bake at Gas Mark 4 (350°F, 180°C) middle shelf for 18 minutes.

Plaice

Use a 10 oz (275 g) plaice cleaned and with head removed and tail chopped off. Set fish, white side uppermost, on oiled piece of foil measuring 12 inch (30 cm) × 15 inch (37.5 cm). Cover with thin slices cut from a firm good-sized tomato. Spread fairly thickly with garlic butter (Basics, p. 24). Close the foil up and bake middle shelf at Gas Mark 4 (350°F, 180°C) for 20 minutes.

When feeling specially self-indulgent, scatter 2 oz (50 g) shrimps over the plaice, then lay on the tomatoes and finally spread with garlic butter.

SAUSAGES WHICH NEVER BURST

Forget altogether that complete nonsense about pricking sausages with a fork before cooking. Just undo them from their plaited bundle. Heat about 2 oz (50 g) of clean dripping in an ordinary meat baking tin over an ordinary gas ring or electric hot plate. When runny, turn the sausages, all joined together, in the liquefied dripping. Cook on the centre shelf at Gas Mark 4 (350°F, 180°C) for 15 minutes. Turn them over in the tin and continue for a further 10 minutes and only then snip them apart. You will find that none have burst.

KIDNEYS IN THE MANNER OF FRENCH BUTCHERS

2 lamb's kidneys still enclosed in their fat jackets of suet
2 good-sized firm tomatoes
1 × 8 inch (20 cm) length of bread cut from a fairly narrow French 'flute' or stick
Salt
Black pepper
English mustard (optional)

Put kidneys into a small meat baking tin and bake at Gas Mark 4 (350°F, 180°C) for 45 minutes or until most of the suet has melted into pan and only a thin, crisp, brown, fatty overcoat remains. Cut each kidney into four slices and spread these out. Cut the tomatoes into eight slices and spread these out. Sprinkle lightly all over both with salt and preferably black pepper.

Slice through the bread down

to the base crust but on no account cut right through. The base crusts should be like hinges when you have made the eight incisions. Slot a kidney slice alternated with a tomato slice into all cuts. Close up so far as you can, return to the oven under a light covering of Alcan Foil for about 4 minutes to make all piping hot. Optionally each slice of kidney can be spread with a little made English mustard.

PISH-PASH

A very pleasant and filling main course casserole.

1 leg and thigh chicken portion
4 oz (100 g) rice
¾ pint (450 ml) milk
1 large peeled onion
Salt
Pepper

Divide the chicken portion into four. Sprinkle a little of the raw rice over base of a small, lidded casserole. Slice onion finely and scatter about a quarter over the rice. Lay in one piece of chicken, season with salt and pepper and repeat until all dry ingredients are used. Pour on the milk and if this does not fully cover casserole's contents, then add a little more until it does. Cover with lid or piece of Alcan Foil and bake in the oven at Gas Mark 4 (350°F, 180°C), middle shelf for 30 minutes. Check it and continue to cook if rice has not become just moist, but with surplus fluid absorbed. Taste and if not fully cooked to *al dente*, continue for a further 15 minutes.

Note

Any left-overs may be moistened with a little extra milk and re-heated in a saucepan while stirring over a low to moderate heat.

CORNED BEEF HASH

4 oz (100 g) corned beef
4 oz (100 g) peeled onions
2 oz (50 g) dripping or real lard
4 oz (100 g) cold cooked cabbage
Salt
Black pepper
5 oz (135 g) cold, cooked
    potatoes
Plenty of bottled tomato sauce

Crumble the corned beef into a roomy bowl. Melt the dripping in a frying pan and fry the thinly sliced onions over a very low heat until soft, making sure they do not crisp up and brown, which they will do if you try to hurry this process. Tip onions onto corned beef. Chop up cabbage and rough-cut the potatoes into coarse dice. Add to the corned beef and sprinkle lightly with salt and black pepper. Pour on at least half the bottle of tomato sauce. Scrub your hands and plunge them in to work up the ingredients to a moist well-blended mixture.

Use the remaining dripping from onion-frying to rub over base and sides of an ordinary meat baking tin. Turn in the hash and pat down evenly. When required bake at Gas Mark 4 (350°F, 180°C) under a light covering of Alcan Foil for 30 minutes.

Serve in fat wedges, with or without a fried egg on the top of each.

HAM AND CHEESE BAKE

2 × ½ inch (1.25 cm) thick slices
    of white or brown bread
Butter or Gold
3 oz (75 g) Mozzarella or Bel
    Paese cheese sliced extremely
    thinly
2 oz (50 g) very thinly sliced
    cooked ham, prosciutto or
    Parma ham

Spread base and sides of a small pie dish with Gold or butter. Spread the bread slices similarly and cut in halves. Then lay down one layer slightly overlapping in prepared dish. Cover with half the chosen cheese slices. Cover with the remaining bread slices, then

Black pepper
4 tbsps (4 × 15 ml spoons) milk

with the remaining cheese. Sprinkle lightly with black pepper, splash with milk and bake on middle shelf of oven at Gas Mark 6 (400°F, 200°C) until top cheese begins to turn colour (approx 12 minutes). Lay on chosen ham, turn oven down to Gas Mark 4 (350°F, 180°C) to heat through for a maximum of 4 minutes. Serve immediately.

SAUSAGE ROLLS

8 oz (225 g) pork sausage-meat
Bought frozen puff paste
  (Jus-rol)
Flour
Cold water
A little top-of-the-milk

Sausage rolls are made in long strips – not singly, as this just about trebles your work. Begin by rolling out the pork sausage-meat on a lightly floured board or working surface. Roll it out of your way.

Re-dust the surface with flour and roll out the pastry paste to a strip of matching length, 5 inch (12.5 cm) wide and ⅛ inch (3 mm) in thickness. Trim each side of the length off neatly. Lay the long sausage down the length about ¼ inch (5 mm) from the nearer lengthwise edge. Wet all edges with cold water. Roll up the paste to enclose sausage-meat and roll it over until the join comes underneath. Press the whole strip out gently to make all even. Prick down the length with a fork at approximately 1 inch (2.5 cm) intervals. Brush the top and sides with top-of-the-milk and lop off with a sharp knife into separate lengths of 3½ inch (8.75 cm). Thus you have the added

105

advantage of proper sausage rolls with sausage-meat right up to each end! Lay them fairly wide apart on a lightly floured baking sheet. Bake high up in the oven at Gas Mark 6 (400°F, 200°C) until well risen and puffy. Reduce the heat to Gas Mark 3 (325°F, 160°C) and continue baking until the pastry is richly browned, thus giving (a) sufficient heat for the paste to rise properly and (b) sufficient time at lower temperature for the sausage-meat to be cooked completely.

Note
If preferred, sausage rolls may be slightly under-baked giving you the chance of re-heating them later without overcooking.

STUFFED TOMATOES

2 good-sized, firm tomatoes
1 oz (25 g) scalded unskinned
    mushrooms and their stalks
    chopped finely
1 No 3 egg
½ oz (10 g) butter or Gold
1 very small onion
Salt
Black pepper

Place chosen fat in a small pan. When hot and melted, stir in grated raw onion and cook over moderate heat for 3 minutes, stirring occasionally. Stir in chopped mushrooms and cook for 3 more minutes.

Slice small 'lids' off the tops of the tomatoes. Hollow out the pips and flesh, leaving only a supporting base and wall of flesh. Beat up the egg and draw in mushroom mixture. Season lightly with salt and black pepper. Stuff into tomatoes, replace little lids and stand in a small, shallow heat-resistant dish. Run a very mean layer of water around. Bake for 25 minutes at Gas Mark 4–5 (350°–375°F, 180°–190°C) on middle shelf of your oven.

STUFFED COURGETTES

1 lb (450 g) topped tailed courgettes

2 tbsps (2 × 15 ml spoons) tomato coulis or bottled tomato sauce

2 oz (50 g) fine soft breadcrumbs

1½ oz (40 g) Gruyère cheese

1½ oz (40 g) Parmesan cheese

1 rounded tbsp (1 × 15 ml spoon) freshly milled parsley heads

2 oz (50 g) mushrooms and their stalks

Salt

Black pepper

A few flakes of butter and a little extra for the butter dish plus 1 tbsp (1 × 15 ml spoon) melted butter

Steam the courgettes until just soft when pinched gently. Remove and cool. Split all lengthwise, scoop out soft pulp carefully into a roomy bowl and arrange the cases side by side on a shallow heat-resistant dish suitable to carry to table.

Mash down the courgette flesh, work in half the cheeses, the parsley heads, finely chopped mushrooms and their stalks, a light seasoning of salt and pepper and work up to a paste with tomato coulis or tomato sauce. Mix remaining cheeses with breadcrumbs, work half into the courgette paste, pack into the cases, sprinkle the remainder over the tops and moisten these with drips of melted butter. Bake at Gas Mark 3 (325°F, 160°C) for 15 minutes just before service.

STUFFED MUSHROOMS

Use only large flat mushrooms, ideally field mushrooms.

2 very large mushrooms

¼ pint (150 ml) simple white sauce (Basics, p. 24)

1 oz (25 g) grated hard cheese

1 oz (25 g) soft brown or white crumbs

1 very small grated onion or shallot

Salt and pepper

A scrap of butter

Butter the base of a small heat-resistant container. Remove the mushroom stalks. Set mushrooms on buttered base. Stir onion, chopped stalks and three-quarters of the cheese into the white sauce. Season with salt and black pepper to taste. Pour over mushrooms to mask completely. Mix remaining cheese with crumbs. Scatter this over the top and bake at Gas Mark 4 (350°F, 180°C) on the centre shelf for 15 minutes.

VEGETABLE PIE

A dish from left-overs.
2–3 cold cooked potatoes
Salt
Black pepper
3 tbsps (3 × 15 ml spoons) finely
    chopped onions
Transparently thin slices of
    ordinary Cheddar cheese
¼ pint (150 ml) top-of-the-milk
1 small nut of butter

Rub butter over base and sides of a little pie dish. Arrange a layer of sliced potatoes and season lightly with salt and pepper. Sprinkle over a third of the chopped onions. Cover with a layer of paper-thin cheese slices. Repeat twice more. Then finish with an extra layer of potatoes. Moisten all over with the top-of-the-milk. Season once more. Dot a few extra flakes of butter on top. Cover with a lid or Alcan Foil and bake at Gas Mark 3 (325°F, 160°C) for 30 minutes. Remove covering and continue to bake until potato topping is lightly browned.

SAUTE OF POTATOES WITH ONIONS

8 oz (225 g) old or new potatoes
1 small onion
Salt
Pepper
Dripping or lard

Slice the potatoes ⅛ inch (3 mm) thick. Spread just enough chosen fat over the base of an ordinary meat baking tin to coat it. Lay half the sliced raw potatoes in the tin. Peel and grate the onion on the coarse side of a grater. Sprinkle thickly over the potatoes in the pan. Cover with remaining sliced potatoes. Season with a sprinkling of both salt and preferably black pepper. Bake on lowest shelf of the oven at Gas Mark 2 (300°F, 150°C) when cooking some other slow cooking item above.

108

JACKET BAKED POTATOES

Use only large ones. Scrub very thoroughly to remove all soil and other possible impurities. (We have seen the Southern Irish sprinkle artificial fertiliser thickly down the rows and then plonk the seed potatoes on top.)

Place on the bars of the middle shelf and bake at Gas Mark 5 (375°F, 190°C) for between 1 hour and 1¼ hours according to size. The potato is cooked when it yields to slight pressure through the skin. Remove, halve lengthwise, season with salt and pepper, then spread with butter, Gold, garlic or any other herb butter.

POTATO BAKE WITH SHRIMPS

1 × 7–8 oz (200-225 g) old potato
1½ oz (40 g) shelled shrimps or any cooked, flaked fish
1 rounded teasp (1 × 5 ml spoon) finely chopped parsley
½ oz (10 g) grated hard cheese ends
Salt
Black pepper
2 tbsps (2 × 15 ml spoons) milk
1 smallest separated egg yolk
½ oz (10 g) butter or Gold

Note
Eat the lot, including the crisp skin.

Bake the potato as described. When cool enough to handle, cut off the top. Scoop out the flour of potato, leaving only ¼ inch (5 mm) thick wall inside. Mash the potato and beat in the shrimps or other flaked fish, egg yolk, milk, half the grated cheese, parsley and chosen fat. Stuff potato with this mixture doming it up a little on top. Sprinkle with remaining cheese. Return the 'lid'. Stand on a heat-resistant plate and return to the oven middle shelf, Gas Mark 5 (375°F, 190°C), for 8–10 minutes to heat through.

POTATO EGGS 1

1 largest possible egg
10 oz (275 g) old potato
1 tbsp (1 × 15 ml spoon) grated hard cheese ends
A walnut of butter
Salt
Pepper

Bake the potato as described. When cool enough to handle, cut off a 'lid' and scoop out the floury potato to leave a hollow inside. Drop in the egg, sprinkle lightly with salt and pepper, add the cheese and butter and replace the 'lid'. Bake at Gas Mark 4 (350°F, 180°C) middle-shelf for 15–20 minutes

109

or until the egg white inside is just nicely set but the yolk is still very moist.

POTATO EGGS 2

1 × 8 oz (225 g) well scrubbed
    old potato
1 No 3 egg
1 eggsp (1 × 2.5 ml spoon) curry
    powder
1 oz (25 g) Gold
Salt
Black pepper to season
1 flat teasp (1 × 5 ml spoon)
    milled or chopped fresh
    parsley heads
1 large egg
1 scant teasp (1 × 5 ml spoon)
    masala paste (from any Indian
    or Pakistani store)

Bake the potato as described. Slice off a lid thinly and lengthwise. Scoop the floury potato into a bowl and mash down with Gold, parsley, curry powder and seasoning. Use as much as possible to re-line hollowed potato case, leaving sufficient room at centre for the raw egg. Break this in. Add a light seasoning of salt and pepper. Cover and dome up slightly with remaining potato mix and return to oven at Gas Mark 4 (350°F, 180°C) on middle shelf for 12–15 minutes if still warm or up to 20 minutes when left to become cold.

POTATO MACAIRE

This is an excellent way of using jacket-baked potatoes.

1 × 8 oz (225 g) old potato
1 de-rinded rasher No 4 cut back
    or streaky bacon
1 dessertsp (1 × 10 ml spoon)
    milled parsley heads
Black pepper
Salt
A little melted butter

Bake the potato as described. When cool enough to handle, split lengthwise and scoop out all the flour into a bowl. Mash finely, then fold in the following: the bacon cut into small dice and fried briskly in a small, dry pan, until the juices run; the parsley heads, black pepper to season and possibly a little salt (used sparingly because of the saltiness of all bacon these days). Mix well into mashed potato, return to case and smooth off doming slightly. Use a little melted butter to brush over

110

before browning under a moderate grill or baking in the oven one shelf above centre Gas Mark 5 (approx 375°F, 190°C) until well browned.

SPINACH AND CHEESE NOODLES

4 oz (100 g) shell noodles
4 oz (100 g) from tin of spinach purée
2 slices of processed cheese
1 oz (25 g) Gold or butter
Salt
Black pepper

Put noodles into fast-boiling water, re-raise to boiling and bubble for 12 minutes. Drain very thoroughly. Rub base and sides of a small pie dish with chosen fat. Put half the noodles onto buttered base, cover with quarter of the spinach, season with nutmeg and pepper, lay a single sheet of cheese in strips on top and repeat. Finish with a few flakes of extra Gold and bake in the oven at Gas Mark 4 (approx 350°F, 180°C) on middle shelf for 20 minutes or until bubbling and lightly browned on top.

CHEAT PIZZAS

½ inch (1.25 cm) thick slice of bread with crust left on
2 oz (50 g) either Mozzarella or Bel Paese cheese
1 chopped anchovy fillet
4 stuffed sliced green olives
1 medium tomato or drips from a bottle of tomato sauce
Oil
Black pepper
½ teasp (1 × 2.5 ml spoon) dried oregano or wild thyme

Shake 1 tablespoon (1 × 15 ml spoon) oil over bread slice. Dot with flakes of chosen cheese. Intersperse with bits of anchovy fillet, then with olive slices, cover with tomato slices or shake little blobs of tomato sauce over. Flick oil on top liberally so that all shines. Bake in oven one shelf above centre at Gas Mark 6 (400°F, 200°C) for 5–7 minutes – just take out when all bubbles and is lightly browned.

111

ADRIATIC RICE (Risi-e-Bisi)

A speciality in and around Venice where pastas give place to rice dishes.

4 oz (100 g) Patna rice
1 pint (600 ml) good meat bone stock (ideal) or substitute 1½ chicken cubes dissolved in boiling water
1 rasher of de-rinded diced streaky bacon
1 very small, peeled diced shallot or onion
1 oz (25 g) butter or oil
3 oz (75 g) cooked fresh (ideal) or substitute frozen peas
Salt
Black pepper

Melt butter or heat oil in a small frying pan. When this begins to sizzle, fry prepared onion or shallot for 1 minute, add rice and stir/turn until well-impregnated and slightly yellow. Turn into a small, lidded heat-resistant container. Add stock or substitute. Cover and cook on middle shelf, Gas Mark 5 (375°F, 190°C) for approximately 40 minutes or until rice is cooked and grain-separate and there is only just enough fluid remaining to make it rather sloppy. Fry and scrape in bacon, the juices and the peas and stir/turn very thoroughly. Taste and correct seasoning with salt and black pepper.

Note
You can also add to this basic mixture 2 oz (50 g) of shelled shrimps just heated in 1 tablespoon (1 × 15 ml spoon) oil in a small pan.

ITALIAN CROSTINI

6 × 2 inch (5 cm) squares of crustless bread cut a scant ½ inch (1.25 cm) in thickness
2½ fluid oz (75 ml) milk
1 No 4 egg
Hot oil in pan or deep-fryer
2½ fluid oz (75 ml) thick simple white sauce (Basics, p. 24)
1½ oz (40 g) finely chopped unskinned mushrooms and their stalks

Beat egg with milk. Slide bread squares through to impregnate and fry immediately in hot oil until puffy and golden brown. Drain and set on a flat heat-resistant dish. Stir prepared mushrooms and garlic into white sauce, season to taste with salt and pepper. Spread over the little squares. Strew cheese equally on tops, drip on melted

1 heaped tbsp (1 × 15 ml spoon)
grated cheese
½ oz (10 g) butter or Gold
¼ clove of crushed garlic
Salt and pepper

butter or Gold and bake high in oven Gas Mark 6 (400°f, 200°C) for approximately 6–8 minutes until cheese has bubbled and browned.

BAKED BANANA

This must be the easiest pudding in the world to make.

1 banana
Soft brown sugar
Lemon juice
Cream

Put the banana onto the rack of the middle shelf at Gas Mark 4 (350°F, 180°C). Bake until the skin is completely black. Remove to find banana is cooked, juicy and soft. Nick the top so as to pull off a strip of skin right down the length. Fold back both sides of the skin, sprinkle on soft brown sugar, moisten with a squeeze of lemon juice and serve with single cream for everyday occasions, whipped double cream or whipping cream for special ones.

BAKED APPLES

Only make these when you can obtain large Bramley cooking apples. Excavate each apple's core with a potato peeler, if lacking an apple corer. With a sharp knife cut a split round the centre of each apple, just going through the skin and making what is tantamount to a meridian line all around. This makes the apple skin contract, not burst out higgledy-piggledy, enabling you to jack off the top half in one piece and thus serve the fruit in its own natural juices which the water has drawn out.

Fill the central cavity with soft brown sugar, or thick honey, or mix either with a rounded teaspoon (1 × 5 ml spoon) roughly chopped sultanas and then use. Stand a single prepared apple in an individual Pyrex sundae bowl or similar type Pyrex dish containing 2 tablespoons (2 × 15 ml spoons) cold water. Bake in the oven at Gas Mark 4 (350°F, 180°C) middle shelf for 40–50 minutes.

Hand extra honey or soft brown sugar.

113

DRIED APRICOTS AND PRUNES

Wash chosen dried fruits in cold water to remove any dust and then tumble into a roomy bowl. Cover with strained, cold Indian tea and leave for at least 12 hours or until swollen and fairly soft. Place the fruit in a lidded heat-resistant container with just enough of the cold tea to cover. Stir in 2 hugely heaped tablespoons (2 × 15 ml spoons) soft brown sugar. When possible add a single strip of thinly cut lemon peel and cook for 40 minutes on a low shelf at Gas Mark 2 (300°F, 150°C).

Note

All the fresh fruits that are normally 'stewed' in England, taste entirely different and infinitely better if cooked in this way.

BAKED APPLE CHARLOTTE

Use the very smallest Pyrex pie dish for this.

1 small cooking apple
Jam
Suet from a packet
1 small teacupful of roughly crumbled white bread
1 small nut of butter

Peel the apple. Then cut it all up paper-thinly, slicing down one side until you reach the edge of the core, then turn and go on slicing paper-thinly until only the core remains. Rub the butter over the base and sides of a little pie dish. Put a ¼ inch (5 mm) layer of breadcrumbs on the base, then a ¼ inch (5 mm) layer of chosen jam. Cover with a quarter of the thinly sliced apples and scatter on a ¼ inch (5 mm) layer of suet. Repeat these layers until pie dish is full, finishing with a layer of crumbs. Bake at Gas Mark 4 (350°F, 180°C) middle shelf for 20–25 minutes or until bubbling at the edges and browned on top.

The whole mixture will have become a delectable goo with the jam and suet lubricating the crumbs and the apple turning to pulp – unless you fail to cut your slices extremely thinly.

BAKED VIENNESE OMELETTE

1 No 3 egg
1 tbsp (1 × 15 ml spoon) caster
  sugar
Pinch of salt
A little warmed apricot jam
1 flat tbsp (1 × 15 ml spoon)
  flour

Separate the egg. Blend yolk with sugar and whip hard until pale and thick. Whip in flour. Whip egg white to a very strong peak and fold gently into yolk mixture. Butter the base of 6–7 inch (15–18 cm) diameter heat-resistant dish. Turn in mixture. Bake at Gas Mark 5 (approximately 375°F, 190°C) until mixture sets lightly – about 15 minutes. Spread top very lightly with warmed jam. Slide spatula beneath and flip over. Dust with sifted icing sugar and serve fast.

FRUIT JUICE RICE PUDDING

3 oz (75 g) Patna rice
½ pint (300 ml) water
2 oz (50 g) caster sugar
½ pint (300 ml) Del Monte
  orange juice *or* fresh strained
  orange juice

Put rice and sugar onto the base of a smallish pie dish. Add mixed juice and water. Bake well below centre at Gas Mark 2 (300°F, 150°C) until fluids are almost completely absorbed. If you dislike that brown tarpaulin on top, cover with a small piece of Alcan Foil while baking.

Basically you cook this until it is the consistency you like best, but if the pudding becomes too dry, just stir in an extra tablespoon or two of both water and orange juice and heat through again for a maximum of 5 minutes.

115

YORKSHIRE PARKIN

6 oz (175 g) golden syrup
10 oz (275 g) Fowler's black
   treacle
8 oz (225 g) pure lard or butter
8 oz (225 g) well-sifted flour
1 pinch of salt
1 lb (450 g) coarse oatmeal
2 oz (50 g) soft brown sugar
2 oz (50 g) ground ginger
1 scant flat teasp (1 × 5 ml
   spoon) soda bicarbonate
3–4 fluid oz (90–120 ml) hot
   water

Heat treacle with syrup. Rub chosen fat into flour, then work in oatmeal, sugar and ginger and the soda stirred with a tablespoon (15 ml spoon) of cold water. Finally stir in hot water just until mixture flops idly from a lifted wooden spoon. Lay a fitting piece of buttered or oiled greaseproof in the base of a standard meat baking tin. Turn in mixture and level off. Bake one shelf below centre at Gas Mark 2 (300°F, 150°C) for 1¼ hours. Mark off into fingers or squares immediately.

When cold divide and store in an airtight tin to keep successfully for several weeks.

GRAN'S HOT BUNS WITH SUGAR GLAZE

These were 'treats' when Fanny was in the nursery. They are still!

6–8 currant buns
2 fluid oz (60 ml) milk
16 lumps sugar

Prod buns all over vigorously with a skewer. Melt sugar lumps in milk over a mere thread of heat. When completely dissolved arrange buns on a small baking sheet and drip sugared milk into those skewer holes. Use up every scrap, being sure to brush tops too. Slip into your small oven at about centre position and heat through at Gas Mark 2 (300°F, 150°C) until piping hot.

Eat immediately.

116

MUM'S YEASTLESS QUICK BREAD

1 lb (450 g) flour
1 hugely rounded teasp (1 × 5
  ml spoon) baking powder
Cold water

Sift flour with baking powder into a roomy bowl. Go to work with a knife gradually cut/stirring in sufficient cold water to make a firm dough. Cut into 2½ oz (60 g) pieces, roughly, just like rock cakes. Dump fairly widely spaced on a floured, flat baking sheet and bake at Gas Mark 5 (375°F, 190°C) one shelf above centre for approximately 15–20 minutes until faintly marked with beige on the knobbly tops. Do this immediately prior to eating these little breads. They are delicious while hot, revolting when cold. Take from the oven, wrap in a clean cloth to keep them warm and enjoy.

HERBY BREADS

Whatever herb is chosen the procedure is identical.

2 oz (50 g) butter or Gold
1 rounded dessertsp (2 × 5 ml
  spoons) fresh, finely-chopped
  chives *or* parsley heads *or* use
  mixed dill and parsley
Miniature Hovis loaves

Slice up each tiny loaf into ¼ inch (5 mm) thick slices *without cutting through the base crust.* Thus when completed, loaves open out like little fans but remain joined together at bases. Mash chosen fat with chosen herb or herb mixture and spread over each slice as far down as possible. Press all buttery slices together to restore shape. Wrap each in a small piece of Alcan Foil and, when required, heat through low down in the oven at Gas Mark 3 (325°F, 160°C) for about 5 minutes or until piping hot.

117

BUN PUDDING

2 stale currant buns, halved
   centrally
3 fluid oz (90 ml) milk
1 smallest possible egg
1 flat pinch powdered cinnamon
2 oz (50 g) chopped, peeled
   sweet apples
1 walnut-sized piece of butter
1 oz (25 g) soft brown sugar
1 oz (25 g) currants *or* seeded
   raisins *or* sultanas

Butter a small, shallow Pyrex dish, using half given butter. Set halved buns on base. Whip egg with milk. Mix sugar, cinnamon, chosen dried fruit and chopped apple together and sprinkle half this mixture over buns. Moisten with half the milk mixture. Then sprinkle on remaining fruit mixture and dot with remaining flakes of butter. Pour over remaining milk mixture and bake at Gas Mark 5 (375°F, 190°C) on middle shelf for 30 minutes, or until just golden brown on top.

SAINDOUX

This is invaluable for brushing waffle irons, griddles and *Croque M'sieu* and *Madame* irons to ensure a perfect surface on both sides of any coated item. It will keep for a very long time in ordinary domestic refrigeration.

The mixture originated in Brittany, home of the famous *Crêpes Dentelles*. The area abounds in *crêperies* where blackwheat flour is used for them and they are made on a griddle and spread with a little wooden skimmer.

2 lbs (900 g) raw, unsalted pork
   fat
2 raw No 3 egg yolks

Use a very sharp knife to cut fat from rind as closely as possible. Cut fat up roughly and place in an ordinary meat baking tin. Leave on the floor of the oven until rendered down or place on the bottom shelf-rack and do so at Gas Mark 1 (275°F, 140°C). Strain through an ordinary sieve. When cold beat very thoroughly with egg yolks and pack into a preferably stone jar. Cover with cling wrap and store in refrigerator. Do not attempt to freeze.

Part 2

Contents

In Your First Home   121
Kitchen Guidance for the Inexperienced   122
Soups   135
Hors d'Oeuvre   155
Fish   171
Eggs   191
Pastas   209
Main Course Dishes:
in a Slow-Cooking Pot   219
with Poultry   229
with Lamb and Beef   235
with Pork and Veal   249
Vegetables   255
Cheese   271
Puddings   283
Brunches and Sandwiches   305
Sunday and Holiday Teas   317
Beginning a Very Modest Wine Cellar   327

Dear Reader,

As you most certainly will know, recipes alone cannot make skilled cooks. We all need far more than just assemblies of ingredients and methods if we are to gain culinary confidence. At every stage along the route to proficiency everyone requires vital, basic knowledge. Therefore we believe it is the *how* of cookery that must be acquired as easily as possible from the moment we begin to cook.

There are two alternatives: either we find out by trial and error, which can prove both costly and time-wasting; or else we must find help and guidance from any cookery book which aims to be comprehensive.

We have scoured our records and memories for some of the professional expertise that has helped us immeasurably over the years. Some of our more modest gleanings are in this Part 2, in the chapter, Kitchen Guidance for the Inexperienced. Some more will be found in Volume Two for the family cook and, on a more advanced culinary level, in Volume Three for the ambitious cook.

Fanny and Johnnie

In Your First Home

This is primarily for those of you whose sole cooking experience up to now has been self-catering at universities or training colleges or with the scant amenities provided in bed-sitting rooms or tiny flats.

We see you as a couple setting up house for the first time, whether two young women, two young men, or a man and woman either married or just having a trial run together before deciding to marry and raise a family. We also assume, hopefully, that you both go out to work during the week. It is unlikely that you will both return simultaneously, so whoever is home first begins preparing the evening meals, leaving the weekends for your shared, simple entertaining and such advance preparations as you decide to do for the following week.

We also suspect your entertaining will centre on Saturday evening suppers and Sunday brunches with possibly a modest bottle or two of 'plonk' or a mixed drink, for which we give some suggestions. There are other drink mixtures in Part 1. We hope the recipes in Part 1 will also help when you are planning a hurried snack before going out again to a theatre, cinema or adult educational group, or conversely to subdue gnawing pangs when you come home afterwards.

Johnnie has also compiled a chapter on How to Begin a Very Modest Wine Cellar, showing how this can be done very well without an actual cellar.

121

Kitchen Guidance
for the Inexperienced

We draw a clear line of demarcation between what we call gadgets – the things you fall for at exhibitions and whose prime function thereafter is to nip your fingers in a kitchen drawer as you rummage for something really useful – and genuine kitchen aids: A Mouli Parsmint and a real cheese mill. The Parsmint is faster than the speed of light at milling herbs instead of wasting all that time chopping.

A cucumber slice because then you can slice up cucumbers swiftly and also cut paper-thin slices of potato for crisps or cheese or meat like the slivers used by the Japanese for beef or chicken *Sukiyaki*.

One professional Sabatier knife. These are costly. The blades range from 3 inch (7.5 cm) to 14 inch (35 cm). Just buy one with a 6–7 inch (15–18cm) blade because you can carve with it as well as cut the peel from an orange so successfully that you can remove the skin and pith together. Sabatier knives are all pointed at the tips, so chefs keep them in knife rolls made of felt, with corks on those tips.
  Never be bamboozled into spending good money on what is euphemistically called a bread knife, with a serrated edge. If you want to cut paper-thin bread and butter, stick to your Sabatier and never let anyone else get their hooks on it. The handles have little

patented flanges on them, which ensure they will never slip. You curve your little finger around the flange and are thus anchored by it securely.

If you invest in a joint of pork and hanker for super crackling, buy a Stanley knife – a decorator and handyman's tool – which we use to score pork rind faster and closer than any butcher we know can do it with a precious Sabatier knife.

'Snips' are not yet very well known. They are small, inexpensive and quite exceptional. Besides cutting through thick and thin wire, they combine the functions of meat and game secateurs, which cost a bomb, so that, provided your pair is kept spotlessly clean, it can be used both out of doors and in the kitchen.

A large rectangular casserole by Aubecq made of vitreous enamel fulfils a double purpose. It is a casserole, but also does super duty as a top-of-the-stove pan for boiling the few things which a good cook ever boils – like salt beef for a dish of boiled beef, carrots, onions and dumplings, or a small bacon joint. You can also boil corn-on-the-cob, kohlrabi, beetroot, globe artichokes and large Spanish onions, but all other vegetables are better steamed.

A deep-fryer can be replaced by the Aubecq casserole, or you can use a Pyrex one or any large saucepan. The displacement of oil is not really as horrendous as it first seems, for in no circumstances whatever must the oil come more than one-third up the chosen pan. Moreover, if using a saucepan with a handle, do be absolutely certain to turn that handle inwards, so that it can never project from the cooker top and thus cause terrible accidents.

With such a utensil you can make your own chips instead of contributing to the wealth of fish-and-chip shopkeepers or, worse still, that of the producer of frozen chips. You can also make your own crisps. We once did a test for our column in the *Daily Telegraph* on home-made versus shop-bought bags of crisps. This was *before* the price escalations of the past few years, yet when we made a giant dishful for the price of one small shop-bought bag we saw the light. Since then we have made our own.

Aim for Pyrex heat-resistant table and cooking ware: colourful, attractive designs and sensible shapes. These can all be used for cooking items and then be brought to table, thus saving washing-up.

Brushes are a pitfall for the unwary. There are two that are in constant use in a pastrycook's kitchen: a glazing brush for painting on anything from egg wash to jelly glazes and a 'sweeper' brush to clear up surplus flour. The glazing brushes sold in ordinary kitchen equipment shops are hard, prickly and soon moult their spikes, thus defacing the surface. Buy a paperhanger's brush for your sweeping operations (this costs very little in comparison with the professional 'sweeper' brush) and an ordinary soft 1 inch (2.5 cm) paint brush for glazing. Just be sure you sterilise both before using for the first time!

Metal meat batters are ideal for batting down veal, turkey or pork slices to turn them into *escalopes*. Such costly implements are for professionals. Do what we did for years: use an old flat-iron, paint it with rust remover, clean off meticulously and then dip the base into cold water to perform the same jobs far more cheaply and equally effectively.

An omelette pan should be made of solid iron, have steep sides and be given a special treatment when new, lest later on, something sticks on the base during use. Put ordinary rock salt into your new pan to a depth of ½ inch (1.25 cm). Set over lowest possible heat and leave undisturbed until it turns beige. Empty out and burnish the pan thoroughly with a clean cloth while it is still warm.

If you hanker for a Mouli Maxima Food Processor, which we say is like having an extra pair of skilled hands in the kitchen but which probably costs too much for you at present, even on HP, you can manage with a modestly priced Braun Multipractic. The manufacturers describe this as a 'blender-on-a-stick'. It makes super mayonnaise and can even be used in a cooking pot or pan. It has a space-saving wall bracket, mixing beaker and recipe leaflet.

There are several types of slow-cooking pot available, but we have found over the years that the Pifco Slow Cooker has proved itself very easy to use and startlingly economical with electricity. It can be left on all day and all night, cooking away gently in perfect safety while you are out at work or play. In some instances you fill it one evening and leave it on until you return the next evening when the contents will be ready to eat.

It has the added virtue of making excellent stock for soups, gravies or sauces, which can be cleared of grease in moments and used immediately instead of having to wait until cold (when the fat sets on top and can be cut away to the clear liquor underneath). You can even cook a creamy rice pudding in a slow cooker like ours, roast a chicken, bake a tongue (marvellous to press and slice for lunch box sandwiches or night starvation), or make a super oxtail casserole. You can steam a featherweight sultana or bread pudding, or a beef and mushroom one, make a dish of good old tripe and onions and even bake large scrubbed old potatoes – just for a few examples.

In some instances pre-preparation is necessary, such as using your frying pan to seal/fry meat or fish for casseroles after turning the divided pieces in seasoned flour. You must also be careful when you prepare casserole vegetables either to dice them or slice them thinly before adding to the pot.

If you have not already invested in a three-tier steamer, do so now. If you also have steamer dividers, you can steam, for example, two vegetables in one tier simultaneously.

Buy three offcuts of wood from a DIY shop, one measuring around 12 inch (30 cm) × 16 inch (40 cm) in hard wood to use as a chopping board; another about 6 inch (15 cm) square which must live in a polythene bag when not in use as a board for crushing garlic (thus it will not impart its pong to anything else); and a 14 inch (35 cm) length of 1½ inch (3.75 cm) diameter dowelling to use instead of a far more costly professional rolling pin. Then you can roll out pastry properly instead of, as with those daft Mrs Beeton jobs with handles on the end, putting all your weight on those handles instead of on the pin.

If you have kitchen units, get one or two pieces of plywood from your DIY shop to make dividers for a base unit. You can then file your metal baking sheets, Swiss roll tins, meat baking tins and Victoria sponge tins *upright* instead of groping about on a shelf for whichever one you want, which is invariably at the bottom of the pile. Johnnie made these for us. He also put a metal rail (of the kind fitted into men's compactums) across the top centre of another floor unit. With hooks attached, this enabled us to hang five saucepans in each unit, with kitchen implements, such as slices, spatulas, basting spoons and sieves on the side walls. The compactum rails pull out enabling cook to see at a glance which pan is wanted.

If you wipe out cake tins and bun tins with a dry cloth while they are still hot from the oven, they do not need washing. Similarly, rolling pins and omelette pans should really never need to be washed.

125

If you are at work all day, you will not be able to spend much time in the kitchen. If you are out of work, your culinary horizons will be restricted by lack of funds. Here at least we have removed temptation as far from you as possible by segregating our recipes into different categories, so that you do not have to read those which make your fingers itch to cook them but which you know you cannot manage yet. We know, because it has happened to us too, and it is wildly frustrating to ambitious cooks.

Many of you will not aspire to freezers yet or other costly items of kitchen equipment intended to make work easier. We have often found we can use substitutes which cost only what we call 'flumpence'. We came across an instance of this the other day when a friend produced a special tiered pot for raising the sprouting seeds which contribute so much to both salads and sandwiches.

The sprouting of such seeds is equally successfully achieved if you buy a small panel of ½ inch (1.25 cm) thick plastic foam, soak it thoroughly in cold water, lay it on an old tray, scatter your chosen seeds over it as evenly as possible and put into a dark cupboard. Just glance at it daily. When the seeds have sprouted – in around 5–7 days – just rinse the sprouts under plenty of running cold water to wash off the seed husks. You can grow any of the highly nutritious sprouting seeds on our list in this way. All are obtainable from Thompson & Morgan, London Road, Ipswich: salad alfalfa, Alphacoco sprouts (sweetest of all), Chinese bean sprouts (mung beans), English tea sandwich, spicy fenugreek, salad sprouts, sweet lupin sprouts (new), white mustard sprouts.

Good cooks thrive on lists. You can pick these people out in shops because they never hum and haw, holding up the assistant while they ask themselves, 'Now I wonder if I have forgotten something?' Stop speculating and make adequate lists.

Good cooks work to just inside their weekly budgets, leaving a little over for building up a store-cupboard.

If you want to be a good cook, always read an unfamiliar recipe from start to finish before you begin to cook. There is no other way of checking that you have all the ingredients and utensils available.

Good cooks are always highly selective buyers, so know not only your onions, but how to select the best and reject the sub-standard in any foodstuffs.

Smell your melons. When ripe they are heavily scented. No scent signifies little flavour, plus, in many instances, unripeness as well.

126

Test runner or French beans. If they snap when bent over, they will be fresh. If either type of bean makes no resistance when turned into croquet hoops, they will be old and weary.

Pea pods should pop open, because they are young and crisp when fresh.

Egg plants (aubergine) and pimentos should be hard and shiny. Never wrinkled or soft.

Globe artichokes should have green moist tips, not browned, shrivelled ones.

Frost bite can be detected easily in carrots, potatoes, turnips, cauliflowers and even scorzonera and radishes. All have a slightly opaque look when frost-bitten.

Choose heavy citrus fruits with brown blemishes on the skins; these are always the best.

Chestnuts are a pitfall for the unwary for they can look perfect and be brown right through inside. Just collect and return. We have never been refused replacement and you won't either unless you are aggressive.

Good cooks always have an eye to the main chance when driving or cycling around the countryside. In spring the ardent seeker may well be rewarded with not more than 3 inch (7.5 cm) long bracken sprouts. If picked and bound with cotton into little bunches, they taste like asparagus when properly cooked. Just place the bunches in a small pan, cover with cold water, raise to boiling fast, drain off water and repeat twice more. Then cook in slightly salted, boiling water until tender (approx 6–7 minutes), dunk in a little melted butter or Gold and eat from the fingers.

Summer gleanings include those best-of-all wild strawberries, the tiny ones which lurk under their pale leaves on shady banks. The flavour is superb and they make the most marvellous jam.

Autumn means mushrooms, best when gathered early – and without trespassing, please. Look for fields where horses graze. Store some mushrooms for winter use. Remove the stalks (use in casseroles and soups). Darn through the middle of the cups with fine string. Tie up taut between two nails and make sure no mushroom touches its neighbour. Leave, preferably where there is a light draught, until they are dry and shrivelled. Then pack into plastic or paper bags and hang up until needed. Soak in cold water and they will swell back to their original size ready for cooking.

Winter's first frosts mean crab apples, gathered in the hedgerows for making into jellies. If you have only a large window box, begin taking (even from under a fall of snow) heads of August-sown corn salad or romaine. It only grows to 6 inch (15 cm) high clumps of delicious leaves and replaces costly green salads in winter.

Real kippers undyed and full flavoured come from the Isle of Man where dyeing is not permitted. Because the colour, instead of being a bright ginger brown with dye is light beige, you, in England, will not buy them. Isn't it a pity?

Learn how to tell fresh fish from stale. The fresh ones have bright shiny scales, firm gills and clear eyes. Dim-scaled, rheumy-eyed fish are stale.

Poultry must have springy breastbones, smooth legs, white flesh and the soft little feather stumps that can only be found under the neck feathers of young birds. Pigeons with discoloured vents are not for you either. Only accept turkeys which are broad and thick with plump breasts, white flesh, smooth black legs and moist, supple feet.

Lamb must have firm, white kidney fat and firm, clear-looking flesh. A small leg will have a far finer flavour than a big one. Go for shoulders which are short and thick rather than large, flat ones. Fanny's father christened mutton 'divorce meat'. We agree.

Pork rind should be thin and delicate, the flesh firm and pale; when pressed, this should spring back.

If you are unaccustomed to buying pork spare ribs, make sure you ask for belly of pork ones. You buy them by the piece very cheaply and you can cut them right through into thin strips, each with a bone in it. Do not be deluded into buying the more costly, more meaty-looking ones. Most of that meat is fat, which melts down during the cooking. It can be used for frying, and when set it makes quite a good pastry paste, but it is superfluous for spare ribs.

With the high cost of oil these days, corn oil does very well for general frying. Olive oil must, however, be used for treating tins and moulds as corn oil tends to stick, particularly when used for the oiled greaseproof paper bases and side linings of cake and sponge tins. Walnut oil is regarded as the best by some connoisseurs for using in oil-based sauces. It is an acquired taste and pure French olive oil is preferred by many.

Butter, frying anything means frying very swiftly. Butter turns black otherwise. The ideal is to use equal quantities of oil and butter as this arrests any blackening, unless you burn the lot.

If you want to fake a grilled sole as we have seen done in a famous kitchen, just heat a very slender poker in the bars of a kitchen range, or over the gas. Fry the sole, turn it onto a wooden surface and criss-cross sear marks with the hot poker. Just remember to do both sides. We spotted one only faked on one side. Dramas followed.

When cleaning mussels, tug off all the beards, scrub under running water and discard any which are *open*. After cooking discard any which are *closed*.

Prawns (or shrimps) shell easily if you open each one out, push head and tail together and thus remove the shells.

To boil meat or poultry, place in a pan, pour on any *boiling* liquid and thereby seal the maximum flavour into whatever it is. Cover with cold water, raise slowly to boiling and simmer to *extract* all the flavour.

Chickens and turkeys, in particular, emerge from the oven beautifully browned when totally enclosed in Alcan Foil, provided the upper parts of bird are first brushed with a little butter, clean dripping or Gold, then sprinkled lightly with ground sea salt and, finally, wrapped up *loosely* with foil. Just remember that tightly wrapped items are *insulated* by this foil, lightly and loosely enclosed ones cook to perfection.

Pigeons are officially vermin. Put the cleaned carcases into a stock pot if you like, but only use the breasts for cooking. Make an incision in each breast to split the skin through the feathers. Chop off head, legs and wing tips. Then rip off skins and feathers easily.

To tenderise poultry while roasting, stuff with peeled raw potatoes. These will steam during roasting and thus tenderise the bird.

Sealing pieces of raw fish, meat, game, poultry or offal is a process designed to lock in the item's precious juices, so that these do not become dissipated in the liquor during casserole cooking. The old traditional method was to turn the pieces first in seasoned flour and then fry briskly before assembling for the actual cooking. Today, the real *Cuisine Nouveau* of the great Paul Bocuse of Lyons has introduced the less fattening and often more flavoursome method of sealing without flouring, adding vegetable purées to thicken thereafter.

To cut new bread, stand the blade of a really sharp knife (one which is certainly not saw-edged) in a tall jug filled with boiling water. Have ready some softened butter or Gold and a table knife for spreading your choice onto each slice. Cut off the end crust. Spread on the chosen fat. Take the knife from the water, shake off the drops and cut, holding the soft new loaf with the other hand but *not* pinching it. You can then slice bread paper-thinly without any difficulty. Return the knife to the water and repeat to obtain transparently thin slices of buttered bread.

This was an old parlourmaid's trick which we watched in a grandparent's house in the days when 'afternoon tea' was served in drawing-rooms. Today, after removing the crusts, we roll up the buttered bread into miniature Swiss roll shapes and layer in Tupperware boxes between waxed papers for picnics and parties.

Day-old French bread is a dead loss – it can only be made palatable if you prod what is left with a skewer, moisten sparingly under a cold tap, wrap loosely in Alcan Foil and heat through in the oven at Gas Mark 2 (approx 300°F, 150°C) for 8 minutes. Unwrap at table.

To have cold butter without refrigeration, dissolve 1 oz (25 g) saltpetre in 1 pint (600 ml) water and immerse the butter container so that the liquid comes two-thirds up the sides.

Cream-off-the-milk comes away best with a fountain pen filler or eye dropper. You may be surprised at how quick and effective this method is and how much cream you can filch.

Cream cheese for sweet uses is best made by pouring soured milk into a bowl, leaving it undisturbed until quite thick and then turning it into an ordinary sieve or *tamis*, first lined out with a few folds of butter muslin. Knot the opposing ends and hang up with the bowl underneath for the drips.

All cooks find peeling very strong onions makes them weep. Try this Spanish trick. Cut off the top and peel down to the root end but do not cut this off until last. We find it works every time. The same chef

130

told us – very solemnly – that putting onion skins on your head stops weeping too. It might explain why we called him 'Fawlty Towers'.

Put a peeled onion on a wooden surface. Slice down to about half-way, keeping the cuts extremely close to each other. Slice across these cuts at right angles. Then turn the onion on its side and slice across your own cuts, thus achieving very small dice. The same may be done with cucumbers and fat carrots. When you reach the end of your first slicings, just repeat as explained.

To obtain onion juice, grate peeled onion on the fine side of a grater. This produces a juicy pulp. Put into a small sieve and just press out the juice. Put the residue into the stockpot.

Large eggplants (aubergines) can be rather bitter. Extract such bitterness by slicing unpeeled into ⅙ inch (4 mm) rounds, scatter with salt and wipe off the brown bubbles which the salt draws out in about 25–30 minutes.

Chicory or *whitloof* as the Belgians call it (or *endive*, its French name) is also prone to taste bitter, which puts people off it altogether. To offset this, place trimmed heads in cold water and boil up with 3 lumps of sugar to every 1 lb (450 g) chicory. Throw water away after 10 minutes' boiling and use chicory as desired.

Green bananas make excellent Caribbean-type cocktail nibbles. Just peel, slice into ⅛ inch (3 mm) thick rounds, fry until golden brown and drain before serving.

Never refrigerate eggs because they are porous and will absorb the smells of any other foodstuffs in refrigeration.

Egg whites only whip to stiff perfection when they are no longer very fresh. When wanting really stiffly-whipped egg white, use 10-day-old eggs or egg whites which have been separated, covered and refrigerated for several days (if uncertain of their age).

Whatever recipe you are using, please drum into yourself that no experienced cook ever takes any cake from the oven before testing it with a skewer. It is madness to rely blindly on a stated time for baking to completion. Gas pressures vary, oven positions are rarely constant from one cooker to another, containers vary too, and if a cake is not completely cooked when taken out of the oven, it will sink in the middle and may be almost raw and certainly inedible. Instead, if the cake looks 'done', just draw it out on its shelf to enable you to

131

push a small skewer or metal knitting needle in about ½ inch (1.25 cm) off centre. If the skewer comes away cleanly, the cake will be ready but if small particles of moist cake are still clinging to it, push the shelf and cake back again and go on cooking.

If you do have a sunken cake, baked for a special occasion and with no time (or funds) to make another, just excavate the sunken, inedible centre very carefully until you reach properly cooked cake. If it is a fruit cake for an anniversary or such like, just fill the centre with almond paste and then ice over the lot. If it is a member of the sponge family, brush the cut centre and top of sponge with a little warm jam and then scatter liberally with milled and chopped nuts.

Nearly all baked confectionery should be transferred to wire cooling-racks until perfectly cold. In the case of fruit and Madeira cakes the surrounding paper lining should be scissored away to the top edge of the cake and then the cake can be turned upside down to become cold. When storing cakes, leave the lining papers around base and sides undisturbed. Wrap securely in Alcan Foil and then store in a tin.

Certain cakes like Angel Food and Devil Food Cakes are never transferred to cooling-racks but are put on the rack above the cooker (where the hot oven heat generates best) to cool down very slowly.

Good cooks bring home their bags of flour and *sift* them into the flour container ready to use later on. They also cut all the rinds from bacon, refrigerating these for flavouring in soups, casseroles and sauces. The de luxe version of this habit is to have a Bayonne ham hanging in your kitchen. Then you slice off a little piece and toss it into the pot. The difference both make is amazing.

Rolling up Swiss Roll sponges: 'Dust greaseproof paper with caster sugar and turn your sponge panel out on this.' We have the words beside us as we write and they are sheer poppycock! Hot sponge impacting on sugar melts it, so when you have spread your sponge and started to roll it up, the surface is torn to bits through sticking to the sugar, making it look frightful. Just dust the greaseproof lightly with flour, and as you do the rolling up bit, brush off the surplus flour and replace it with a little sifted sugar when the rolling is completed.

If using slices of citron peel on top of a plain Madeira cake, do remember not to arrange them on top of the raw mixture and then pop all into the oven to bake. As the heat penetrates, the mixture will melt until, by the time the cake is cooked, no trace of peel will remain on top – it will be found buried in the cake. Lay on the peel *only* when the top of the cake is *firm* to a light touch.

Sweet almonds pop out of their brown overcoats if first placed in a small bowl of boiling water and left 5 minutes.

Please understand chocolate before wasting money on it for cooking. There are two ways in which you can buy proper cooking chocolate: in 7 lb (3.5 kg) slabs, milk or plain, which is ridiculous for you, or as chocolate chips or drops which *are* professional cooking chocolate couverture and sold in 4 oz (100 g) and 5 oz (135 g) packs to meet the requirements of home cooks. Sweet-shop chocolate cannot be used successfully for an enormous number of chocolate items as it forms into granules in the pan and has to be thrown away.

Again, as you will discover later on in this book, cane sugar is an absolute *must* for using with cooking chocolate. We learned this to our cost when we made, in Southern Ireland, another in a very long line of Sachertortes. When it came to the icing, which we could make with one hand tied behind our backs, it simply turned to inedible grits because we added a syrup made with *beet* sugar. Avoid this at all times. It represents a kind of culinary halitosis or plague to cooks. Tate & Lyle supply cane sugars.

Place chocolate chips in a heat-resistant bowl. Put on lowest oven shelf at Gas Mark ¼ (approx 240°F, 110°C) and prop oven door open slightly with a crumpled piece of Alcan Foil. Leave until collapsed. Beat with a wooden spoon very vigorously indeed before using.

There are three different ways of imparting vanilla flavouring to sweet items such as cakes, biscuits, puddings and ices. We need say little about bottled vanilla essence or other bought essences. Suffice to share with you the observation made to us by a Cockney 'daily' with French origins. Said she, 'Them bottled essences, Madam, taste to me like the smell of a tatty actress's 'andbag. All cheap perfume and powder.'

Use vanilla pods. These are not cheap, but one lasts for many months and imparts the true flavour to sweet fluids. Heat the chosen liquid *slowly* with the vanilla pod immersed, thus giving the pod time to impart its delicious flavour and fragrance. Remove it, wipe it, and store it to use over and over again, thus justifying the initial expenditure. When at last the pod becomes exhausted for this purpose, chop it up into 1 inch (2.5 cm) pieces and bury these in a tin of sugar. If you do this with caster, icing or granulated sugars, they will be vanilla-flavoured, ready for you to use in all kinds of cake, biscuit and sponge making. Alternatively you can buy little envelopes of real vanilla-flavoured sugar which will do the same job for you. On the luxurious level, you can buy little pots of black powder, highly concentrated and marked on the bottles Sainte-Lucie *Le Vrai Vanille en Poudre*. Just add a pinch or two to whatever you are making.

Good cooks wash citrus fruits before using as a great many are painted with a preservative before shipping. You then save the peel, strew it over a baking sheet and put it on the floor of your oven until crisp and dry. Then put it through a clean coffee grinder or, failing this, slip between several folds of brown paper and roll it down to a powder. It is a marvellous flavouring for soups, sauces and casseroles and only needs storing in a small screw-topped jar.

Good cooks wash, dry and hoard cherry stones to use instead of pulses when baking pastry cases 'blind'. Better cooks make a fat pad of Alcan Foil to fit inside, remembering to brush the base and sides with oil so that it does not stick to the paste during baking. It saves time, labour and money.

Please hoard cold tea. It is ideal for oven-cooking dried fruits like prunes, peaches, apricots and pears with just soft brown sugar and a leaf of lemon peel. Cook covered, on lowest shelf at Gas Mark 2 (approx 310°F, 150°C) until fruit is swollen and deliciously tender. Just rinse chosen fruit before using as it is sometimes *very* dusty!

Apples will not burst when baked if a meridian line is first run around each with a sharp, point-ended knife. The skins will contract in the heat so that top halves can be jerked off and lower halves eased away from the flesh very easily.

If stamping rolled-out puff paste (bought or home-made) into individual shapes, do remember to dip the cutter into boiling water and shake off the drops before using. Put the shapes onto a flat baking sheet, which has been wetted under a cold tap. Lay over a piece of greaseproof or Alcan Foil. Bake for 10 minutes, brush with chosen glaze and discard covering. The combination of steaming baking sheet below and covering above draws all puff paste to its fullest height while baking.

Soups

Chervil soup (from two packets)
Emergency celery soup
A simple corn soup
Mixed vegetable soup
All-the-year-round vegetable soup
A meal-in-itself soup
Our slimmers' soup
Scots barley broth
Haricot bean soup
A stockpot even if you are out all day
Pea and pork soup
Potato soup
Simple chestnut soup
Egg soup
French quick soup
Mrs Marshall's remarkable quick soup
Watercress soup
Watercress and spring onion soup
Portuguese white cabbage soup
German grape harvest soup
Honeymoon soup
Courgette soup

Iced cucumber soup no 1
Iced cucumber soup no 2
Iced tomato soup
Iced health soup
Iced spinach and yoghurt soup
Iced beetroot soup
Iced lettuce soup
Spanish gazpacho
Cold shrimp and watercress cream soup
Iced beer soup
'Cheat' consommé en gelée
Herby bread
Garlic bread
Croûtons
Toast Melba
Pulled bread

Hurrying home on cold winter nights makes everyone's thoughts turn to brimming bowls of tum-warming, nose-tingling, flavoursome, piping hot soups. Many require a little time and patience to make; but we play a culinary game using our ingenuity, mix-matching some of the very best packet soups, blending a little of this one and a little of that and varying the fluids with which they are made up. Instead of just tap water we dilute ours with milk, cleared stock, water and a bit of crumbled bouillon cube, or sometimes add a little red or white 'plonk'-type cooking wine, or cider to enliven them still further. Just remember, when using either of these last, to stir them into the blended powders and heat the milk before adding.

Once they are made up and poured into heated bowls, soups benefit further from a spoonful of cream or a blob of whipped cream at top centre, with a sprinkle of herbs overall. They also fill you more and are enhanced by an accompanying bowl of small, diced, fried croûtons.

We offer you a packet soup example, hoping that by so doing you will be stimulated to creating your own mix-match brews from some of the very good packets available.

136

CHERVIL SOUP FROM TWO PACKETS

¼ pkt Dulfrance's chervil soup mix (*Potage de Cerfeuil*)
¼ pkt Dulfrance's asparagus soup mix (*Potage des Asperges*)
1¼ pints (750 ml) milk or ½ pint (300 ml) stock or water and half a chicken bouillon cube with ¾ pint (450 ml) milk or 4 fluid oz (120 ml) dry white 'plonk' wine or cider with milk or stock, to make total 1¼ pints (750 ml)

Empty given amounts of both soup powders into a bowl and blend with a little cold milk, wine or cider, just sufficient to stir to a thin paste. Heat remaining chosen fluid, pour onto soup mix, stir until blended, return to pan and stir over a moderate heat until thickened. Remember that if the soup is then too thick for you, just dilute with a little extra milk or stock, or stock substitute.

EMERGENCY CELERY SOUP

An emulsifier or liquidiser is needed.
1 small tin celery hearts
¾ pint (450 ml) milk
2 oz (50 g) grated hard cheese
Salt
Black pepper

Empty the contents of the tin into an emulsifier or liquidiser, switch on to full and reduce to pulp. Alternatively, rub through an ordinary sieve. Stir into milk, raise to boiling point, stir in cheese and seasonings until completely blended.

If possible run a little single cream over a dessertspoon (10 ml spoon) onto the surface of each filled bowl.

A SIMPLE CORN SOUP

1 small tin corn
1 pint (600 ml) thick white sauce
Pepper
Flick of caster sugar
A few flakes of softened butter
5 fluid oz (150 ml) single cream
5 fluid oz (150 ml) milk

Tip corn and its liquid into a pan, add the milk and simmer for 20 minutes. Emulsify or sieve into sauce. Stir over low heat until well-blended. Stir in butter flakes and cream, correct seasoning with pepper and sugar and serve piping hot.

MIXED VEGETABLE SOUP

A meal-in-itself soup made in a slow cooking pot.

4 thinly sliced savoy cabbage
  leaves
3 oz (75 g) scraped,
  coarse-grated carrots
3 oz (75 g) coarse-grated onions
1 fat, thinly-sliced leek
2 oz (50 g) dried peas soaked
  overnight
1 rounded dessertsp (1 × 10 ml
  spoon) concentrated tomato
  purée
1 flat teasp (1 × 5 ml spoon)
  crumbled, dried sage
4 bacon rinds
Optional garlic clove
1 rounded teasp (1 × 5 ml
  spoon) sea salt
1 mean flat teasp (1 × 5 ml
  spoon) freshly milled black
  peppercorns
1 faggot of herbs (*bouquet garni*)
Cleared pork, veal or beef bone
  stock

Wash prepared vegetables carefully. Pack down into a slow cooking pot. Insert herb bag, crushed garlic and bacon rinds. Strain and add soaked peas. Now fill with boiling stock to pot's capacity, replace lid and plug in to Low. Leave undisturbed from 8 a.m. to 6 p.m. or for any other convenient span of 10 hours. Excavate bacon rinds and herbs. Taste and make any desired adjustments with salt and pepper seasoning.

Please remember that only thinly sliced or coarsely grated vegetables cook satisfactorily over this period.

ALL-THE-YEAR-ROUND VEGETABLE SOUP

2 pints (1.20 litres) bone stock or
  water (with 2 crumbled
  chicken bouillon cubes)
2 oz (50 g) diced raw potatoes,
  and the same of carrots and
  onions
1 faggot of herbs (*bouquet garni*)
2 trimmed, finely sliced leeks
1 oz (25 g) butter or Gold
Salt
Black pepper
1 stick celery, chopped small
1 tbsp (1 × 15 ml spoon) soy
  sauce
Grated hard cheese

Place stock or substitute stock in a roomy pan. Wash and stir in all prepared vegetables, add herb faggot and raise to boiling. Simmer steadily for 40 minutes, taste and adjust flavour with salt and pepper. Stir in soy and serve in soup bowls with 1 heaped tablespoon (1 × 15 ml spoon) grated cheese in the base of each bowl.

138

A MEAL-IN-ITSELF SOUP

3 oz (75 g) overnight-soaked, red beans
4 oz (100 g) ribbon noodles
2 celery sticks, chopped small
1 unsalted pig's trotter
3 large, peeled, diced old potatoes
1 large, peeled, crushed-to-pulp garlic clove
Salt
Black pepper
2½ pints (1.5 litres) pork bone stock

Put the stock (or substitute water and a bouillon cube) into a roomy pan. Add the trotter, together with all the prepared vegetables. Season lightly. Stir in garlic clove. Simmer for 2½ hours. Throw in the broken-up noodles, stir until re-boiling and cook giving an occasional stir for a total 30 minutes. Taste and adjust seasoning with salt and plenty of black pepper.

After a large bowlful just eat cheese or fruit.

OUR SLIMMERS' SOUP

3 lb (1.5 kg) small, meaty beef bones, but *not* marrow bones
5 pints (3 litres) water
6 oz (175 g) roughly shredded, tight, white cabbage
3 oz (75 g) red cabbage
2 large rough-chopped onions
6 leaves de-stalked spinach
4 large, skinned and de-seeded ripe tomatoes
1 faggot of herbs (*bouquet garni*)
1 peeled garlic clove
6 bacon rinds or 1 strip bacon rind which has *not* been soaked to remove its saltiness
1 peeled, cored, rough-chopped cooking apple
1 large leek, trimmed, washed and sliced thinly
Black pepper

Put the bones into a baking tin and bake on second shelf for 45 minutes at Gas Mark 4 (approx 350°F, 180°C). Drain off fat and put bones into a casserole. Cover with cold water and lid. Return to oven on lowest shelf Gas Mark 1 (approx 275°F, 140°C) and leave for 3 hours. Remove bones, skim off any remaining fat. Tumble in all remaining ingredients, cover and simmer in the oven or on a top burner for 1 hour. Remove bacon rinds and herb faggot. Ladle with well-stirred vegetables into a large bowl.

Taken at night at the beginning of a really austere, fatless, starchless, sugarless diet, this soup provides the necessary roughage and may be used for several meals if refrigerated in between.

139

SCOTS BARLEY BROTH

Another meal-in-itself soup.

1 lb (450 g) fatless scrag end of mutton or lamb
1 peeled, sliced turnip
3 oz (75 g) overnight-soaked pearl barley
3 pints (1.80 litres) mutton or lamb bone stock
1 oz (25 g) flour
1 oz (25 g) dripping
1 heaped teasp (1 × 5 ml spoon) sea salt
1 flat teasp (1 × 5 ml spoon) black pepper
1 oz (25 g) overnight-soaked dried peas and 1 oz (25 g) white beans
1 trimmed, cleaned celery root
A fat sprig of thyme
1 medium-sized leek, sliced thinly
1 medium onion (can be stuck with 4 cloves)
3 oz (75 g) carrots
A sprig of parsley

Chop up chosen meat roughly. Place in roomy container with turnip, carrot, celery, leek and onion. Cover with stock, raise to boiling point, skim and steady off at a good simmer. Maintain for 2 hours. Excavate meat, remove all bones and chop small. Add soaked peas, beans and barley to pan and simmer for further 30 minutes.

Meanwhile heat dripping in a small pan, stir in flour to soft-ball stage and dilute with a small ladleful of the soup. Stir until perfectly smooth and then stir into the soup. Fish out and chop onion, then return with thyme and parsley. Simmer gently for 10 minutes. Taste and correct seasoning. Remove thyme and parsley for service.

HARICOT BEAN SOUP

Very warming on cold nights.

4 oz (100 g) dried white beans, soaked for 12 hours
1¼ pints (750 ml) clear pork bone, or bacon and bone stock
1 medium onion and carrot, both coarsely grated
1½ oz (40 g) pork fat or dripping
6 fluid oz (180 ml) top-of-the-milk or single cream
Salt
Black pepper
Nutmeg to season

Melt chosen fat in a saucepan over a lowish heat, toss in the prepared onion and carrot, then fry/turn for 5 minutes. Add stock, beans and a generous grate or pinch of nutmeg. Simmer until beans collapse. Either sieve or emulsify back into pan. Stir in milk or cream, taste and correct seasoning with salt and pepper.

Optionally sprinkle each bowl with finely scissored chives.

140

A STOCKPOT EVEN IF YOU ARE OUT ALL DAY

If you have no slow cooking pot, and no time, you can still have good flavoursome stock to give a lift to any tin or packet soup, quite apart from all its other uses.

2 lb (900 g) beef, pork or lamb bones, or 2 lb (900 g) pork bones with 1 lb (450 g) bacon bones (in this case use *no* salt until after tasting)
A faggot of herbs (*bouquet garni*)
1 peeled onion
Cold water
Piece of dried, crisp orange peel, if possible (Kitchen Guidance, p. 133)

Put the bones into any kind of roomy, heat-resistant casserole; cover liberally with cold water and sink in the herbs, onion and orange peel. Raise to boiling. Skim off the rather disagreeable foam which forms on top. Discard this and add a further tumbler of cold water. Cover with the lid and put into the oven on the bottom shelf. Set heat at Gas Mark ½ (250°F, 120°C).

Leave this to cook overnight, so that when you come down the next morning you have a jolly good pot of stock. Just lift from the oven and leave on the stove top to become cold during the day. When you return home again, a crust of fat will have set on the top. Remove it and your stock is ready to use.

Should you cook the stock during the day instead and find you want to use some immediately, you can remove the liquid fat quite easily too. Just two pieces of absorbent kitchen tissue (or old scraps of hoarded tissue paper) over the stock's surface. The fat is thus blotted off in moments, leaving the clear stock underneath ready for you to use.

141

PEA AND PORK SOUP

8 oz (225 g) dried peas, soaked
  overnight in cold water
8 oz (225 g) fresh belly of pork
Salt
Pepper
8 oz (225 g) trimmed white and
  green of a fat leek
1 bouquet garni (comprising
  thyme, bay leaf, parsley
  stalks)
8 oz (225 g) trimmed carrots
1 lb (450 g) peeled old potatoes
1 heart of cos lettuce
12 inch (30 cm) stick of stale
  French bread sliced into
  thinnish rounds
3½ pints (2.10 litres) white stock

Cut the pork belly into dice. Slice the trimmed and washed leek into ¼ inch (5 mm) rounds. Put pork and leeks into a roomy pot with strained peas and *bouquet garni*. Cover with the stock, season lightly with salt and pepper and maintain at a steady simmer under a lid for 2 hours. Add the carrots, cut into thin rounds, the potatoes and the well-washed lettuce heart torn small. Cook till tender.

Meanwhile line a soup tureen with bread slices and keep warm. Taste soup. Adjust seasoning with extra salt and pepper. Stir well, pour over the bread in the tureen and provide (optionally) hand grated hard cheese in a separate bowl and croûtons or pulled bread.

POTATO SOUP

1½ lb (750 g) peeled old potatoes
8 oz (225 g) peeled, thinly sliced
  onions
3 pints (1.80 litres) beef bone
  stock (or if this is impossible
  use water and chicken Oxo
  cubes)
1 level teasp (1 × 5 ml spoon)
  salt
½ pint (300 ml) milk
1 oz (25 g) butter or Gold
1 generous tbsp (1 × 15 ml
  spoon) milled fresh parsley
  (optional)

Rough-cut the potatoes and chop sliced onions. Put in a roomy pan with stock (or substitute), raise to boiling point and simmer for 30 minutes or until onions are perfectly tender. Rub through a coarse sieve, return to pan, stir in milk, taste and add extra salt and black pepper if necessary. Finally stir in butter in small flakes. Optionally add parsley and serve with pulled bread (p. 154) made from a new crusty loaf.

SIMPLE CHESTNUT SOUP

1 lb (450 g) chestnuts
1 medium onion
2 small cloves
3 pints (1.80 litres) pork or veal
  bone stock
Salt
Pepper
Celery salt
4 oz (100 g) peeled old potatoes
Extra stock or milk

Nick or prick chestnuts. Place on a baking sheet and roast in the oven at Gas Mark 7 (approx 425°F, 220°C) until skins burst open with loud reports (approx 7 minutes). Remove skin as soon as the chestnuts can be handled, rough chop and place in a roomy pan with the onion stuck with the cloves. Add stock. Simmer down hard until reduced to 2 pints (1.20 litres). Then add rough-cut potatoes. Simmer until chestnuts and potatoes are tender. Sieve or emulsify into a clean pan. Dilute to required soup consistency with extra stock or milk. Taste and correct seasoning with salt, black pepper and celery salt.

EGG SOUP

2 No 2 eggs
1 rounded dessertsp (1 × 10 ml)
  concentrated tomato purée
1 oz (25 g) grated stale cheese
1 extra small, chopped,
  hard-boiled egg
Salt
Pepper
Celery salt
1 oz (25 g) crumbled vermicelli
1½ pints (900 ml) boiling milk
2 fluid oz (60 ml) top-of-the-milk
  or single cream

Simmer milk with vermicelli for 5 minutes. Stir in cheese and stir/simmer until clear. Turn into top of a double or porage saucepan with boiling water in base pan. Blend the eggs with the cream or top-of-the-milk and tomato purée. Stir both into bulk mixture and continue stirring until piping hot and thickened. Correct seasonings to taste, pour into heated bowls and scatter the chopped hard-boiled egg equally over the filled bowls.

FRENCH QUICK SOUP

2 rounded tbsps (2 × 15 ml spoons) semolina
1 flat teasp (1 × 5 ml spoon) celery salt
1 hard-boiled No 3 egg
A pinch each of parsley, chervil, tarragon and sage (fresh or dried)
2 separated No 2 egg yolks
2 pints (1.20 litres) water
1 tbsp (1 × 15 ml spoon) cream or tinned unsweetened milk
Salt
Black pepper

Season the water with salt and black pepper, raise to boiling point, scatter on the semolina and stir for 5 minutes, or until thickened, then remove from heat. Stir egg yolks with cream or tinned milk, then add celery salt. Turn into soup while stirring carefully. Scatter on coarsely chopped herbs and finally stir in the very finely chopped hard-boiled egg.

Warning
If intending to make in advance and then reheat, please do so in a double or porage saucepan lest the egg yolk content cause your soup to curdle.

MRS MARSHALL'S REMARKABLE QUICK SOUP

You will need to use only *the given ingredients* without deviation. *You must also accept our guarantee that* this works, *though it defies all the generally accepted rules for sauce making.*

1 oz (25 g) flour
2 oz (50 g) finely grated stale, hard cheese
1½ oz (40 g) butter or Gold
2 raw separated No 3 egg yolks
Pinch salt
Generous pinch black pepper
7½ fluid oz (225 ml) cold milk
2 tbsps (2 × 15 ml spoons single cream or top-of-the milk
10–12 fluid oz (300–360 ml) extra boiling milk

Put flour, cheese, butter, egg yolks, salt, pepper and cold milk into a thick pan. Stir very carefully over moderate heat. Once butter melts and blends, add 2½ fluid oz (75 ml) of hot milk gradually. Keep stirring please, increasing your speed until mixture becomes perfectly smooth and very thick. Dilute with remaining extra hot milk until a desirable soup consistency is achieved. Remove from heat, beat in cream and serve with little fingers of hot buttered toast.

144

WATERCRESS SOUP

1 sturdy bunch watercress
1 heaped dessertsp (1 × 10 ml
  spoon) flour
3 medium, peeled old potatoes
1½ oz (40 g) butter or Gold
Salt
White pepper
1 pint (600 ml) milk
1 pint (600 ml) water

Wash and pick over watercress carefully. Melt chosen fat in a saucepan. Add watercress, cook and stir over a moderate heat until it collapses and the stalks are tender. Sprinkle on flour and work in carefully. Add milk and water gradually, beating well after each addition. Chop the potatoes, stir into the soup and simmer for 15 minutes. Either rub through an ordinary sieve, or emulsify. Then return to pan. Raise once more to boiling point, adjust flavour with salt and pepper and serve.

WATERCRESS AND SPRING ONION SOUP

1 bunch watercress, washed
  with all browned leaves
  discarded
8 slim spring onions, trimmed
  and chopped small
6 oz (175 g) raw diced old
  potatoes
½ pint (300 ml) milk
½ pint (300 ml) strong bone
  stock (or ½ pint (300 ml) water
  and 1 bouillon cube)
Salt
Pepper
3 fluid oz (90 ml) single cream or
  top-of-the-milk (optional)

Remove all the leaves from the watercress and put only the rough-chopped stems into a pan with given stock or substitute. Simmer for 15 minutes before adding spring onions and watercress leaves. Simmer for 5 minutes. Then either sieve or emulsify. Correct seasoning with salt and pepper. Optionally add cream or top-of-the-milk.

145

PORTUGUESE WHITE CABBAGE SOUP

The secret of success with this simple, excellent soup lies in the cutting of the cabbage which must *be in hair-thin strips. The rest is easy!*

1 large peeled, rough-cut potato
1 medium-sized, peeled, grated
  onion
Salt
Black pepper
1 large breakfastcupful of very
  finely sliced tight, white
  cabbage
1 generous tbsp (1 × 15 ml
  spoon) olive oil
1½ pints (900 ml) chicken stock
  or water and 1 chicken
  bouillon cube

Simmer the potato until soft in chosen liquor. Rub through an ordinary sieve, return to pan, taste and correct seasoning. Stir in cabbage. Raise heat to simmer hard for 3 minutes precisely, then stir in oil and serve.

GERMAN GRAPE HARVEST SOUP

1 lb (450 g) red or white wine
  grapes – the little ones which
  are eaten from their bunches,
  pips and all
2 pints (1.20 litres) preferably
  rain water
1 No 4 egg yolk
2 tbsps (2 × 15 ml spoons)
  tapioca
Salt
1 oz (25 g) caster sugar

Peel and de-pip grapes. Emulsify or sieve in their own juice. Place in a pan with 2 fluid oz (60 ml) of given water and caster sugar. Simmer down slowly to a syrupy pap. Stir in remaining water. When this bubbles, sprinkle over the tapioca and stir carefully until boiling. Spoon a little soup over the egg yolk, stir fast, then stir into soup which must not be allowed to boil again or it will curdle.

Optionally, a few extra peeled grapes are scattered into each serving and a light dusting of extra caster sugar sprinkled on top.

HONEYMOON SOUP (Soupe de la Nuit de Noce)

2 medium onions
2 fat, peeled garlic cloves
1 rounded tbsp (1 × 15 ml
    spoon) crushed vermicelli
Salt
Black pepper
4 slices cut from a flute of French
    bread

Crisp bread slices in the oven. Chop peeled onions finely. Fry with tomatoes and crushed garlic in chosen hot fat until onions are soft and yellow. Stir in water, raise to boiling point and then maintain at a steady simmer for 30 minutes. Taste and correct seasoning with salt and pepper. Place 2 crisp bread slices in each heated soup bowl. Pour soup over bread and serve – naturally – *in bed*!

Note
Garlic is believed to be a specific against evil spirits and also an aphrodisiac.

COURGETTE SOUP

1 lb (450 g) topped, tailed,
    unskinned courgettes
2 pints (1.20 litres) stock, or
    water and 1 chicken bouillon
    cube
4 fluid oz (120 ml)
    top-of-the-milk, or single
    cream
Salt
Black pepper
A small handful of fresh or 1 flat
    teasp (1 × 5 ml spoon) dried
    chervil
2 oz (50 g) peeled chopped onion
    or shallot

Put stock or water and cube, into a pan with roughly sliced courgettes, chervil and prepared onion. Simmer until all is tender. Liquidise, emulsify or put through a Moulinex Maxima. Switch on and off for 10-second bursts until a purée. Return to pan, stir in cream or top-of-the-milk and taste. Correct seasoning with salt and black pepper. Reheat when required.

EASY COLD SOUPS

Cold soups must always be icily chilled, otherwise more than half their distinctive character is lost. To achieve this, just make the soup in advance, turn into a jug and refrigerate until a few minutes before service. Put an ice cube or two into each bowl, pour the soup over and serve after 5–10 minutes.

ICED CUCUMBER SOUP No 1

1 small unskinned cucumber
Salt
Black pepper
1 pint (600 ml) best possible milk
5 fluid oz (150 ml) single cream
Finely scissored chives

Grate the cucumber on the coarse side of an ordinary grater. Scoop the pulp into a bowl. Scatter over about 1 rounded teasp (1 × 5 ml spoon) salt, sprinkle with pepper and leave for 1 hour. Turn into the milk, stir well, then stir in the chives and refrigerate.

At the moment of serving stir in the cream (also refrigerated). Pour the soup into bowls containing ice cubes. Hand a small bowl of chives to accompany, each person shaking a generous teaspoonful over their portion.

ICED CUCUMBER SOUP No 2

1 small peeled cucumber
2 peeled, rough-cut ripe
   tomatoes
4 fluid oz (120 ml) dry white
   cooking wine
1 pint (600 ml) best milk
5 fluid oz (150 ml) single cream
1 heaped teasp (1 × 5 ml spoon)
   milled or chopped fresh
   parsley heads
1 heaped dessertsp (1 × 10 ml
   spoon) finely scissored or
   chopped chives
Salt
Black pepper

Coarse-grate the entire cucumber. Put juices and pulp into an emulsifier or liquidiser, add wine and reduce to purée. Add all remaining ingredients except seasoning. Taste, correct with salt and pepper. Refrigerate in a jug until using. Then pour into small bowls over an ice cube apiece. Optionally scatter with extra chives or parsley.

148

ICED TOMATO SOUP

8 oz (225 g) very ripe tomatoes
1 rounded teasp (1 × 5 ml
  spoon) celery salt
1 flat eggsp (1 × 2.5 ml spoon)
  dried or fresh savory
1 pint (600 ml) milk
2 generous pinches of white
  pepper
1 level tbsp (1 × 15 ml spoon)
  concentrated tomato purée
Half crushed garlic clove
  (optional)
1 oz (25 g) butter
Spring onion (optional)
Ice cubes

Turn tomatoes into boiling water, leave 4 minutes, plunge into cold water and thus remove skins fast. Melt butter in a small pan and stir in skinned tomatoes. Cook over a low heat until collapsed and tender. Add garlic and rub through an ordinary sieve. Then blend with all remaining ingredients except ice. Stir thoroughly, tip into a jug and refrigerate until 5–10 minutes before service. Put two ice cubes into each bowlful and, optionally, scatter finely chopped white and green of spring onion on top.

ICED HEALTH SOUP

No cooking – but emulsifier or liquidiser is needed.

1 bunch picked, trimmed,
  well-washed watercress
1 pint (600 ml) tinned or
  home-bottled tomato juice
1 rounded teasp (1 × 5 ml
  spoon) celery salt
4–5 drops Lea and Perrins
  Worcestershire Sauce
Salt
Pepper
Either ½ pint (300 ml) cold,
  cleared, well-reduced pork or
  bacon bone stock or milk
1 generous eggsp (1 × 2.5 ml
  spoon) crumbled savory
  (whenever possible)

Emulsify or liquidise the watercress with half the tomato juice. Tip into a roomy bowl. Add all remaining ingredients except seasonings. Taste, season with salt and pepper and celery salt. Pour soup over two ice cubes in each serving bowl. Optionally sprinkle extra crumbled dried savory on top.

ICED SPINACH AND YOGHURT SOUP

No cooking – but emulsifier or liquidiser needed.

8 oz (225 g) spinach leaves, weighed after removing all stalks
6 oz (175 g) celery sticks, chopped small
4 oz (100 g) grated, raw carrot
2 × 5 fluid oz (150 ml) cartons plain yoghurt
A little milk
Salt
Pepper
Celery salt
Fresh parsley (optional)

Place prepared spinach with half the yoghurt in an emulsifier or liquidiser. Add the prepared celery. Switch on full and maintain until all is creamy. Rub through an ordinary sieve into a roomy bowl. Add carrot, remaining yoghurt and seasonings to taste. When well-blended, stir in milk to bring down to desired consistency. Optionally sprinkle fresh parsley on top of each after pouring soup over ice cubes in each bowl.

ICED BEETROOT SOUP

No cooking – but emulsifier or liquidiser needed

4 oz (100 g) cooked, coarse-grated beetroot
4 oz (100 g) white of celery, chopped small
16 fluid oz (480 ml) strong, clear stock or milk
4 fat heads parsley, with stalks left on
5 fluid oz (150 ml) soured cream
8 fluid oz (240 ml) stock or milk
Salt
Pepper

Emulsify or liquidise parsley including stalks and half the stock (or milk). Then mix beetroot with remaining stock (or milk) and prepared celery. Blend beetroot and parsley mixtures together. Beat in soured cream, correct seasoning with salt and pepper. Refrigerate in a jug. Put two ice cubes into each soup bowl, pour chilled soup over and so serve.

ICED LETTUCE SOUP

No cooking – but emulsifier or liquidiser needed.

1 heart of cos or cabbage lettuce
1 oz (25 g) raw, shredded white cabbage
1 × 5 inch (12.5 cm) stick celery
1 × 2 inch (5 cm) chunk unskinned cucumber
1 small, peeled, crushed-to-pulp

Emulsify or liquidise cabbage and chopped celery with tomato juice. Switch on to full and reduce to a fine pulp. Tip into a roomy bowl. Repeat process with rough-chopped cucumber, watercress and crushed garlic

150

garlic clove
1 sprig watercress
1 medium-sized pimento (red or green) de-pipped and de-pithed
Salt
Pepper
1 teasp (1 × 5 ml spoon) celery salt
Strained juice of 1 small thin-skinned orange and half a small lemon
½ pint (300 ml) tinned or home-bottled tomato juice
½ pint (300 ml) milk

and half given milk. Add to bowl contents. Repeat with remaining milk and pimento. Blend all emulsified mixtures together. Add lemon and orange juices, celery salt and salt and pepper to taste. Chill in refrigeration and serve poured over two ice cubes in each bowl.

SPANISH GAZPACHO

We include this although the making of it is dreary. Do not attempt it unless you are prepared to dice the following:

Half a small unskinned cucumber
1 fat green and 1 red pimento (mixed together)
2 fat ripe but firm tomatoes (skinned and de-seeded)

Arrange these separately in small bowls and fill a fourth with cold croûtons.

1 large Spanish onion
8 oz (225 g) rough-cut tomatoes
2 crushed garlic cloves
5 bacon rinds
7½ fluid oz (225 ml) dry cooking sherry
1 tbsp (1 × 15 ml spoon) tarragon wine vinegar
Salt
Black pepper
Celery salt
4 tbsps (4 × 15 ml spoons) oil
1 *bouquet garni* or herb faggot

Slice up the skinned onion very thinly and put into a roomy pan with the oil, rough-cut tomatoes, garlic and bacon rinds. Cover liberally with tap water, immerse herbs, raise to boiling and then simmer for 1 hour. Remove bacon rinds and herb faggot and rub the soup through a coarse sieve. Correct seasoning with salt, pepper and celery salt, and refrigerate.

Gazpacho must always be served icily chilled. Set prepared dishes of vegetables on the table and let each person stir a spoonful of all three and of the croûtons into soup. This is ideal for a summer brunch.

COLD SHRIMP AND WATERCRESS CREAM SOUP

1 large bunch watercress
4 oz (100 g) shelled, chopped
   shrimps
5 fluid oz (150 ml) soured cream
8 fluid oz (240 ml) best possible
   milk
Salt
Pepper

Wash, drain and pick over watercress thoroughly, removing any browned leaves. Rough chop the rest, put into emulsifier with milk and switch to full. Leave until all is smooth and creamy. Remove, add shrimps, stir in with soured cream, taste and correct seasoning. Refrigerate overnight.

The next evening serve in soup bowls, with an ice cube dropped in each 5–10 minutes before meal begins.

ICED BEER SOUP

1½ pints (900 ml) light ale
1 dessertsp (1 × 10 ml spoon)
   caster sugar
1 tbsp (1 × 15 ml spoon) strained
   lemon juice
12 fluid oz (350 g) chicken stock
   (or water and bouillon cube)
A fat pinch of cinnamon powder
1 stiffly whipped No 3 egg white

Place all ingredients in a cocktail shaker, fill the upper part with crushed ice and shake very vigorously indeed. Really work at it, then pour into glass bowls and serve immediately.

'CHEAT' CONSOMME EN GELEE

1 × 15 oz (425 g) tin chicken or
   beef consommé
Scant ½ oz (10 g) powdered
   gelatine
2 tbsps (2 × 15 ml spoons) dry
   sherry
Generous squeeze of lemon juice
1 chicken or beef bouillon cube
5 fluid oz (150 ml) water
Finely chopped parsley

Shake gelatine over cold water; stir with chosen bouillon cube until both cube and gelatine are melted and fluid is clear over a low heat. Blend with consommé, add sherry, stir in lemon juice and turn into a bowl to refrigerate until almost set and rather wobbly. Beat to a froth with a fork, divide into soup bowls or small glass dishes, sprinkle with parsley and leave in refrigeration.

152

HERBY BREAD

1 heaped teasp (1 × 5 ml spoon) thyme, parsley heads, tarragon leaves, chervil and chopped chives
3 oz (75 g) soft butter or Gold
1 crushed garlic clove
1 flat eggsp (1 × 2.5 ml spoon) salt
Either miniature Hovis brown loaves or long *flutes* of French bread

Chop or mill all herbs. Add chosen fat with garlic and salt. Beat until well blended. Put into a small pot and cover tightly with Alcan Foil for insulated storage in refrigeration.

Slice miniature brown loaves ¼ inch (5 mm) thick from end to end *without* severing the base crusts so that each then opens out like a fan. Slice French bread at the slant in 1 inch (2.5 cm) thick slices from end to end, again being sure not to sever any at base. Spread chosen butter over each slice with a small table knife. Re-assemble these by pressing firmly together to restore original shape. Wrap fairly loosely in Alcan Foil and 10 minutes before serving heat through at the equivalent to Gas Mark 1 (approx 275°F, 140°C) on floor of oven, possibly over heating plates and under most of the meal.

Take to table in a basket, unwrap and tear pieces off as required, thus keeping the rest hot.

GARLIC BREAD

1 tbsp (1 × 15 ml spoon) milled or chopped parsley heads
3 crushed-to-pulp garlic cloves
4 oz (100 g) soft butter or Gold
1 flat eggsp (1 × 2.5 ml spoon) salt
Either miniature Hovis brown loaves or long *flutes* of French bread

Prepare and use as for Herby Bread.

153

CROUTONS (herb-flavoured)

1 generous tbsp (1 × 15 ml
   spoon) oil
1 × ¼ inch (5 mm) thick slice
   from a sandwich loaf (white or
   brown) and, if liked,
1 flat teasp (1 × 5 ml spoon)
   either garlic or parsley butter
   (see preceding recipes)

Heat the oil in a small frying pan. Cut the bread, including crusts into ¼ inch (5 mm) dice. Add chosen herb butter to oil and scatter the bread dice into pan. Step up heat to fullest, and stir/turn giving the pan handle an occasional shake until croûtons are crisp and richly browned. If necessary keep warm in their serving bowl under a covering of Alcan Foil.

Note
Variations: Mix croûtons with a diced rasher of No 3 cut streaky bacon, fried dry until frizzled or fry in an equal quantity – 1 tbsp (1 × 15 ml spoon) to 1 slice – of chicken, rendered-down pork fat or bacon fat.

TOAST MELBA

Totally unskilled labour!

Cut slices of bread a bare ¼ inch (5 mm) in thickness. Cut off all crusts. Toast each slice on both sides. Then with a sharp knife split through each one and toast the untoasted sides, so one slice makes two pieces of toast Melba. It should always be made freshly and immediately prior to service, not made in bulk and left to get hard and horrid in a tin.

PULLED BREAD

When cutting crusts from a sandwich loaf tear these into rough pieces, set on a dry flat baking sheet and heat to crisp, low down in oven for about 10 minutes.

Hors d'Oeuvre

Raw cabbage salad
Quick cole slaw dressing
Beetroot salad
Simple cucumber salad
Real potato salad
Raw vegetable salad
Raw mushroom salad
Tomato salad
Egg salad
Egg and herring salad
Salade Niçoise no 1
Salade Niçoise no 2
Cauliflower salad
Cheese and potato salad
Kidney bean and apple salad
Russian salad
Dandelion salad
Watercress and mushroom salad
Jerusalem artichoke salad
Italian salad
Simple cream cheese mayonnaise
Stuffed eggs

Stuffed tomatoes
Onion-stuffed tomatoes (hot)
Stuffed celery sticks
Melon boats
Orange and cream cheese starters
Hot baked grapefruit
Anchovy butter
A simple pork pâté
A simple rabbit pâté
A very simple pâté maison

As so many of the salads we offer here form the basis of good, simple hors d'oeuvre assemblies, we have included them in this chapter. This is an area where we can learn a thing or two from the Americans, whose cooking generally appals us, and whose salad dressing mixtures often exceed the bounds of palatability for Europeans. For extenuation we suggest you study their Thousand Island Dressing – but not in this book! Nevertheless the average American housewife puts up a salad to accompany her main courses as automatically as her English counterpart boils some potatoes. So here the Americans are wiser than we.

One of the least known and little understood salads is Cole Slaw. This, contrary to popular belief, is *not* made with raw, sliced tight white cabbage but with raw celeriac, sometimes mixed with matching shredded or slender-cut matchsticks of celery heart. Swill first with the strained juice of half a lemon and an equal quantity of water to avoid blackening. Toss well, then give them their own special dressing.

We offer here a raw cabbage salad, because celeriac is not easily obtained and is expensive.

RAW CABBAGE SALAD

Quarter of a tight white cabbage with outer damaged leaves and hard core removed

½ teacupful raw, scraped or peeled, grated carrots, using only the outer part and not the cores (use them up for soup)

1 given quantity of Quick Cole Slaw Dressing

1 flat teasp (1 × 5 ml) caraway seeds (optional)

Shred cabbage very finely; then, if shop bought, toss into iced water to re-invigorate before using. Drain, pat dry and turn into a salad bowl. Mix well with raw grated carrot. Unlike any other classic salad you may dress this one ahead of service because it actually improves by being so treated. Sprinkle with caraway seeds if liked.

QUICK COLE SLAW DRESSING

Whip 4 heaped tbsps (4 × 15 ml spoons) plain yoghurt with 2 tbsps (2 × 15 ml spoons) well-shaken French dressing together at full speed.

BEETROOT SALAD

This reverses the English cutting method and we submit it tastes much nicer.

8 oz (225 g) cooked, skinless beetroot

1 small, raw onion, sliced into fine rings

1 teasp (1 × 5 ml spoon) fresh, chopped parsley heads

Red wine vinegar

Slice beetroot into ¼ inch (5 mm) thick rounds, then reverse-slice into ¼ inch (5 mm) thick strips. Arrange neatly in a shallow dish, moisten with wine vinegar, sprinkle with parsley and lay an overlapping line of raw, separated onion rings down the centre.

SIMPLE CUCUMBER SALAD

Half a small, unskinned cucumber

Salt

Grate unskinned cucumber on coarsest side of grater. Spread over a shallow dish. Sprinkle liberally with salt and refrigerate for 1 hour. Drain away drawn liquor which is now like brine. Serve the cucumber well-chilled in a small bowl.

REAL POTATO SALAD

Try for soapy rather than floury potatoes, please.

1½ lb (750 g) old or new potatoes
1 small ladleful strong, clear
   stock
1 peeled, crushed garlic clove
1 very thin crust cut from a
   sandwich loaf
1 heaped teasp (1 × 5 ml spoon)
   French mustard
1 fluid oz (30 ml) wine vinegar
4 fluid oz (120 ml) oil
Chives

Scrub chosen potatoes. Steam until cooked but still firm, plunge into cold water, wipe and skin. Make dressing in a salad bowl by putting in French mustard and working it up with wine vinegar and a slow trickle of oil. Lay crust crumb-side downwards on a working surface and work in garlic pulp very vigorously. Cut crust into very slender matchsticks. Cut the potatoes – rough cubes are best but do not cut them small. When these are ready, toss matchstick crusts into the salad bowl, tumble potatoes in fast and turn and blend very quickly too. Sling in the boiling stock and turn again.

Serve heaped into a shallow dish with scissored chives scattered on top or mix in any of the following gently: torn leaves of curly endive, scraps of torn lettuce or chicory, little leaves from sprigs of corn salad (*romaine*), milled parsley heads, tiny diced or matchstick-cut strips of any charcuterie meats, and even a small handful of cooked peas. Serve icily chilled from the salad bowl.

RAW VEGETABLE SALAD

1 large scraped carrot
1 small heart of celery
4 inch (10 cm) piece of
    unskinned cucumber
1 small teacupful raw,
    coarse-grated red cabbage
1 small teacupful raw,
    coarse-grated tight white
    cabbage
2 pieces of washed, finely-diced
    crystallised ginger
4 fluid oz (120 ml) well-shaken
    French dressing and the same
    of classic mayonnaise
1 small endive or bunch of
    watercress

Place a small bowl and ladle in the centre of a large platter. Coarse-grate the carrot into two mounds on the platter. Cut the celery heart in two lengthwise, shred down into matchsticks and place in two mounds next to the carrots. Divide the red and white cabbages into two mounds apiece, being careful to leave a fraction of space on either side of the red cabbage, lest it stain its neighbours. Halve and cut the unskinned cucumber into matchsticks and arrange between the other vegetables. Border with carefully washed, drained and picked endive or watercress. Sprinkle with diced ginger. Then beat the French dressing and mayonnaise together and pour into the little central bowl for ladling over each serving at the table.

RAW MUSHROOM SALAD

4 oz (100 g) unstalked
    mushrooms
Powdered paprika
4 fluid oz (120 ml) soured cream

Scald the unskinned mushrooms in boiling water. Wipe, slice very thinly, mix with the cream, arrange in a shallow dish and sprinkle liberally with powdered paprika.

TOMATO SALAD

6 firm, ripe, even-sized skinned
    or un-skinned tomatoes
1 flat teasp (1 × 5 ml spoon)
    crushed dried or chopped
    fresh basil leaves
Oil
Wine vinegar

Slice tomatoes thinly. Lay in overlapping lines down a shallow dish. Sprinkle with basil. Flick lightly with wine vinegar and more liberally with oil.

159

EGG SALAD

2 thinly sliced hard-boiled eggs
1 finely diced gherkin
2 heaped tbsps (2 × 15 ml
  spoons) mayonnaise
1 tbsp (1 × 15 ml spoon) single
  cream or top-of-the-milk
Diced gherkin

Lay eggs in a small dish. Mix the mayonnaise with the cream or top-of-the-milk. Pour over eggs and scatter diced gherkin on top.

EGG AND HERRING SALAD

This needs a little patience.

Soused herring (from a
  delicatessen or see Fish, Part
  3)
3 oz (75 g) well-drained
  sauerkraut from a delicatessen
1–2 hard-boiled No 3 eggs
1 dessertsp (1 × 20 ml spoon)
  tomato sauce
1 rounded tbsp (1 × 15 ml
  spoon) real mayonnaise
Sufficient of any available green
  salad to form a base

Check the herrings over patiently to ensure there are no bones remaining and then break into small pieces. Wash, drain and spread chosen salad over a plate. Mix some herring pieces with sauerkraut and spread on top. Scatter with more herring pieces. Garnish with crescents of hard-boiled egg. Dress with mayonnaise into which tomato sauce has been blended.

SALADE NICOISE No 1 (classic)

This has changed over the years from a simple salad to a dog's dinner assembly. We give the two versions and leave you to choose.

4 oz (100 g) cooked, cold thinly
  sliced new potatoes
4 oz (100 g) peeled, de-seeded,
  quartered, ripe tomatoes
4 oz (100 g) cooked, French
  beans cut into 1 inch (2.5 cm)
  lengths
Cos or cabbage lettuce heart torn
  small
1 peeled coarse-grated-to-pulp
  shallot or very small onion
1 rounded teasp (1 × 5 ml
  spoon) finely milled or
  chopped chervil
French dressing

Mix the vegetables in a salad bowl and scatter with chervil. Moisten with French dressing and turn well at moment of serving.

SALADE NICOISE No 2 (modern)

This contains all the ingredients of real Salade Niçoise as in No 1 plus:

4 oz (100 g) tuna fish in oil
12 mixed black and green olives
2 well-wiped anchovy fillets
1 No 3 hard-boiled egg
8–10 drained capers

Break the tuna into small pieces and arrange over No 1 salad in a salad bowl after the dressing has been turned in. Scatter mixed olives over, slice shelled egg and arrange against the side of the bowl. Chop anchovy fillets and scatter over with the capers.

CAULIFLOWER SALAD

1 smallest possible head of cauliflower with all green removed
French dressing
5 oz (135 g) red or green pimento

Separate the flowerets or small sprigs from the white 'head'. Divide any large ones to ensure their being evenly sized. Arrange stems to centre, in a circle on a flat, round dish. Shake bottle of French dressing and drip over. Leave to steep for 30 minutes. Cut the top off the pimento and with a grapefruit cutter or potato peeler excavate all white pith, eject seeds and cut into fine rings. Pile over the cauliflower at centre. Hand extra French dressing in a small jug or sauceboat.

CHEESE AND POTATO SALAD

2 lb (900 g) old potatoes
6 tbsps (6 × 15 ml spoons) sharp cider
Salt
Black pepper
Wine vinegar
Oil
Parsley
Chervil
1 shallot, finely grated
1 teacupful diced Cheddar cheese

Scrub potatoes and steam until just firmly cooked through. Drain, wipe and remove skins while still very warm. Slice fairly thinly into a salad bowl. Immediately add the cider and turn over thoroughly. Add the diced Cheddar, grate finely and work in the peeled shallot. Make a dressing with salt, pepper, vinegar and herbs.

161

KIDNEY BEAN AND APPLE SALAD

2 oz (50 g), kidney beans soaked overnight in cold water, then drained, boiled in salted water until tender and chilled

1 large tart apple, peeled, cored and diced

2 oz (50 g) finely shredded tight white cabbage

2 heaped tbsps (2 × 15 ml spoons) basic mayonnaise

1 tbsp (1 × 15 ml spoon) thin cream or top-of-the-milk

1 eggsp (1 × 2.5 ml spoon) salt

A flat coffeesp (1 × 2.5 ml spoon) scissored chives and the same of milled or chopped parsley heads

Green salad

Paprika powder (optional)

Mix together the beans, apple and cabbage. Beat cream or top-of-the-milk into mayonnaise with parsley, chives and salt. Fold/turn into salad mixture. Line a shallow dish with any chosen green salad. Shape bean mixture into a centre mound. Optionally scatter a very light sprinkling of paprika powder on top. Serve well chilled.

RUSSIAN SALAD

3 oz (75 g) each of cooked diced new potatoes, carrots and French beans

3 oz (75 g) chopped heart of celery

3 tbsps (3 × 15 ml spoons) basic mayonnaise

1 teasp (1 × 5 ml spoon) raw grated onion juice

1 rounded teasp (1 × 5 ml spoon) powdered gelatine

3 tbsps (3 × 15 ml spoons) cold water

Turn mayonnaise into a roomy bowl. Put water into a very small pan, shake gelatine on top and stir over a mere thread of heat until mixture clears and becomes slightly syrupy. Beat fast into mayonnaise, then blend in all given vegetables. Rinse a 2 lb (900 g) pudding basin under a cold tap. Shake off surplus moisture, tip in the salad mixture, smooth off top and refrigerate until set. Unmould onto a shallow dish, surround at base with overlapping, thinly cut slices of unskinned cucumber and serve with soused herrings.

162

DANDELION SALAD

Invert flower pots over growing dandelions and leave until the leaves are well blanched.

8 oz (225 g) blanched young
  dandelion leaves
2 tbsps (2 × 15 ml spoons)
  chopped fresh tarragon heads
1 tbsp (1 × 15 ml spoon)
  chopped fresh chervil
1 small bunch of trimmed,
  picked and washed watercress
4 pale young nasturtium leaves
4 peppercorns
1 small flat teasp (1 × 5 ml
  spoon) salt
1 flat eggsp (1 × 2.5 ml spoon)
  dry mustard
3 tbsps (3 × 15 ml spoons) oil
1 tbsp (1 × 15 ml spoon)
  tarragon vinegar
1 flat teasp (1 × 5 ml spoon)
  sugar
A squeeze of lemon juice

Discard stems and tear dandelion and nasturtium leaves into small pieces. Mix in a salad bowl with watercress sprigs.

Make the dressing but do not use until moment of service. Crush down the peppercorns in a wooden bowl with salt, mustard and vinegar. Beat in sufficient oil to thicken mixture slightly. Draw in sugar and lemon juice and beat in remaining oil. At moment of service beat once more, pour over mixture in salad bowl and turn religiously until every piece of every leaf is coated.

Note

Tiny matchsticks of bread crust, rubbed with crushed garlic, may be added optionally at the last.

WATERCRESS AND MUSHROOM SALAD

1 large bunch watercress
4 oz (100 g) unskinned,
  thinly-sliced mushrooms
4 fluid oz (120 ml) oil
2 fluid oz (60 ml) wine vinegar
1 dessertsp (1 × 10 ml spoon)
  double or whipping cream
1 flat eggsp (1 × 2.5 ml spoon)
  salt and half the same of black
  pepper
1 smallish, very thinly-sliced
  onion
1 peeled, cored, very
  thinly-sliced eating apple
1 teasp (1 × 5 ml spoon) finely
  scissored fresh chives

Slices unskinned mushrooms and their stalks very thinly. Turn into a roomy bowl. Beat oil and vinegar together, then beat in salt, cream, black pepper and chives. Add the prepared onion and apple. Pour the dressing overall and marinade for 1 hour. At moment of service blend lightly and evenly with the prepared watercress and serve.

163

JERUSALEM ARTICHOKE SALAD

1 lb (450 g) peeled Jerusalem artichokes
1 chopped, hard-boiled egg
1 rounded teasp (1 × 5 ml spoon) mixed scissored or chopped chives and the same of milled parsley heads
Sour cream dressing (No Cooking, Part 1 p. 30)
Heart of lettuce
The strained juice of half a lemon mixed with an equal amount cold water
Powdered paprika

Slice artichokes thinly into a bowl. Add lemon water, leave 10 minutes, drain and add all remaining ingredients except lettuce and paprika. Turn thoroughly to blend. Wash, drain and shake separated lettuce leaves in a salad basket or tea towel. Use to line out base and sides of a salad bowl reserving the small central heart. Turn in artichoke mixture and shape into a mound at centre. Stab the top with the lettuce heart, dust lightly with powdered paprika and serve well chilled.

ITALIAN SALAD

2–4 oz (50–100 g) red pimentos
6 medium tomatoes
French dressing or French dressing with herbs

Split pimentos centrally from stem to base. Eject all seeds and remove white pith. Slice into narrow strips across each of the four halves. Skin the tomatoes, then slice thinly. Mix the two together in a shallow dish. At the moment of eating moisten with chosen dressing.

SIMPLE CREAM CHEESE MAYONNAISE

3 oz (75 g) cream cheese
2 oz (50 g) skinned Camembert cheese
4 heaped tbsps (4 × 15 ml spoons) thick mayonnaise
2 fluid oz (60 ml) yoghurt
2 fluid oz (60 ml) single cream
1 flat teasp (1 × 5 ml spoon) paprika powder

Put cream cheese into a bowl. Peel crust carefully from the Camembert, mash down with a fork and add with mayonnaise and paprika. Whip down to obtain a far too thick cream. Bring down gradually with the yoghurt while still whipping. Finally blend in cream, chill and serve.

STUFFED EGGS

4 No 3 hard-boiled, shelled eggs
1 tbsp (1 × 15 ml spoon) basic
  mayonnaise
6 drops anchovy essence
2 well-wiped anchovy fillets split
  lengthwise and then halved
1 dessertsp (1 × 10 ml spoon)
  single cream
Black pepper
A mere pinch of salt

Halve eggs lengthwise being sure to take a sliver from the white base of each to ensure they stand steadily. Eject the yolks into a small bowl. Fork down thoroughly, work in all remaining ingredients with salt and pepper to taste. Pack back into hollowed egg whites and fork up. Alternatively put mixture into an icing bag with a No 7 crown pipe and pipe rosettes into white shells. Finish each with a tiny coil of anchovy fillet at top-centre.

STUFFED TOMATOES

Remove tops and skin required number of medium, ripe tomatoes. Scissor out cores carefully, avoiding making a hole at bases. Fill with cucumber salad. Scatter with powdered paprika and replace lids at an angle. Serve with an equal number of stuffed hard-boiled eggs, on a small bed of carefully washed, picked and stem-shortened watercress. At moment of serving sprinkle watercress lightly with salt and black pepper.

ONION-STUFFED TOMATOES (hot)

2 large ripe tomatoes
A little Onion Sauce (Eggs,
  p. 202)
A little grated cheese

Slice small lids from the tomatoes and hollow them out with the aid of a small pair of point-ended scissors. Fill with onion sauce, scatter with grated cheese, replace lids and bake one shelf above centre at Gas Mark 5 (approx 375°F, 190°C) in a shallow tin with a trickle of water in the base for 10 minutes. Serve on small rounds of buttered toast as a hot first course or plain as an accompanying vegetable to grilled steak, chops or cutlets.

165

STUFFED CELERY STICKS

6 inside celery sticks trimmed neatly, washed and wiped
4 oz (100 g) cream cheese
1 oz (25 g) finely chopped nuts
1 very small flat teasp (1 × 5 ml spoon) capers pressed to expel all moisture then chopped finely
1 flat teasp (1 × 5 ml spoon) powdered paprika
2 oz (50 g) butter or Gold

Whip cheese with chosen fat and paprika. Fork in the nuts and prepared capers and spread into the celery sticks. Chop with a sharp knife into 1½ inch (3.75 cm) lengths and arrange on a d'oyley covered dish.

MELON BOATS

Run a very sharp knife between base skin and flesh of each cut melon crescent. Slice through flesh down to skin base at 1 inch (2.5 cm) intervals along the whole length. Push alternate slices away from you for ½ inch (1.25 cm) and push the remaining towards you in the same way.

Hand a little dish of powdered ginger and another of soft brown sugar for sprinkling over – if liked!

Alternatively, make rolls from halved or quartered paper-thin slices of Parma ham and insert one in each of the spaces left by the way you have pushed the slices apart, or put a skinless segment of tangerine into each space and again hand a small bowl of sugar separately.

166

ORANGE AND CREAM CHEESE STARTERS

4–6 crustless squares white or
  brown ¼ inch (5 mm) thick
  bread
Butter
Cream cheese
2 oranges
6–8 sliced, stuffed olives

Butter the bread squares and spread thickly with cream cheese. Peel oranges with a small, sharp knife, removing skin and pith together. Slice to yield 4–6 slices. Eject all pips and excavate central pith. Lay slices over cream cheese, put a small extra blob or piped rosette of cream cheese at centre of each. Garnish with sliced olives and optionally arrange on a small bed of either cress or watercress.

HOT BAKED GRAPEFRUIT

For each half grapefruit allow:
2 flat teasps (2 × 5 ml spoons)
  soft brown sugar
1 pinch ginger
1 pinch cinnamon

Separate the fruit segments carefully from the skin partitions as nothing is nastier than encountering these. Invert each half grapefruit in its bowl and leave overnight. In the morning turn cut side uppermost. Drain off juice, scatter mixed sugar and spices over the fruit, moisten overall with drained juices and bake for 10–12 minutes one shelf above centre at Gas Mark 4–5 (approx 350°–375°F, 180°–190°C). These swell up surprisingly during baking.

ANCHOVY BUTTER

2 oz (50 g) butter
Anchovy essence
Black pepper
2 small, wiped anchovy fillets

Work butter with drops of anchovy essence to taste. Crush anchovy fillets to pulp with the tip of a small knife. Work thoroughly into prepared butter. Press into a little pot and cover with Alcan Wrap or Alcan Foil. Store in refrigeration.

A SIMPLE PORK PATE

1 lb (450 g) pigs' liver
Raw, unsalted pork fat
2 fluid oz (60 ml) dry Madeira
   from a miniature bottle
1 eggsp (1 × 2.5 ml spoon) black
   pepper
1 level teasp (1 × 5 ml spoon)
   salt
½ eggsp (1 × 2.5 ml spoon)
   powdered nutmeg
1 small teacupful fine soft,
   brown breadcrumbs
1 small garlic clove
1 tbsp (1 × 15 ml spoon) brandy
   from a miniature bottle
Milk

Make sure the liver has been sliced thinly for you. Put into a bowl, cover – just – with lowest grade milk and leave overnight. By morning milk will be a dark plum colour. Drain off and give to the cat. Wipe the liver slices, then mince with pork fat and peeled, rough-cut garlic. Turn into a roomy bowl, add all remaining ingredients and rub through a sieve with either a wooden roller or a pusher. Alternatively the mixture can be emulsified and then sieved.

Cut narrow strips of extra pork fat and lay criss-crossed over base and sides of a small terrine or casserole. Turn pâté onto this, level off, cover with lid or Alcan Foil and stand in a meat baking tin half-filled with boiling water. Cook at Gas Mark 4 (approx 350°F, 180°C) for 1 hour before testing as explained in preceding recipe for Simple Rabbit Pâté. Total cooking time must never exceed 1¼ hours.

Note
This pâté is of a creamier texture and suitable for re-pressing into individual pots for serving at a Saturday night supper party. Hand plenty of toast or toast Melba in a toast box (Brunches, page 307).

A SIMPLE RABBIT PATE

8 oz (225 g) raw flesh cut from
   rabbit pieces
1 peeled, crushed-to-pulp garlic
   clove
1 small shallot or onion
1 fluid oz (30 ml) sherry
Raw unsalted pork fat
1 flat teasp (1 × 5 ml spoon) salt
½ flat teasp (1 × 2.5 ml spoon)
   black pepper
2 oz (50 g) lean raw ham or
   well-soaked raw gammon

Cut up the rabbit. Add half the weight in rough-chopped pork fat. Mince with rough-cut shallot or onion and garlic. Add salt and pepper and stir in sherry, being careful to blend all very thoroughly. Turn mixture into a small terrine or casserole, which has been well-rubbed with extra rendered down pork fat. Level off the mixture, cover terrine securely with Alcan Foil and stand in an ordinary meat tin. Pour boiling water in to come half way up sides of terrine. Cook for 40–50 minutes on centre shelf at Gas Mark 4 (approx 350°F, 180°C).

Test after 40 minutes by driving the tip of a small knife into pâté at centre. Press down a little. If the juice which oozes out is a strong pink, cook for further 10 minutes. If the juice is beige but just faintly tinged with pink, remove. Take the terrine from outer tin, set on working surface, put a buttered paper over the surface and press down with heavy scale weights. Lacking these, use any heavy tins from store cupboard. The next day remove weights and papers.

Optionally run ¼ inch (5 mm) layer of melted pork fat over the top surface, and refrigerate until set before serving.

169

A VERY SIMPLE PATE MAISON

5 oz (135 g) minced, raw, unsalted pork fat cut from the rind
4 oz (100 g) minced stewing veal
4 oz (100 g) lean pie pork
4 oz (100 g) pork sausage-meat
1 peeled, crushed garlic clove
1 small peeled onion or shallot grated finely
1 scant, small teasp (1 × 5 ml spoon) mixed spices, the same of salt
1 flat eggsp (1 × 2.5 ml spoon) black pepper
Either ½ teacup strong bone stock and 4 tbsps (4 × 15 ml spoons) cooking-type sherry or use all stock
A little extra melted pork fat

Put all prepared ingredients into a roomy bowl and work up until thoroughly blended. Turn into a small terrine or pie dish which has been brushed on base and sides with extra melted pork fat. Press down, cover with a piece of Alcan Foil and stand in an ordinary meat baking tin two-thirds filled with boiling water. Put in the oven, one shelf below centre and cook at Gas Mark 4 (approx 350°F, 180°C) for about 45 minutes or until, when a test-skewer is driven in just off centre, the hole oozes the very palest pinky-beige juice.
Remove from oven, cover with a butter paper, place a heavy weight on top and chill in refrigerator.

Note
Optionally run a ¼ inch (5 mm) layer of liquefied pork fat over the cold pâté's surface.

Fish

Crisp batter for fish frying
Fried fillets of whiting
Hot shrimps cooked in sea water
Whitebait
Conger steak parcels
Mackerel parcels
Mackerel and mussel pie
Kedgeree
Grilled mackerel with gooseberry sauce
Haddock and mushroom pie
Smoked haddock with spinach purée
Haddock mornay
Bornholmer herring and egg cake
Swedish herring bake
Herring roes in puff pastry
Kipper pâté
Kipper crusts
Stuffed baked whiting
Baked hake steaks
Baked plaice with cheese and tomato
Poor man's Russian fish pie
Dripping pastry paste

Fish puffs
Skewered mussels with saffron rice
Steamed fish pudding
Fish faggots
Queenie pie
Monkfish cream
Fish cakes

CRISP BATTER FOR FISH FRYING

4 oz (100 g) sifted flour
2 generous pinches of salt
1 tbsp (1 × 15 ml spoon) oil
Water at blood heat
1 stiffly whipped egg white

This batter will not coat successfully if beaten. Just stir, please.

Stir flour in a basin with salt. Make a well at centre, tip in oil, then resume stirring while giving very slow additions of water. Stir to a thick, smooth coating consistency. Rest for 30 minutes. When oil in deep fryer is hot, fold whipped egg white into batter until this blends perfectly. Then use.

FRIED FILLETS OF WHITING

Draw whiting through flour and tap off surplus. Tow through fish batter (see preceding recipe) until thickly coated. Slide into oil at slightly smoking (390°F, 195°C). Fry until puffed and pale golden only. Turn off heat and complete frying in slowly diminishing heat until well-browned all over. Drain on absorbent kitchen tissue.

Note
Other suitable fish for this treatment include ling or plaice fillets, or cod and hake steaks.

HOT SHRIMPS COOKED IN SEA WATER
(Crevettes chaudes)

Half-fill a roomy pan with sea water taken from a calm untroubled pool or the smooth open sea, to ensure no sandy particles. If nervous, pour water through a butter muslin-lined sieve into the pan. When hot, slide in live shrimps and simmer strongly with one or two sprigs of fennel and half a dozen peppercorns. As soon as the shrimps turn either brown or pink, depending upon which type you have taken, strain and eat at once.

The best method is to hold the head and tail of each shrimp and bite off the middle. All that shelling is pointless and time-wasting as even the little shells are quite soft when cooked this way straight from the sea.

173

WHITEBAIT

Whitebait (allow 4 oz (100 g) per person)
Flour
Oil for deep frying
Parsley sprigs (optional)
Salt
Black pepper
Quartered lemon
Cayenne pepper

The secret of cooking these tiny fish is to fry only a fat handful at a time. Turn each handful in flour, place in a sieve and tap off the surplus flour. Then scatter the fish over slightly-smoking hot oil and stir with a perforated spoon or 'spider' slice until lightly browned and crisp. Lift out and drain on absorbent kitchen paper, season lightly with salt and pepper and keep warm at Gas Mark ¼ (approx 240°F, 110°C) while frying successive batches.

Toss parsley sprigs into hot oil for just long enough for each little sprig to frizzle and crisp and therefore become edible. Lift out with kitchen tongs and use to border the mound of little fishes. Hand round lemon and cayenne pepper separately with thin brown bread and butter in England, with crisp-crusted bread in Europe because the Continental brown bread is terrible.

CONGER STEAK PARCELS

2 × 6 oz (175 g) conger steaks
2 oz (50 g) onion purée
2 fluid oz (60 ml) top-of-the-milk or single cream
Salt
Black pepper
2 medium tomatoes
2 × 15 × 10 inch (37.5 × 25 cm) pieces of lightly oiled Alcan Foil

Lay each steak in centre of lightly oiled piece of foil. Mix onion purée with milk or cream. Season both this and steak lightly with salt and pepper. Skin the tomato, slice very thinly and lay on top of steak. Add another flick of salt and pepper. Then pour over mixed purée and milk or cream. Cook for 15 minutes, one shelf above centre

174

at Gas Mark 6 (approx 400°F, 200°C).

Note
Make sure steaks are cut for you from the thick part of the conger. Thus the given weight of each steak is not too thick to cook well in the time stated.

MACKEREL PARCELS

2 good-sized mackerel, topped, tailed and with spine bones removed
A little oil
2 small 'leaves' of lemon peel
2 oz (50 g) mushroom stalks
1 flat dessertsp (1 × 10 ml spoon) milled fresh parsley heads
3 oz (75 g) fine soft breadcrumbs
2 fluid oz (60 ml) cider
Salt
Black pepper
2 × 16 inch (40 cm) pieces of standard width Alcan Foil

Brush dull side of foil lightly with oil. Lay one mackerel centrally on each piece. Give each a leaf of lemon peel on top, scatter each with half the crumbs, moisten with half the cider and season lightly with salt and black pepper. Bring outside edges together over top centres and make small folds, thus allowing the essential air pocket between foil and fish. Pinch ends together. Set on an ordinary oven baking sheet and when required bake at Gas Mark 4 (approx 350°F, 180°C) one shelf above centre for 15–20 minutes depending upon size of chosen fish. Open both parcels and slide contents onto heated plates. During cooking they will have sauced themselves.

MACKEREL AND MUSSEL PIE

4 large or 8 small mackerel
    topped, tailed and with spine
    bones removed
8 oz (225 g) mussels in shell
1 heaped dessertsp (1 × 10 ml
    spoon) milled, fresh parsley
    heads
5 fluid oz (150 ml) cider
5 fluid oz (150 ml) fish stock*
5 fluid oz (150 ml) milk or single
    cream
1½ oz (40 g) flour
1½ oz (40 g) butter or substitute
Salt
Black pepper
1½ lb (750 g) cooked, creamed
    potatoes

*Use the head, tails and
    spinebones of the mackerel
    simmered with:
    1 pint (600 ml) cold water
    1 sliced shallot
    1 'leaf' of thinly pared lemon
    rind
    Parsley stalks
    3 peppercorns

Place the open mackerel on grill pan rack in low position and grill for 5–6 minutes depending upon size. Cool, remove any remaining bones, turn over, pull away skin and fins and then divide centrally. Scrub and beard the mussels, then steam for 30 seconds under a lid. Cool, then extract mussels and pull them all in halves.

Make fish stock from mackerel trimmings. Melt butter in a thick pan. Stir in flour to form a roux. Cook and stir for 3 minutes to dispel flour taste. Add cider over a fairly strong heat. Wait until this begins to boil. Stir first to blend roughly, then beat very vigorously until smooth and far too thick. Add the fish stock, repeat the procedure and repeat again after adding milk or cream. When a smooth, thick sauce results, taste and correct seasoning with salt and pepper.

Draw in halved mussels and parsley. Put down a spread of sauce over a lightly buttered medium pie dish. Lay in a quarter of the mackerel strips, cover with another layer of sauce and so continue until all fish is laid in and covered with a last layer of the sauce. Cover all with a thick layer of seasoned, creamed potatoes. Bake in the oven at Gas Mark 3 (approx 325°F, 160°C) one shelf above centre for 20 minutes.

KEDGEREE

Originally an Indian dish called Kitcheree which was hot enough to bring tears to European eyes. This is popular when having a few friends in on Sunday.

1 lb (450 g) Patna rice

4 hard-boiled No 3 eggs

4 heaped dessertsps (4 × 10 ml spoons) freshly milled, or chopped parsley

Salt

Black pepper

1 lb (450 g) faked haddock, dyed yellow, or real smoked haddock

5 oz (135 g) butter or Gold

4 oz (100 g) unskinned mushrooms and their stalks, sliced very thinly

Optionally 12 shelled prawns or large shrimps with their heads left on

Note

You can keep it hot if necessary without deterioration in oven at Gas Mark ¼ (approx 240°F, 110°C) one shelf below centre under a complete tenting of Alcan Foil.

Have ready a large saucepan two-thirds filled with boiling water. Stir in 1 heaped tablespoon (1 × 15 ml spoon) salt, then stir in rice and keep stirring until mixture re-bubbles. Cook for exactly 11 minutes. Turn immediately into a strainer or colander. This large amount of water ensures that the surplus starch is satisfactorily washed off during cooking time and after straining. Thus rice will be grain separate. Turn into a roomy bowl. Add the given butter or Gold and work up until every grain is impregnated with it.

Have ready the steamed fish, boned, skinned and flaked. Fold into the rice with the mushrooms. Taste and correct seasoning with salt and black pepper. Turn onto a heated dish – a rectangular Pyrex one is ideal. Shape up into a long panel which rises to a ridge on top.

Separate the yolks from the whites and chop both finely. Put a narrow border of the chopped yolks right around the base of the panel. Make an outer border of the parsley, and a final one of the chopped egg whites. If using the prepared prawns stab their tails in a line down the top ridge and so send to table.

GRILLED MACKEREL WITH GOOSEBERRY SAUCE

The less you do to really fresh mackerel, the better. Just get the fishmonger to top, tail and gut for you and ask if he will split them and remove the spine bone.

2 good-sized, spit-fresh mackerel

A very light seasoning of salt and white pepper

Gooseberry Sauce (our recipe, Volume Two)

Lay the opened fish, head end to tail end, on a heated grill rack and grill on one side only. We allow between 5 and 7 minutes depending upon size. After this, fish will be found to be perfectly cooked and bubbling slightly with their own natural oil. Hand the sauce separately.

HADDOCK AND MUSHROOM PIE

8 oz (225 g) bought, frozen Jus-rol puff paste

4 oz (100 g) cold, cooked rice

4 oz (100 g) very thinly sliced, scalded mushrooms and their stalks

2 heaped tbsps (2 × 15 ml spoons) from a small carton of soured cream

2 heaped tbsps (2 × 15 ml spoons) cream cheese (home-made or bought)

Black pepper

8 oz (225 g) smoked haddock or cod fillet steamed, skinned, boned and flaked

Milk or raw, beaten strained egg

Roll out puff paste thinly and line a medium pie dish. Trim off all surplus to use for lid. Mix together all remaining ingredients and turn in over paste lining. Gather up trimmings and re-roll paste until just large enough to provide the lid. Lay on and trim off edges neatly, pinching these between thumb and second finger to flute. Brush top with either milk or a little raw, beaten strained egg. Bake at Gas Mark 6 (approx 400°F, 200°C) one shelf above centre for 15 minutes. Then move to centre shelf, reduce heat to Gas Mark 4 (approx 350°F, 180°C) and continue baking until pastry has risen well and is a rich golden brown.

Note
This pie is greatly enhanced by the following quick sauce. Soften 4 oz (100 g) Gold over a very low heat, stir in the strained

juice of 1 lemon and stir on to blend. Optionally add 1 heaped tablespoon (1 × 15 ml spoon) finely scissored chives, replaced by milled parsley heads for those who dislike onion flavouring.

SMOKED HADDOCK WITH SPINACH PUREE

1 lb (450 g) smoked haddock
   fillet
1 lb (450 g) fresh spinach
Salt
Black pepper
1 lemon
5 fluid oz (150 ml) single cream
Powdered nutmeg
½ pint (300 ml) milk

Wash and remove stems from spinach leaves. Pack into a saucepan without any water. Set over a low heat and ease from sides and across base with a wooden spoon until pan contents yield their own juices and thus subside. Cook for an absolute maximum of 7 minutes. Emulsify and then sieve to reduce to a fine smooth purée. Beat in half the given cream, with two fat pinches of both nutmeg and black pepper.

Scissor the haddock fillet into 1 inch (2.5 cm) wide strips. Heat the milk in a wide, shallow pan. Keep warm. Lay in the haddock strips and poach until just cooked. Let the milk form a bubble or caul over the fish in preference to turning the strips over and possibly causing them to break up.

When the haddock is ready, make a spinach purée bed on a heated dish, lay fish pieces over and drip on the remaining cream. Cut the lemon into eighths and arrange as a border round the dish at moment of service.

179

HADDOCK MORNAY

1 lb (450 g) smoked haddock
   (skinned, boned weight)
1 lb (450 g) creamed old potatoes
Black pepper
1 pint (600 ml) thick simple
   white sauce
Salt
2½ oz (60 g) grated stale cheese
1 oz (25 g) butter
Milk

Place haddock in a roomy bowl, cover with boiling water and leave for 5 minutes. Drain, wipe and place in a saucepan with just sufficient milk to cover. Raise to boiling, reduce heat and poach until just tender. Strain, skin, bone, then check weight and flake coarsely. Taste milk in which haddock was cooked as this may be sufficiently salty already. If so use only pepper to flavour but use the milk to make the sauce. Beat in 2 oz (50 g) of the cheese.

Pipe or fork a high border of creamed potato around the edges of four buttered deep scallop shells. Fold haddock into cheese sauce. Divide equally inside the four potato borders. Scatter remaining ½ oz (10 g) of cheese on top. Dab remainder of butter in small flakes over the top. Bake one shelf above centre Gas Mark 6 (400°F, 200°C) for 14 minutes.

BORNHOLMER HERRING AND EGG CAKE

Made and served in a frying pan.
1 fat smoked herring or mackerel
4 No 3 eggs
1 teasp (1 × 5 ml spoon)
   chopped chives
1 rasher lean bacon

Set a thick frying pan to heat over a very low burner, while opening up the chosen fish, removing skin and picking apart small pieces of the bone-free flesh. Accumulate these in a saucer. Set bacon rasher to fry in dry pan and when cooked, drain, take off rind and dice coarsely, being sure to leave bacon fat in pan. Draw this slightly away from heat now.

Beat eggs with a fork. Check that bottom heat is low. Pour in eggs, set pan over heat and allow eggs to run and settle over pan base. Run the top of a metal spatula occasionally around outer edges, then tip pan slightly to make unset egg run underneath. As soon as egg begins to set over base, scatter over the pieces of herring flesh. Repeat with bacon dice and sprinkle chives overall. Allow egg cake to continue cooking just until set all over but *not* dry. Serve from the pan with plenty of ideally black bread and butter or Gold.

SWEDISH HERRING BAKE

12 oz (350 g) fishmonger-boned
  fresh herrings
Old potatoes cut into small
  matchsticks – peeled weight
  12 oz (350 g)
A scrap of butter or Gold
Salt
Black pepper
Milk or top-of-the-milk or single
  cream

Cut the herrings into slim strips, removing any stray bones. Cut very thin slices of peeled potato into matchsticks and check weight. Grease a pie dish. Cover base with a layer of herring strips, then of matchstick potatoes and season lightly with salt and black pepper. Repeat until all ingredients are used, ending with a potato layer. Pour in chosen fluid slowly until this becomes visible through the last layer of potatoes. Cover with Alcan Foil and bake on middle shelf at Gas Mark 4 (approx 350°F, 180°C) for 20 minutes. Remove foil and bake for a further 10 minutes so that top potatoes are slightly crisp.

Note
If liked, 2 No 3 eggs can be whipped up with milk before pouring over potatoes.

HERRING ROES IN PUFF PASTRY

8 oz (225 g) thawed Jus-rol puff
   paste
8 oz (225 g) herring roes
Black pepper
3 very thin rashers of de-rinded
   streaky bacon
Milk

Roll out puff paste very thinly using little jerky movements. This encourages the paste to rise. Cut into rectangles measuring 6 × 4 inch (15 × 10 cm). Lay a single roe upon each. Season lightly with black pepper only. English bacon is very salty anyway. Halve the bacon rashers, and cut each half into two strips to lay over the roes. Wet the edges of each paste rectangle with cold water. Fold the two lengthwise edges over and then roll each one up. Rinse a flat baking sheet under the cold tap, shake off any surplus moisture. Then lay rolls on wet surface. Bake one shelf above centre at Gas Mark 6 (approx 400°F, 200°C) until golden brown and serve piping hot in a napkin.

KIPPER PATE

8 oz (225 g) kipper fillets
1 × 1 inch (2.5 cm) thick
   crustless slice cut from a large
   brown loaf
Approx 1 fluid oz (30 ml) cider
Freshly milled black
   peppercorns
1 scant flat teasp (1 × 5 ml
   spoon) concentrated tomato
   purée
1 scant flat eggsp (1 × 2.5 ml
   spoon) anchovy purée

Grill the kipper fillets with grill rack at low position for approx 4 minutes without the necessity of turning them. Cool sufficiently to remove skins, then flake into a roomy bowl and check for any stray remaining bones. In a separate small bowl moisten the bread with the cider and work down to a paste. Work up with flaked kipper flesh and then work in all remaining ingredients. Pot up and refrigerate under a butter paper.

KIPPER CRUSTS

2 fat crusts cut from the base sides of a small cottage loaf
Kipper pâté (see previous recipe)
4 thin slices of packet processed cheese
A little butter or Gold

Toast the crumb side of both slices. Spread the chosen fat, put into two small heat-resistant dishes, cover liberally with kipper pâté, lay cheese slices on top and slip under the grill to bubble and brown.

STUFFED BAKED WHITING

2 × 1 lb (450 g) whiting, topped, tailed and cleaned
4 oz (100 g) fine soft brown breadcrumbs
4 oz (100 g) shelled shrimps
1 dessertsp (1 × 10 ml spoon) fresh milled or finely chopped parsley
Salt
Black pepper
2 teasps (1 × 10 ml spoon) strained lemon juice
2 No 3 eggs
2 firm tomatoes – skinned, seeded and chopped finely
1 large chopped shallot or small onion
1–2 tbsps (1–2 × 15 ml spoons) oil
1 rounded tbsp (1 × 15 ml spoon) flour
1 eggsp (1 × 2.5 ml spoon) anchovy purée
9 fluid oz (270 ml) milk

Chop half the shrimps fairly finely. Place in a bowl with the crumbs, parsley, lemon juice, a generous two pinches of black pepper, the anchovy purée and the tomato flesh. Beat in 1 egg to make a firm but moist stuffing. Hard-boil the other egg and chop fairly finely. Heat oil in a small pan and fry onions slowly until soft and golden.

Meanwhile divide stuffing into two equal parts and stuff back into the two fish. bring the two flaps up over the stuffing and press down lightly. Set in a lightly buttered heat-resistant dish with stuffing side uppermost. When onions are tender, stir in flour to form a roux and dilute gradually with given milk. Add remaining shrimps and shelled, chopped, hard-boiled egg. Finally season very lightly with salt, strongly with pepper and pour mixture right over the fish. Cover lightly with foil and bake Gas Mark 4 (approx 350°F, 180°C) one shelf above centre for 30 minutes.

Fish of the given weight provides ample for four people.

183

BAKED HAKE STEAKS

2 thick hake steaks
1 medium tomato
1 small onion, peeled and sliced
   very thinly
Salt
Black pepper
Squeezed juice from half a
   lemon
1 walnut-sized piece of butter
1½ fluid oz (45 ml) water or cider

Rub the inside of a small heat-resistant container such as a Pyrex 6 inch (15 cm) fairly shallow dish with a small piece of butter or Gold. Sprinkle hake steaks lightly on each side with salt and pepper. Lay in the little dish.

Skin and slice the tomato. To do this, just spear the tomato with a fork and hold it over a fairly strong flame until the skin pops. Then peel easily and cut into four neat slices. Put two over each steak. Season again, very lightly with salt and black pepper. Squeeze lemon juice over both. Dab with flakes of the chosen fat. Swill with either water or cider. Cover with Alcan Foil and bake on middle shelf of oven at Gas Mark 3 (approx 325°F, 160°C) for 25 minutes.

Note
When time allows scrub one or two 8 oz (225 g) old potatoes and put on the same shelf 1¼ hours before the fish. Then both will be done simultaneously.

BAKED PLAICE WITH CHEESE AND TOMATO

2 large plaice fillets
Salt
Black pepper
4 skinned tomatoes
A small section of cut lemon
1 small onion, grated to pulp
1 heaped tbsp (1 × 15 ml spoon)
   grated Cheddar cheese
1½ oz (40 g) soft white or brown

Rub the interior of a small fireproof dish with chosen fat. Roll up the two fillets and set them on the base, side by side. Squeeze with lemon juice. Season lightly with salt and pepper. Cover with half the onion pulp, then half the sliced tomatoes, repeat and season

184

breadcrumbs
1 pinch cayenne pepper
1 oz (25 g) butter or Gold

again. Mix crumbs and cheese with cayenne and spread overall. Dab with remaining flakes of chosen fat and bake at Gas Mark 4 (approx 350°F, 180°C) for 30 minutes on middle shelf.

POOR MAN'S RUSSIAN FISH PIE

In Volume Three you will find the famous Coulibiac made with sturgeon, visega and served with slices of smoked salmon on top. This is the 'peasant' version, deliberately scaled down to very modest proportions. For a family dish given quantities should be doubled.

4 oz (100 g) cooked Patna rice
1 fluid oz (30 ml) oil
2 No 2 hard-boiled eggs
12 oz (350 g) hake or other white
    fish
1 heaped tbsp (1 × 15 ml spoon)
    milled parsley heads
1½ oz (40 g) butter or Gold
Salt
Black pepper
4 oz (100 g) finely chopped,
    cooked green cabbage
2 fluid oz (60 ml) rough, sharp
    cider
12 oz (350 g) dripping pastry
    paste (see overleaf)

Take off sufficient of pastry paste to form a lid to a small to medium pie dish. Roll out the rest on a lightly floured working surface to line pie dish on base and sides.

Heat oil in a small frying pan. Cut hake into boneless fingers. Stiffen by frying in oil very fast until flesh contracts. Cover pastry lining with a third of the cabbage, then a third of the rice, then a third of the fish strips, the same of parsley and of chopped egg. Season lightly with salt and black pepper. Repeat twice more, thus using up all the ingredients except chosen fat and cider. Melt butter or Gold and flick overall. Drip in cider and use remaining pastry paste to form a lid. Bake one shelf above centre at Gas Mark 6 (approx 400°F, 200°C) for 25–30 minutes. Optionally hand a little more melted chosen fat with a squeeze of lemon juice to pour over each serving.

Serve either hot or cold.

DRIPPING PASTRY PASTE

1 lb (450 g) sifted flour
1 flat teasp (1 × 5 ml spoon) salt
½ flat teasp (1 × 2.5 ml spoon)
    white pepper
6 oz (175 g) clean dripping
Cold water
1 No 3 egg

Rub dripping into flour until very fine-grained. Beat up egg and pour into central well in flour. Add salt, pepper and a splash of cold water and work up gradually to a good rolling consistency with a knife, adding more water sparingly. Rest for 1 hour in refrigeration before using.

FISH PUFFS

To use up left-overs of cooked rice and fish.

3 oz (75 g) cold cooked rice
3 oz (75 g) cold cooked fish
1 teasp (1 × 5 ml spoon) strained
    lemon juice
4–5 drops anchovy purée
1 oz (25 g) finely grated hard
    cheese ends
1 chopped hard-boiled egg
2 tbsps (2 × 15 ml spoons)
    top-of-the-milk
8 oz (225 g) Jus-rol frozen puff
    paste

Roll out puff paste very thinly on a lightly floured surface. Then cut into four 7 inch (18 cm) squares. Run an ordinary oven baking sheet under a cold tap. Shake off the drops and space paste squares widely apart on moistened baking sheet. Mix up flaked fish and all given ingredients and divide in equal mounds in the centre of each square. Wet the edges with cold water. Bring all four corners over, one at a time to overlap the filling. Press them down a little. Brush the top surface with a little milk. Bake at Gas Mark 6 (approx 400°F, 200°C) one shelf above centre for 20–25 minutes until pastry is well puffed up and a rich golden brown.

SKEWERED MUSSELS WITH SAFFRON RICE

2 pints (1.20 litres) mussels
4 oz (100 g) de-rinded bacon
    pieces
2 very small shallots
4 small bay leaves

Wash and beard the mussels meticulously. Discard any that are open – they are either dead or dying. Place tightly closed mussels in a pan, cover with

1 No 4 egg
Soup plate of fine soft
  breadcrumbs
1 lemon
2 oz (50 g) butter
Salt
Pepper
2 fluid oz (60 ml) oil
6 oz (175 g) rice
1 thimbleful of saffron
1 tbsp (1 × 15 ml spoon) salt

boiling water and boil for 1½ minutes or to a slow count of ninety. When they are cool enough to handle, remove from their shells.

Pick over a bag of bacon pieces and select those suitable for cutting into 1½ inch (3.75 cm) squares. Tear bay leaves in halves. Boil peeled shallots for 8 minutes in fast boiling, slightly salted water. Drain and cool.

Assemble metal skewers, oil in a saucer, crumbs in one soup plate and the beaten egg in another. Push each item on to skewers alternately. Draw the load through the beaten egg, then bury in the crumbs. Drip all over with oil flicked from a pastry brush. Set on a grill rack to cook. Moisten the lemon juice while grilling. Turn carefully to grill all over. Season lightly with salt and pepper and serve with Saffron Rice.

To cook Saffron Rice
Use abundant boiling water in a large pan with saffron and 1 tbsp (1 × 15 ml spoon) salt stirred in. When water bubbles fiercely, tip in the rice, stir until mixture re-bubbles and allow 11½ minutes from this point, thus obtaining yellow, grain-separate rice which only needs straining and is *al dente* or firm to the teeth. Mound on a dish in a neat rectangle and lay the skewered mussels on top.

187

STEAMED FISH PUDDING

Suet crust
12 oz (350 g) cod
2 tbsps (2 × 15 ml spoons) fine
  soft crumbs
1 dessertsp (1 × 10 ml spoon)
  chopped parsley heads
1 dessertsp (1 × 10 ml spoon)
  raw grated onion pulp
A generous pinch of salt and of
  white pepper
1 No 2 egg
4 drops anchovy essence
1 eggsp (1 × 2.5 ml spoon)
  grated lemon peel

Roll out suet crust to line a 1½ lb (750 g) pudding basin, leaving a sufficient overlap at rim to trim away, gather up and re-roll for the lid.

Steam fish for 10 minutes, then skin, flake and remove any stray bones. Mix with parsley, onion pulp, grated lemon peel, salt and pepper and work up to a paste with beaten egg. Fill into prepared basin. Wet dough's rim with cold water and re-roll remaining suet crust to form a lid. Press this over wetted edge. Cover first with a butter paper and then with Alcan Foil, making a pleat at centre to allow for the dough's expansion during cooking.

Stand in base pan of a steamer on a 1 inch (2.5 cm) folded strip of Alcan Foil long enough to go over base, continue up both sides and meet over the top of the pudding. Thus the basin can be lifted out with ease. Pour in boiling water to come two-thirds up the basin's sides. Have more boiling water available to top up during cooking. Cover with lid and simmer steadily for 2 hours. Unmould and serve with Anchovy and Egg Sauce (our receipe, Volume Two). Either pour sauce over unmoulded pudding on its heated dish or serve separately in a small jug or sauceboat.

FISH FAGGOTS

6 oz (175 g) steamed white fish
 with skin and bones removed
6 oz (175 g) cold, mashed
 potatoes
1 level eggsp (1 × 2.5 ml spoon)
 celery salt
A flick of cayenne pepper
A grate, or pinch, of nutmeg
1½ oz (40 g) crumbled vermicelli
A few drops of anchovy essence
1 No 2 egg
A little butter or Gold
Salt
A little milk
Fine soft breadcrumbs
Oil to fry
White pepper

Mix mashed potato with flaked fish and work in a generous pinch of salt with cayenne pepper, white pepper, nutmeg and anchovy essence used sparingly. Work up with milk into a firm paste and shape into 1¼ oz (30 g) sausages. Dip these in egg, bury in crumbs and pat these in thoroughly. At the moment of frying pass again through the beaten egg and roll in the vermicelli. Deep fry in very hot oil until richly browned. Drain on absorbent kitchen paper. Serve with Anchovy and Egg Sauce (our recipe, Volume Two).

QUEENIE PIE

Queenies are the name given to small succulent scollops from the Isle of Man.

1 lb (450 g) creamed, seasoned
 potatoes
½ pint (300 ml) thick white sauce
Salt
Pepper
1 oz (25 g) grated strong
 Cheddar or ½ oz (10 g) grated
 Parmesan
1 No 3 egg
2 fluid oz (60 ml) Long Life
 single cream
1 lb (450 g) queenies
I hard-boiled egg

Chop up the hard-boiled egg and fold into the sauce with a seasoning of both salt and pepper to taste. Work in the chosen cheese. Finally rough-chop the well-washed little scollops and be sure to pick off any little bits of black found clinging to them. Fold and blend into sauce mixture. Turn into a lightly greased small pie dish. Make potato mixture really creamy so that you can spread it right over the sauce mixture. Bake at Gas Mark 4 (approx 350°F, 180°C) one shelf above centre for 15 minutes and eat while bubbling hot.

MONKFISH CREAM

8 oz (225 g) monkfish, skinned
  and boned
5 fluid oz (150 ml) shelled
  shrimps, fresh or frozen and
  thawed
1 smallest tin Libby's
  unsweetened milk
3 fluid oz (90 ml) cold water
1 dessertsp (1 × 10 ml spoon)
  powdered gelatine
4 fluid oz (120 ml) dry white
  wine
Black pepper
3–4 parsley stalks (whenever
  possible)

Cut raw fish into bite-sized pieces. Poach in the wine and water with the parsley stalks. Simmer for 10 minutes. Leave to become cold in the liquor, then remove parsley stalks. Take sufficient liquor to soften gelatine in a very small pan over a low heat. Add the unsweetened milk and raise to boiling while stirring over a gentle heat. Strain, add the monkfish mixture, taste and correct seasoning with pepper. The mixture is unlikely to need more salt than is already in the shrimps; but add a pinch or two if really necessary. Pour into a shallow, wetted mould and refrigerate. Serve well-chilled with a mixed or tossed green salad.

FISH CAKES

These must be moist and soft inside.
8 oz (225 g) rock salmon fillet
4 oz (100 g) cooked potatoes
2 tbsps (2 × 15 ml spoons) very
  thick white sauce
1 smallest egg
Salt
White pepper
1 flat teasp (1 × 5 ml spoon)
  curry powder

Steam the fish until sufficiently cooked to flake finely. Work in white sauce with sieved potato, curry powder and a seasoning of salt and white pepper. Beat in egg and refrigerate for a few moments to make firm enough to shape into flat rounds, approx ¼ inch (5 mm) deep and 2½ inch (6.25 cm) in diameter. Turn in flour, dust off surplus and shallow fry in a little oil in a frying pan. When well browned on undersides turn over and repeat. Serve with tomato sauce.

190

Eggs

The egg white soufflé
The three-egg soufflé
Basic economical soufflé mixture (savoury)
Basic economical soufflé mixture (sweet)
Spanish tomato and croûton omelette
Onion and croûton omelette
Emmeline's eggs
Herb sauce
Waffle fillings or spreads
Coconut butter
Egg and spinach cocottes
Spinach and egg cocotte
Egg-stuffed tomatoes
Eggs on rice with corn
Florentine eggs
Savoury custard tartlets
Highland eggs
Onion sauce
Poached eggs with onion sauce
Egg and sweet corn flan
Egg and bacon pasty-pie
Spanish eggs

Savoury Spanish torrijas
Egg and sardine pâté
Egg bake
Grandfather's special
Oeufs à la Bruxelloise

Every time we eat what used to be called a 'standard' egg we take in the equivalent of 2½ oz (60 g) steak. This is a particularly important comparison if we remind ourselves that even at their highest price, eggs are still one of the least costly nourishing food items we can buy today.

Eggs are porous so we should never keep them in refrigerators where they absorb the odours and flavours of other foodstuffs. The extreme proof of this fact concerns a luxury we are very unlikely to produce. When the thrifty French put Truffle Omelette on a restaurant menu at a modest price, they are able to do this with what is known as the black diamond of French gastronomy because – in truffle-growing regions – they pack a dozen or more fresh eggs with one truffle – unwashed and straight from the ground – into an airtight container together. After a few days the eggs have absorbed the flavour of the truffle through their shells. Then the truffle is cleaned and used for astronomically expensive dishes, while only a few tiny truffle trimmings are added to the egg mixture for those omelettes.

Both separated egg yolks and egg whites keep very well in refrigeration, if they are stored either in little plastic Tupperware bowls with gripping plastic lids, or covered securely with Alcan Foil or transparent cling wrap. Yolks keep this way for a week and egg whites much longer. As we know, it is always best to use 8–10-day-old egg whites for anything which calls for stiffly whipped egg whites. There is never any need to add that ubiquitous pinch of salt some cooks direct, but should a drip of water, or a sliver of egg yolk, get into those whites, they will seldom whip as successfully. In very hot weather it is always advisable to whisk at an opened door or window to pass the ultimate test: just tip the bowl up over your head and if the whites do not slip out, they are perfectly whipped.

Fresh eggs sink in cold water, very stale ones float. When making a brine of salt and water, you never need to know the exact proportion of coarse salt to water. Just put a raw fresh egg into the water and keep on stirring in more salt until the egg floats.

THE EGG WHITE SOUFFLE

This is the easiest soufflé of all.

5 separated No 3 egg whites
12 oz (350 g) any chosen jam
Butter

Whip egg whites as stiffly as possible. Rub chosen jam through an ordinary sieve. Fold/turn the resultant purée into the stiff egg whites until well, but gently blended. Level off in a 6 inch (15 cm) diameter, buttered soufflé mould and bake one shelf above centre at Gas Mark 7 (approx 425°F, 200°C) for exactly 13 minutes.

Note 1

This mixture, if liked, can be filled into 6 small aluminium individual pudding basins that have been well oiled immediately before so that the oil does not trickle back into the base. Draw a metal spatula right across, thus locking in the mixture. Set on a baking sheet and bake for 8 minutes one shelf above centre at Gas Mark 7 (approx 425°F, 220°C). Have an oven glove and a small sharp knife ready. Take each soufflé basin in one hand, run the knife around the inside edge carefully and invert onto a heated dish.

The remarkable thing is that they not only turn out without collapsing, but also hold their shape and remain perfectly edible when completely cold.

Note 2

A most impressive soufflé is made with 2 tins of Heinz Peach and Apricot Junior Foods and the 5 egg whites. Use one tin instead of the given jam to fold into the stiffly whipped whites. Then while the soufflé is baking for 8 minutes, turn contents of second tin into a tiny saucepan and heat very slowly. When piping hot, add half a miniature bottle of peach or apricot brandy and pour a little over each little dome on its dish.

These are good enough for any dinner party.

THE THREE-EGG SOUFFLE

This is the second easiest soufflé.

3 No 3 eggs
4 rounded dessertsps (4 × 10 ml spoons) caster sugar
A pinch of vanilla powder
Butter

Separate the eggs. Place the yolks in a small bowl and whip with the caster sugar until well-blended. Whip the egg whites until very stiff. Stir yolk mixture into the stiff whites with a gentle fold/turn movement until well-blended. Butter the sides and base of a 6 inch (15 cm) diameter soufflé mould. Turn in the mixture, level off and bake at Gas Mark 7 (approx 425°F, 220°C) one shelf above centre for exactly 13 minutes. Serve immediately.

Variations on the above mixture:
Spread the buttered base of the soufflé mould with a 1 inch (2.5 cm) layer of apple and sultana mixture (Puddings, p. 298), or with sliced tinned fruit, such as pears, apricots or peaches using only a few drops of the syrup. Turn the given soufflé mixture on top, level off and bake as above.

194

BASIC ECONOMICAL SOUFFLE MIXTURE (Savoury)

1½ oz (40 g) sifted flour

1½ oz (40 g) butter

3 oz (75 g) grated hard cheese (ideally Parmesan)

7 only fairly stiffly whipped No 3 egg whites (*no* egg yolks, please)

¾ pint (450 ml) milk *or* 5 fluid oz (150 ml) dry white cooking wine and ½ pint (300 ml) milk

1 flat eggsp (1 × 2.5 ml spoon) salt

1 flat eggsp (1 × 2.5 ml spoon) black pepper

1 flat eggsp (1 × 2.5 ml spoon) dry English mustard

Make a roux with the flour and butter but do not bother to stir for the 3–4 minutes needed when making sauces in order to expel the taste of flour. The baking does that for you. Switch on an electric mixer at full speed and leave to whip the egg whites while you add the chosen fluids to the roux gradually, drawing in the cheese as you do so and giving a very thorough beating after each addition. Work in the salt, pepper and dry mustard. Remove from the heat. Give one final vigorous beating. Switch off the mixer and then draw in a big blob of the egg white and blend fast with a plastic spatula. Add more, repeat with remaining egg white, beat in and turn into a 7 inch (18 cm) diameter Pyrex soufflé mould which has been buttered and floured. Bake at one shelf above centre Gas Mark 7 (approx 425°F, 220°C) for 15 minutes by which time the soufflé will have soared to a flat hugely risen brown top and the mixture will remain very moist at centre.

BASIC ECONOMICAL SOUFFLE MIXTURE (Sweet)

The recipe is really constant so all you have to change now is the flavouring. Replace the cheese with 3 oz (75 g) vanilla-flavoured caster sugar. Omit salt, pepper and mustard and use sweet white wine instead of the dry one needed for savoury mixtures. Otherwise proceed exactly as before. If you have no vanilla sugar available, heat milk very slowly with a vanilla pod. Remove, wipe and store to use over and over again until the flavour diminishes.

SPANISH TOMATO AND CROUTON OMELETTE

4 No 3 eggs
1 large, peeled tomato
3 thinly cut slices from a
    sandwich loaf
1 fluid oz (30 ml) oil and 1 oz
    (25 g) butter or 2 oz (50 g)
    dripping
Additional 1 oz (25 g) butter
Salt
Black pepper

Remove all seeds from the tomato and chop up the flesh. Break eggs into a bowl and add tomato dice. Cut bread slices into dice. Heat oil and butter or dripping in a small frying pan. When hot turn in bread dice and stir/fry until dice have taken up all the fat and become crispy and browned. Turn into egg bowl. Beat all lightly with a fork, beating in a seasoning of both salt and black pepper.

Have ready two heated medium-sized plates. Add additional butter to frying pan to set over a low heat. When melted and turning slightly brown at edges, turn in the egg mixture and stir fairly gently over the low heat, easing up the sides so that the fluid runs underneath until omelette is well formed and only just beginning to set on upper surface. Divide in the pan and lift half of this flat omelette onto each plate. Serve immediately. Remember that all omelettes go on cooking even on a warm plate!

ONION AND CROUTON OMELETTE

The best way of handling this is to have ready a bowl of soft-fried, drained onions and another of little diced fried croûtons so that a spoonful of each can be added to each beaten egg. We give the recipe as for one serving.

1 No 3 egg
Half a thin-cut slice from a
    sandwich loaf, diced small
1 oz (25 g) diced, raw onion
Salt

Heat the oil, fry the onion gently. Drain and set aside, fry croûtons in the pan residue until crisp and brown. Fold both onion and croûtons into lightly

Black pepper
1 tbsp (1 × 15 ml spoon) oil
Butter

beaten egg, season with salt and pepper and make into a flat omelette fast over a buttery surface (Eggs and Cheese, Part 1 p. 44).

EMMELINE'S EGGS

4 No 2 or 3 eggs
2 oz (50 g) butter or Gold
4 round pieces of bread stamped out with a fluted 3 inch (7.5 cm) diameter pastry cutter
Herb sauce

Melt the butter in a chafing dish over a low heat. When hot slide in the eggs and leave over a low light until set. Stamp out neatly with a pastry cutter and lift each onto a croûton (fried in the residue butter from cooking the eggs). Spoon the herb sauce liberally over the top.

HERB SAUCE

1 small, finely chopped shallot
1 small sprig of thyme
A pinch each of finely scissored chives, savory, marjoram, sage and basil
2 peppercorns
A grate of nutmeg
7 fluid oz (210 ml) consommé (tinned or fresh)
1 tbsp (1 × 15 ml spoon) butter
1 tbsp (1 × 15 ml spoon) flour
1 teasp (1 × 5 ml spoon) mixed, chopped chervil and tarragon
Strained juice of quarter of a very small lemon

Put shallot, thyme, chives, savory, marjoram, sage, basil, peppercorns and nutmeg into a small pan and cover with boiling consommé. Cover with a lid and leave to infuse over a low heat for 10 minutes. Strain and set liquor aside. Make a roux with given butter and flour. Add strained consommé, beating well between each addition. When all is absorbed, smooth and devoid of any flour taste, stir in the mixed herbs and lemon juice and use.

WAFFLE FILLINGS OR SPREADS

Instructions for making waffles are given in Eggs, Part 1 p. 52.
1   De-rinded, grilled bacon and the fat from cooking this in a completely dry pan poured on top.
2   Sprinkle 1–2 tbsps (1–2 × 15 ml spoons) of finely diced fat and lean ham or gammon over surface after spreading this out on iron. Dab butter flakes over finished waffle.
3   Add 4 oz (100 g) any chopped nuts to completed batter and serve

with maple syrup or, less costly, Tate & Lyle's golden syrup.

4   Add 4 oz (100 g) fine-grated hard cheese to otherwise completed batter and dot finished waffle with extra butter flakes.

5   Add 1–2 teasps (1–2 × 5 ml spoons) finely grated lemon or orange zest to completed batter. Serve with butter flakes and orange or lemon preserves.

6   Follow instructions for adding zest in No 5 but top with orange ice cream or lemon sorbet.

7   Add 4 oz (100 g) shredded fresh or dried coconut to batter and spread with Coconut Butter.

8   Serve plain and hand maple syrup (or golden syrup) in a jug with butter or Gold to dab on in flakes.

COCONUT BUTTER

4 oz (100 g) unsalted butter or Gold

4 oz (100 g) sifted icing sugar

4 oz (100 g) desiccated coconut

Whip butter until light and fluffy and then work in sugar and coconut. Spread over hot waffles and serve.

EGG AND SPINACH COCOTTES

If wanted for a supper dish, bake four. If just for a first course, bake two. For each one you will need:

1 rounded tbsp (1 × 15 ml spoon) cooked, sieved spinach

Pinch of nutmeg

Pinch of black pepper

½ oz (10 g) butter or Gold

1 No 3 egg

1 rounded teasp (1 × 5 ml spoon) grated hard cheese

Rub chosen fat over base and sides of each 3 inch (7.5 cm) diameter cocotte. Mix each portion of spinach with the nutmeg, pepper and half the given cheese. Spread half over cocotte base, break in an egg, cover lightly with remaining spinach mixture and sprinkle with remaining cheese. Stand in a shallow pan with sufficient boiling water to come half way up the cocottes' sides. Cover pan. Set over a very low heat for 11–12 minutes.

Note
If left to go cold thereafter the gradually diminishing heat will set the eggs before service!

198

SPINACH AND EGG COCOTTE

1 small teacupful fresh, or
  tinned, cooked spinach
4 No 2 eggs
Salt
Black pepper
A pinch of nutmeg
1 tbsp (1 × 15 ml spoon)
  top-of-the-milk
1½ oz (40 g) grated Parmesan or
  other hard cheese
1 dessertsp (1 × 10 ml spoon) oil

Oil a shallow cocotte dish. Chop spinach and season with salt and black pepper. Add nutmeg to taste. Beat in top-of-the-milk and turn onto the base of the dish. Whip eggs with 1 oz (25 g) of given cheese and a pinch each of salt and pepper. Pour over spinach, sprinkle with remaining cheese and bake one shelf above centre at Gas Mark 6 (approx 400°F, 200°C) for 8 minutes. Serve immediately with hot brown or white toast.

EGG-STUFFED TOMATOES

2 large tomatoes
2 very small eggs
Salt
Pepper
2 tbsps (2 × 15 ml spoons)
  simple cheese sauce (Basics,
  Part 1)

Slice small lids from tomatoes and hollow them out with the aid of a small pair of point-ended scissors. Put a teaspoonful of sauce into the base of each tomato. Break an egg over the sauce. Sprinkle with salt and pepper. Cover with remaining sauce, replace lids and bake in a little tin with a trickle of water in the base, for 12 minutes one shelf above centre at Gas Mark 6 (approx 400°F, 200°C). Serve with buttered toast as a first course.

EGGS ON RICE WITH CORN

2 oz (50 g) cold, cooked Patna
  rice
1 smallest tin Green Giant corn
  with pimentos
4 small eggs
Salt
1 oz (25 g) butter or Gold

Heat corn in its own liquor, work in rice and chosen fat and keep warm. Hard-boil and shell eggs, halve centrally and keep warm. Turn half corn and rice mixture into a small, shallow dish. Press in halved eggs to half their depth. Turn remaining mixture over all and reheat.

FLORENTINE EGGS

1 small tin or thawed, frozen
    pack of spinach
12 triangular croûtons
4 No 4 eggs
2 oz (50 g) grated Emmenthal
    cheese
5 tbsps (5 × 15 ml spoons) oil
1½ slices crustless bread
2 oz (50 g) butter or Gold
Salt
Black pepper
A pinch of nutmeg

Rub chosen fat over base and sides of a small chafing dish. Empty spinach into a small pan, stir until hot and then rub through a sieve into dish. Season to taste with salt, black pepper and nutmeg. Smooth off top surface.

Heat 3 tablespoons (3 × 15 ml spoons) oil in a small frying pan. Break and slide in the eggs and let them set very slowly over a low heat, just flicking a spoon over the tops for a moment or two to veil them delicately with egg white. Slip a metal slice underneath and lift onto spinach bed. Cover with grated cheese. Slip under a fierce grill to bubble and brown very fast.

Add remaining oil to residue in frying pan and fry bread briskly until browned and slightly crisp. Cut whole slice in halves, then cut into small triangles, do the same with the half-slice and prod broad end of each into spinach to form a border.

SAVOURY CUSTARD TARTLETS

4 oz (100 g) yoghurt pastry paste
2 oz (50 g) cooked, chopped
    gammon or lean pork or
    chicken
Salt
White pepper
1 heaped tbsp (1 × 15 ml spoon)
    grated hard cheese ends
1 rounded teasp (1 × 5 ml
    spoon) chopped parsley

Roll out paste to a mean ⅛ inch (3 mm) thickness. Lay over a six-indent bun tin and roll rolling pin over, thus filling all at once. Cut away surplus pastry with a sharp knife. Fill with dried pulses or dried cherry stones. Bake for 10 minutes at Gas Mark 5 (approx 375°F, 190°C). Tip out pulses or stones

1 No 4 egg
4 fluid oz (120 ml) milk
Dried pulses or cherry stones

and press down base firmly.
Whip egg into warmed milk, stir
in chosen meat dice, parsley and
a light seasoning of salt and
pepper. Fill into little pastry
cases. Bake at Gas Mark 4
(approx 350°F, 180°C) until risen
and set. Serve hot or cold.

HIGHLAND EGGS

8 oz (225 g) Finnan haddock
½ oz (10 g) butter or Gold
5 fluid oz (150 ml) and a little
    extra milk
Oil in pan or deep-fryer
2 hard-boiled No 3 eggs
1 small beaten egg
A shallow dish of fine, soft
    breadcrumbs
½ oz (10 g) flour

Place fish in a pan with chosen
fat and 5 fluid oz (150 ml) milk.
Allow milk to bubble up and
seethe over fish, then reduce to a
simmer, turning fish after 5
minutes to complete on reverse
side. Drain, remove all skin and
any stray bones. Flake finely
(scrubbed fingers are best!).

Pour the fishy milk into a
measuring jug and bulk up again
to 5 fluid oz (150 ml). Use a little
to stir the flour into a smooth
paste. Boil the rest, pour over
the paste, stir well and return to
the pan. Stir until boiling and
thickened. Work in the fish and
again mix well. Correct seasoning and divide into two equal
parts. Press a shelled egg into
each and mould fish up to cover
completely – like Scotch eggs.

Turn in raw, beaten egg, then
in crumbs and pat in very firmly.
Lower into slightly smoking hot
oil and fry to a strong golden
brown all over. Drain on
absorbent paper. Halve each
with a sharp knife and serve
with Onion Sauce either
separately or turned over eggs in
a small dish.

ONION SAUCE (Sauce Soubise)

We give this in a larger quantity than will be needed for Highland Eggs because it keeps for a week in ordinary refrigeration and is very versatile.

1 lb (450 g) peeled, thinly-sliced
   onions
1 pint (600 ml) milk
Salt
Black pepper
5 fluid oz (150 ml) whipping or
   double cream (whenever
   possible)

Put onions into a medium-sized pan, add milk, raise to boiling, then level off to a simmer and maintain until onions are tender. Strain, then emulsify or sieve using as little of the milk as possible. Meanwhile return remaining milk to a small pan and reduce by steady simmering to 5 fluid oz (150 ml). Stir in the onion purée. Add cream, taste and season with salt and black pepper.

Serve with roast lamb, or to give a tremendous lift to a plain grilled cod-steak, or with any of the egg dishes so indicated in this chapter.

POACHED EGGS WITH ONION SAUCE

2 rounds of buttered toast
2 No 4 eggs
5 fluid oz (150 ml) Onion Sauce
   with 1 fluid oz (30 ml) double
   or whipping cream added
Salt
Black pepper
1 oz (25 g) hard grated cheese

Break eggs into a saucer and thus slide into a frying pan containing slightly heaving hot water to which a spoonful or two of wine vinegar has been added. Flick over with a spoon (away from yourself please) until a thin white film sets on top. When ready lift with a metal slice onto absorbent paper and allow to drain before sliding onto the toast set on medium, heat-resistant plates. Blend cream into given sauce. Spoon over the eggs, sprinkle the tops with given cheese and just bubble up very fast under a full grill. Eat immediately.

EGG AND SWEET CORN FLAN

1 uncooked 8 inch (20 cm)
   diameter short paste flan case
4 No 3 eggs
1 small tin of Green Giant corn
   with pimentos
Herb sauce (p. 197)
1 oz (25 g) butter or Gold
2 rashers of de-rinded back
   bacon cut into ½ inch (1.25
   cm) strips

Spread half the herb sauce over
the base of the flan case evenly.
Make four indents with an oiled
tablespoon – evenly spaced out
over the sauce. Break a single
egg into each indent. Season
with salt and white pepper.
Cover with the drained sweet
corn, spreading it lightly but
evenly on top. Trellis with bacon
strips. Cover with remaining
sauce. Dot with flakes of butter
or Gold and bake at Gas Mark 4
(approx 350°F, 180°C) on centre
shelf until lightly browned on
top. Serve hot or cold.

EGG AND BACON PASTY-PIE

5 oz (135 g) sifted flour
2 oz (50 g) clean dripping or lard
Water
3 rashers de-rinded streaky
   bacon
2 No 2 eggs
1 oz (25 g) raw, fine-grated onion
   pulp
Black pepper to season
1 oz (25 g) grated hard cheese
   ends

Bind flour in a small bowl with
sparing additions of cold water
to make a firm paste. Roll out to
¼ inch (5 mm) thickness on a
cold, floured surface. Cut
chosen fat into flakes and spread
over the surface. Roll up and roll
out again twice more until fat is
evenly incorporated. Lay in a
6–7 inch (15–18 cm) chafing dish.
Scissor off surplus and re-roll to
⅛ inch (3 mm) thickness. Cut
into ½ inch (1.25 cm) strips.
Spread onion pulp over paste
base. Cut bacon into strips.
Break eggs over onions. Trellis
with bacon strips and scatter
liberally with grated cheese.
Season with black pepper.
Arrange paste strips on top and
bake on middle shelf at Gas
Mark 5 (approx 375°F, 190°C) for
20 minutes. Serve hot or cold.

203

SPANISH EGGS (Huevos Flamenca)

1½ fluid oz (45 ml) oil

4 medium peeled onions chopped small

12 oz (350 g) raw, peeled diced old potatoes

1 large peeled, crushed garlic clove

1 good-sized pimento

4 large No 3 eggs

Ideally, 4 oz cooked diced Spanish *chorizo* or just use pork sausage-meat

A little extra oil

4 × 3 inch (7.5 cm) squares of bread cut from a thin cut sandwich loaf

Heat oil and soft-fry onions until almost tender but not browned. Work in potato dice and fry until nearly tender adding an extra spoonful of oil if considered necessary. Halve pimento lengthwise, place halves skin uppermost under a moderate grill. When skins blister and begin to brown, peel them off easily. Remove pips and pith, then dice and work into pan contents with the prepared garlic. Fry until just soft. Add the chosen diced sausage.

Fill mixture into 4 small heat-resistant dishes. Press the back of a soup spoon down at centre to form a little egg nest. Break an egg into each. Moisten each bread square with a few drops of extra oil. Place one over each egg and bake at Gas Mark 6 (approx 400°F, 200°C) one shelf above centre for 12–14 minutes.

SAVOURY SPANISH TORRIJAS

1 inch (2.5 cm) thick slices of new bread

4 fluid oz (120 ml) cold water

2½ fluid oz (75 ml) cooking-type sherry

2 No 3 eggs

Oil for deep-frying

Grated stale cheese ends

1 tbsp (1 × 15 ml spoon) paprika powder

Stamp out 2½ inch (6.25 cm) rounds of bread. Mix water with sherry in a shallow dish. Beat eggs and strain into another shallow dish. Mix the grated cheese and paprika in a third. Pass bread rounds through sherry mixture, then through egg and slide into hot oil (390–400°F, 195–200°C). Allow them to puff up and turn a rich golden brown. Lift out instantly and bury in cheese mixture. Serve with a hot cheese sauce.

EGG AND SARDINE PATE

A quickie with next-to-no cooking.
6 No 3 eggs
2 teasps (2 × 5 ml spoons) soy
    sauce
Salt
Pepper
4½ oz (115 g) tin Marie Elisabeth
    sardines in oil
2 heaped tbsps (2 × 15 ml
    spoons) single cream
1 teasp (1 × 5 ml spoon) red
    wine vinegar
Lea and Perrins Worcestershire
    Sauce to taste

Hard-boil, shell and rough-cut
the eggs. Put everything
pell-mell into a Moulinex
Maxima and switch on, switch
off, for slow counts of ten until
the mixture becomes smooth
and creamy.

Alternatively, rub chopped
eggs through a sieve into a
roomy bowl. Mash sardines and
add with vinegar, soy sauce and
Worcestershire sauce. Beat
down until smooth or rub
through a fine sieve. Beat in the
cream.

Turn into a shallow
straight-sided dish measuring 6
inch (15 cm) diameter and 1½
inch (3.75 cm) deep.

For service chill well and run a
thin border of milled fresh
parsley heads around the inside
top.

Note
This pâté also makes an excellent
filling for very thinly rolled 7
inch (18 cm) × 5½ inch (11.25
cm) isosceles triangles of thawed
frozen Jus-rol puff paste. These
are then egg-washed and either
baked to a puffed-up golden
brown or slid into faintly
hazed-with-heat oil in a fryer
and turned when puffed and
browned on one side to repeat.
Drain and serve.

205

EGG BAKE

4 hard-boiled eggs
1 tbsp (1 × 15 ml spoon) melted
    butter or Gold
1 rounded dessertsp (1 × 10 ml
    spoon) milled or chopped
    parsley heads and of grated
    raw onion pulp
5 heaped tbsps (5 × 15 ml
    spoons) stale white crumbs
Salt
Black pepper
½ pint (300 ml) thick white sauce
4 oz (100 g) grated hard cheese,
    choosing from Gruyère,
    Comté and Emmenthal, in
    that order or making do with
    hard, strong Cheddar
A little extra butter or Gold

Shell and halve eggs crosswise. Remove yolks into a bowl. Mix with chosen melted fat, parsley and onions. Add 1 heaped tablespoon (1 × 15 ml spoon) crumbs, a generous pinch of both salt and pepper and sufficient of the white sauce to bind to a paste. Stuff back into the egg white halves.

Rub a little extra chosen fat over base of two small earthenware dishes.

Mix half given cheese into plain white sauce, taste and adjust seasoning with salt and pepper. Spoon a little sauce over the prepared base of each dish. Set 4 halved, stuffed eggs on this in each one. Add all but 2 tablespoons (2 × 15 ml spoons) crumbs to remaining sauce and beat well and pour or spoon round and finally just over the remaining eggs. Sprinkle with crumbs. Dot with flakes of extra butter and bake on middle shelf at Gas Mark 4 (approx 350°F, 180°C) for 15 minutes.

Variations
These include folding 2 oz (50 g) shelled shrimps into the sauce before pouring over the eggs, or adding 2 heaped tablespoons (2 × 15 ml spoons) of cooked fresh or frozen peas around the eggs before adding remaining sauce, when wanting to make a slightly more filling supper dish.

GRANDFATHER'S SPECIAL

Fanny's grandfather, born in the Victorian era and a renowned wine connoisseur, had this mixture every day of his life for tea which he took alone in the breakfast room, while Gran regaled her afternoon tea callers with cucumber sandwiches, sand cake and jumballs. Grandfather had already eaten a Victorian English breakfast, an eight-course luncheon and fully expected a nine-course dinner!

A large tin of Marie Elisabeth
    sardines *in oil*
2 soft-boiled eggs
2 slices of very new, ¼ inch (5
    mm) thick crust and crumbs of
    a white loaf, torn into small
    pieces
Wine vinegar
Freshly milled black pepper

Remove spine bones and tails from the required number of sardines. Mash roughly, moisten with flicks of wine vinegar, sprinkle on freshly milled black pepper and mix with bread pieces. Then cut the tops from the soft-boiled eggs, spoon the yolks and whites onto the sardine mixture, work up like a dog's dinner and eat with a dessertspoon with plenty of extremely thin bread and butter.

Note
Occasionally the old boy would ring the changes, using chopped-up slices of the fat and lean of a York ham which always appeared on the sideboard at breakfast time. This replaced the sardines and vinegar and was often eaten by him at breakfast.

Given that a piece of fatty gammon has been sufficiently soaked in cold water to make it sweet and not like a slice off Lot's posterior, this can be used instead of ham.

207

OEUFS A LA BRUXELLOISE

2 heads of chicory
½ pint (300 ml) simple cheese
   sauce (Basics, Part 1 p. 24)
3 oz (75 g) butter
3 lumps of sugar
4 No 3 eggs
Salt
White pepper

First prepare the chicory by placing it with the lumps of sugar in a pan and covering with boiling water. When re-boiling, steady off at a strong simmer and maintain for 5 minutes. Drain, discard the water and slice the chicory heads small. Place in a pan with the butter. Finish cooking until collapsed over a low heat. Season with salt and white pepper and spread over a lightly buttered chafing dish.

Boil the eggs for precisely 2¾ minutes. Lift out fast. Tap gently against side of sink, then peel with care under a very thin trickle of tap water. Pour one-third of the sauce onto the chicory and spread out. Make four indents in the sauce with an oiled tablespoon. Lower one shelled, soft-boiled egg into each indent and cover with remaining sauce. Finally dot with flakes of extra butter and brown fast under a very strong grill.

Pastas

Spaghetti with Italian sauce
Sicilian spaghetti
Spaghetti with chickens' livers
Vegetable spaghetti
Maize flour polenta
Substitute polenta with semolina and processed cheese
Spaghetti pie
Italian fonduta
Tortellini with cream
Vermicelli kedgeree
Cheese gnocchi

If you like your pastas to be soft, then by all means cook them for a few minutes longer than our given times. Just understand that strictly speaking all pastas should only be cooked until they are *al dente* or firm to the teeth, not like stewed knitting.

Do not be tempted to buy large quantities of packet pastas to leave languishing in the store cupboard. When you become family cooks, for whom Volume Two has been compiled, you will find what an enormous advantage there is in making your own pastas. For some types of pasta a little machine is needed – in addition to more time than you, who may be out all day, can possibly spare.

All pastas require abundant, salted boiling water for cooking them properly. And remember that all members of the long, slim and not-so-slim spaghetti family are best paid slowly into the boiling water. They soften instantly on impact so there is really little point in breaking them up for immersion.

For any pastas which you intend serving plainly, there are certain small, very beneficial attentions to give them *after* cooking and *immediate* straining. Wipe the hot cooking pan, return the chosen pasta, add 2 tablespoons (2 × 15 ml spoons) oil to every 8 oz (225 g) of pasta and swirl round with a fork before turning into a roomy bowl. Hand a small bowl of grated cheese separately. The high cost of living in Italy has made it hard for the average person to afford Parmesan with their chosen pasta, so many content themselves just with oil and well-crushed garlic. A good way of doing this is to put the given oil into a small frying pan with the crushed garlic, leave over a moderate heat for 1 minute and then tip over the pasta and stir in.

You may also like to know that as a general rule 3–4 oz (75–100 g) per head is adequate unless you are cooking for gannets!

HOW TO COOK SPAGHETTI

Two-thirds fill a large pan with fast boiling water. Stir in 1 flat tablespoon (1 × 15 ml spoon) Maldon sea salt, French *gros sel* or rock salt. When bubbling steadily lower 8 oz (225 g) spaghetti into the water. Stir with a wooden spoon until the bubbling recommences, then allow 11½ minutes and strain. Return to dried hot pan. Add 2 tablespoons (2 × 15 ml spoons) of best possible oil, or, if preferred, butter or Gold instead. Swirl pasta around to impregnate and serve.

HOW TO FLAVOUR SPAGHETTI (AND OTHER PASTAS)

Especially when served on its own, spaghetti needs herbs. These can be powdered sage leaves, scissored chives mixed with milled or chopped parsley heads or, best of all, the wild thyme (*oregano*) which abounds in the entire Mediterranean area.

If visiting this region take along a large polythene bag. Stamp a few air holes in it with a hole-puncher – as otherwise there is a danger that the herbs will go mouldy in their container during the return journey. Once home give the bag an almighty thwacking to dislodge the bulk of herbs from their stems. Store in an earthenware jar with a lid cut from a piece of cork, or in a glass jar with a well-fitting glass stopper.

SPAGHETTI WITH ITALIAN SAUCE

8 oz (225 g) lean beef minced with 3 oz (75 g) lean and fat of ham
4 oz (100 g) chopped chickens' livers
1 inner stick of finely chopped celery
1 medium, coarsely grated carrot
1 fairly large coarsely grated onion or 3 shallots
4 skinned tomatoes
6 fluid oz (180 ml) dry white Chianti
12 fluid oz (360 ml) stock or water
Salt and pepper to season
1½ oz (40 g) butter
3 fluid oz (90 ml) oil
A generous grate of nutmeg
Extra walnut of butter
1–1½ lb (450–750 g) cooked spaghetti
5 fluid oz (150 ml) double cream (optional)

Note
If liked, tagliatelle may be used in this manner instead of spaghetti.

Heat oil and butter in a fairly deep pan. Put in carrot, celery and onion, shake until the mixture begins to colour slightly, add minced meats and work down with the back of a wooden spoon turning steadily until juices begin to run. Meanwhile place rough-cut tomatoes in a very small pan with a walnut of butter and allow to reduce to pulp. When meat is beginning to colour, sieve in tomato purée and add chickens' livers, pepper and nutmeg. When the beef is definitely losing the last glimpse of pink, add wine and work in thoroughly. Then add stock, simmer for about 2 minutes, taste, add salt sparingly and cover pan. Reduce heat to very low and simmer, occasionally shaking the covered pan, for between 25–30 minutes.

If liked, add double cream now. At the moment of serving stir in cooked spaghetti so that this is well impregnated with sauce. Turn into a wide, heated bowl and hand finely grated Parmesan cheese separately.

211

SICILIAN SPAGHETTI

8 oz (225 g) spaghetti
Half a small, peeled, crushed
  garlic clove
Salt
Black pepper
2 oz (50 g) stoned black olives
4 oz (100 g) tinned tomatoes
1 heaped tbsp (1 × 15 ml spoon)
  milled or chopped parsley
  heads
2 tbsps (2 × 15 ml spoons) oil
1 teasp (1 × 5 ml spoon) drained,
  chopped capers

Cook spaghetti as already
explained in plenty of salted
water. Heat oil in a small pan,
add garlic and parsley, stir, then
work in tomatoes and cook
gently for 5 minutes. Work in
capers and chopped olives.
Season to taste. Simmer for a
further 5 minutes. Turn over
strained spaghetti in a fairly
shallow bowl. Work up with two
forks to distribute thoroughly.

SPAGHETTI WITH CHICKENS' LIVERS

8 oz (225 g) spaghetti
4 oz (100 g) chickens' livers
2 fluid oz (60 ml) oil
1 coarse-grated onion (largest
  possible)
1 teacupful canned tomatoes
  chopped finely
1 teacupful coarse-grated
  Cheddar cheese
Salt
Black pepper

Cook spaghetti as already
explained, drain and return to
pan. Heat half the oil in a frying
pan and soft-fry onions for 5–6
minutes. Stir in chopped
tomatoes and their liquor. Then
add cheese. Work over low heat
until all is piping hot. Blend into
spaghetti. Heat remaining oil,
turn in livers and sauté for just
long enough to cook through.
Chop coarsely, fold into main
mixture, taste and adjust
seasoning to suit with salt and
black pepper.

VEGETABLE SPAGHETTI

12 small shallots
8 oz (225 g) spaghetti
6 oz (175 g) strained tinned peas
1 streaky bacon rasher cut
  thinly, de-rinded and diced
1 teasp (1 × 5 ml spoon) soft
  brown sugar
Salt
1 tbsp (1 × 15 ml spoon)

Cook spaghetti as already
explained in plenty of fast
boiling salted water. Peel and
quarter shallots or very small
onions, put into a small pan and
stir over low heat with oil or
butter until just tender. Strain
cooked spaghetti into a roomy
bowl. Add onions and fry bacon

concentrated tomato purée
½ pint (300 ml) strong cleared
  stock
4 oz (100 g) Parmesan (ideally)
  cheese
1 flat dessertsp (1 × 10 ml spoon)
  milled parsley heads
4 oz (100 g) diced, steamed
  carrots
3 oz (75 g) butter *or* 3 fluid oz (90
  ml) oil

in oil residue. Stir in peas and a light seasoning of salt. Dilute with stock after simmering hard until this is reduced by half. Stir in half the grated Parmesan. Add parsley, then taste and adjust seasoning with salt and pepper. Turn into a heated dish, scatter remaining cheese on top, slip under a strong grill to brown a little and then serve.

THE POLENTA OF NORTHERN ITALY

As many of our escaping prisoners in the Second World War knew through receiving the hospitality of the Resistance in Italy among the mountain villages of the north, polenta constitutes a charming ritual as well as a life-giving meal for the very poorest peasant families. Mama goes to work with a large, very blackened pot into which she throws boiling water, then stirs in salt and maize flour, stirring very probably with a stick of wood taken from vine-prunings. First the polenta, when thick but runny, is poured slap onto a scrubbed wooden table, where it spreads out over quite a wide area. Depending on how poor Mama, Papa and their brood of children are, a handful of dried fruits is then scattered over the polenta, when in funds some chopped meat or chopped sausage is also added. Each person has a fork, generally two-pronged, and they all gather round the table standing up to eat from sides to middle, quenching their thirsts with a rather thin wine made from Papa's sparse vines, or else just icy cold spring water collected by a couple of the children in a jug.

This is a regular mid-day meal for the mountain people, at which there is much laughter, chatter and friendliness to enhance the sparse rations. Incidentally plenty of steaming polenta, given the celebration treatment, is delicious eaten in the open air. Make the polenta, season with salt and pepper, pour onto the table and then go to town with handfuls of dried fruit, nuts and diced assorted sausages. When the polenta is liberally bestrewn, dot with butter flakes and drink Antinori Chianti as an accompaniment.

In some areas the polenta is poured over a handleless plaited wicker basket which is inverted at the centre of the table. We found some plaited trays at the Lord Roberts Memorial Shop opposite Harrods which did very well too.

213

MAIZE FLOUR POLENTA

2 pints (1.20 litres) boiling water
½ oz (10 g) salt
5 oz (135 g) maize flour
2 oz (50 g) butter or Gold
2½ oz (60 g) hard, finely grated
   cheese (ideally Parmesan)
2 tbsps (2 × 15 ml spoons) oil
A little extra oil
A little extra grated cheese

Raise water to boiling over a fairly strong heat. Stir in salt, then scatter maize over the surface and stir in fast with a wooden spoon. Reduce heat as mixture bubbles but stir until perfectly smooth. Then over a very low heat, allow paste to bubble and blow gently for a total of 25 minutes with only an occasional stir. Pour mixture onto a very lightly oiled marble or laminated plastic slab and let it spread out to a generous ½ inch (1.25 cm) depth.

Leave until quite cold. Stamp out into rounds or ovals with plain pastry cutters, or just cut into 1½–2 inch (3.75–5 cm) squares. Melt chosen fat with the 2 tablespoons (2 × 15 ml spoons) oil in a large frying pan and fry the polenta pieces briskly until browned. Pile into a side dish, trickle the remaining butter/oil mixture overall and scatter with a little extra grated cheese.

Alternatively, instead of pouring mixture onto a marble slab, tip into a buttered, heat-resistant dish and bake at Gas Mark 6 (approx 400°F, 200°C) for 12–15 minutes. Then put onto heated dish and pour Fonduta (preceding recipe) over.

SUBSTITUTE POLENTA, WITH SEMOLINA
AND PROCESSED CHEESE

1 pint (600 ml) milk
2½ oz (60 g) semolina
1 oz (25 g) grated stale cheese
1 flat small teasp (1 × 5 ml
  spoon) salt
1 small pkt Kraft processed
  cheese
2 oz (50 g) butter or Gold
1 rounded eggsp (1 × 2.5 ml
  spoon) black pepper

Rub sides and base of a 1 inch (2.5 cm) deep, heat-resistant container with chosen fat. Boil the milk, add pepper and salt and stir in the semolina, just dusting it over the top and drawing it in until completely blended. Keep stirring for 10 minutes, ideally with a wooden spoon, by which time the mixture will have thickened considerably. Stir in grated cheese until this has disappeared into the mixture. Pour onto a large shallow dish. Leave until cold.

Cut into squares and lay over the greased base of any 2 inch (5 cm) deep heat-resistant container. Cover with fingers cut from slices of processed cheese. Repeat these layers until all ingredients are used, finishing with a layer of processed cheese. Spread lightly with chosen fat. Bake at Gas Mark 4 (approx 350°F, 180°C) middle shelf for 30–35 minutes or until nicely bubbling and browned at top and edges. Hand tomato sauce separately.

SPAGHETTI PIE

Half a small tin tomato soup
12 oz (350 g) raw, minced beef
1 level teasp (1 × 5 ml spoon)
  black pepper
1 level dessertsp (1 × 10 ml
  spoon) powdered dried sage
Half a tin spinach purée
4 fluid oz (120 ml) strong stock or
  water with a meat cube, if you
  must
6 oz (175 g) spaghetti
2 pints (1.20 litres) cold water
2 fluid oz (60 ml) oil
3 oz (75 g) grated hard cheese
1 level teasp (1 × 5 ml spoon)
  and 1 tbsp (1 × 15 ml spoon)
  salt

Put a tablespoon (1 × 15 ml
spoon) salt into the water, raise
to boiling and pay in spaghetti,
unbroken. Cook fast for 9
minutes only. Then drain.
  Rub base and sides of a
medium pie dish with a little of
the oil. Put in half the spaghetti,
then half the spinach, the cheese
and the tomato soup. Repeat.
Season lightly with salt and
pepper, spread out spinach and
soup and finally scatter with
remaining cheese. Moisten with
flicks of remaining oil and bake
at Gas Mark 6 (approx 400°F,
200°C) for 30 minutes one shelf
above centre.

ITALIAN FONDUTA

This is a very modest Italian version of a Swiss cheese fondue made with Fontina cheese.

8 oz (225 g) diced Fontina cheese
Milk to cover
2 rounded tbsps (2 × 15 ml
  spoons) butter or Gold
4 No 3 egg yolks
¼ teasp (1 × 2.5 ml spoon) white
  pepper

Place diced cheese in a smallish
pan. Pour on milk to cover.
Leave overnight to steep. Place
half chosen fat and separated
egg yolks in the top of a double
or porage saucepan, with hot
water half-filling the outer base
pan. Turn in the cheese and milk
mixture and begin whisking
ideally with an electric mixer,
otherwise with a rotary whisk.
The cheese will melt and
thereafter, while you continue
whisking, it will harden a little.
When it is quite firm, remove
from heat, whisk in pepper and
remaining butter and either
serve on toast or with Polenta or
rice.

216

TORTELLINI WITH CREAM

This is the pasta that looks like little hats.

12 oz (350 g) tortellini
2 oz (50 g) unskinned
    mushrooms
1 oz (25 g) butter or oil
3 oz (75 g) grated hard cheese
2 fluid oz (60 ml) thick cream
2 oz (50 g) cooked, diced
    gammon

Cook the pasta in fast-boiling salted water until *al dente*. Heat chosen fat in a small pan. Slice in unskinned mushrooms after blanching by pouring over some boiling water. As soon as the mushrooms collapse in the pan, stir in cheese, half the diced gammon and, after whipping stiffly, add half the cream. Stir well to blend. Turn strained pasta onto a heated dish. Scatter with mushroom mixture, then add small spoonfuls here and there of the residue gammon, cream and cheese.

VERMICELLI KEDGEREE

14 oz (400 g) unbroken vermicelli
10 oz (275 g) smoked haddock
    (weighed after steaming and
    removing all skin and bone)
2 No 3 hard-boiled eggs
Black pepper
1 heaped tbsp (1 × 15 ml spoon)
    milled, fresh parsley heads
1 eggsp (1 × 2.5 ml spoon)
    powdered ginger
3 oz (75 g) shelled shrimps
3 oz (75 g) Gold or butter
1½ oz (40 g) grated cheese
Grated rind and strained juice of
    1 large lemon (wash carefully
    before using)

Steam, flake and weigh haddock. Separate whites from yolks of hard-boiled eggs and chop separately. Cook vermicelli in abundant salted, boiling water for 7–8 minutes. Drain very thoroughly, chop small and keep hot. Mix the haddock, the rough chopped shrimps and the chosen fat in a roomy bowl. Season strongly with black pepper, add the powdered ginger and stir/turn until totally blended. Add lemon juice and rind, mix well and heap into a mound on a heated, preferably long, narrow dish. Border with (a) chopped egg yolk, (b) milled parsley and (c) chopped egg white. Serve in bowls and eat with spoons and/or forks. Hand grated cheese separately.

CHEESE GNOCCHI

It is better to work with a bowlful of grated cheese of your choice for this dish which can be made well in advance for a filling supper dish of considerable excellence.

3 oz (75 g) fine semolina
1 pint (600 ml) milk
Salt
White pepper
Nutmeg
2 separated No 3 egg yolks
Oil
Butter or Gold
Parmesan or other hard grated
  cheese

Begin by boiling the milk, mixing in the semolina and stirring until a smooth thick paste results. Beat in a dessertspoon (1 × 10 ml spoon) of butter or Gold, remove from the heat and then beat in the egg yolks. Turn onto a cold oiled surface and smooth out to a ¾ inch (1.75 cm) thickness. Stamp into 1½–2 inch (3.75–5 cm) diameter rounds with a plain cutter or a small glass.

Brush the base and sides of a shallow heat-resistant dish with oil. Arrange a layer of the gnocchi in the dish, sprinkle with chosen grated cheese, dot with butter or Gold, and cover with a second layer of the gnocchi. Repeat, finishing with a generous layer of grated cheese and plenty of softened butter or Gold.

When required bake on centre shelf at Gas Mark 5 (approx 375°F, 190°C) for long enough for the assembly to bubble cheerfully and turn brown on top.

Main Course Dishes: in a slow-cooking pot

North country hot pot
Slow-cooking pot beef and mushroom pudding
Gammon cooked in a slow-cooking pot
Slow-cooking pot stock
Slow-cooking pot casserole of pork and rabbit
Slow-cooking pot roasted chicken
Boiled chicken with onion sauce
Slow-cooking pot tripe and onions
Slow-baked tongue
Pasta pie
Boned rib of beef
Lamb paysanne

NORTH COUNTRY HOT POT

1½ lb (750 g) boned and
    fat-denuded breast of lamb
1½ lb (750 g) old potatoes
2 large onions
1 pint (600 ml) strong lamb bone
    stock or water with bouillon
    cube
Salt
Black pepper

Cut the boned meat into neat pieces not more than 2 inch (5 cm) square. Slice onions very thinly after peeling. Do the same with the potatoes. Remember that vegetables must be cut very thin, or in very small dice to cook well in a slow-cooking pot. Put in a base layer of meat pieces, then onions, then potatoes and season with salt and pepper. Continue thus until all ingredients are in the pot with a good layer of potatoes on the top, repeating seasonings with each layer. Pour in chosen fluid, replace lid and switch on to Low just before going to bed. Leave until returning home the next evening. This should cover a span of midnight until 6 p.m. when the top layer of potatoes should be creamy underneath and crisp and browned on top. Serve from the pot.

Note
This can also be made with lean, raw pieces cut from a lamb shoulder.

SLOW-COOKING POT BEEF AND MUSHROOM PUDDING

1 lb (450 g) cubed, lean beef skirt
4 oz (100 g) unskinned
    mushrooms and their stalks
1 slender, trimmed leek sliced
    finely
1 bay leaf
3 fluid oz (90 ml) red 'plonk'
    wine
Beef bone stock or water and

Slice mushrooms, chop stalks and blend with carrot and torn-in-halves bay leaf. Melt sufficient dripping to coat base of a medium frying pan thinly. Turn meat pieces thickly in seasoned flour. Fry, turning briskly in hot fat until browned and sealed. Mix with vegetables

bouillon cube
2 good shakes from a bottle of
   real Worcestershire sauce
Seasoned flour
A little dripping
3 oz (75 g) very thinly sliced
   carrots
8 oz (225 g) sifted flour
4 oz (100 g) Atora suet
1 flat small teasp (1 × 5 ml
   spoon) salt
1 large heaped teasp (1 × 5 ml
   spoon) baking powder
Cold water

and turn into a slow-cooking
pot. Add wine, sufficient chosen
fluid and Worcestershire sauce
to cover – just. Switch on to Low
and cook for 6 hours or until
vegetables are tender. Switch
off, remove lid and make suet
crust.

Mix flour, salt, suet and
baking powder thoroughly in a
basin. Bind to a good dough
consistency with cold water
using an ordinary table knife.
Turn dough onto a floured
surface. Cut away and set aside
one quarter. Roll out the rest to
line out a 2 lb (900 g) pudding
basin. Turn in the cold meat
mixture. Push dough edges well
over this filling. Wet the
fold-over all round with cold
water and roll out remaining
dough for the lid. Lay over
wetted dough edge underneath.
Pinch edges well together.
Lower into inner pot, replace lid
and cook at High for 3½ hours.

GAMMON COOKED IN A SLOW-COOKING POT

Unless you like salty gammon, soak for at least 12 hours before cooking.

2½ lb (1.25 kg) piece of corner
   gammon
Cold water

Place soaked gammon in a slow-
cooking pot and pour in cold
water to come two-thirds up the
pot. Replace lid, switch on to
Low and leave for 9½ hours.

On removal, our test piece
was sweet and tender. When left
to go cold it could be cut
extremely thinly without any
crumbling.

221

SLOW-COOKING POT STOCK

Use only small bones; if asked nicely, your butcher will oblige. Put bones into a roomy saucepan and add a faggot of herbs, 3–4 fat parsley stalks and a couple of bacon rinds. Raise to boiling, transfer to slow-cooking pot, cover, switch to Low and leave to simmer for 12 hours, either overnight to switch off in the morning or during the day. When quite cold, skim off all fat and strain stock into a jug for refrigerator storage.

SLOW-COOKING POT CASSEROLE OF PORK AND RABBIT

1 lb (450 g) lean pie pork
1 lb (450 g) rabbit pieces divided
   into 2–3 each
5 oz (135 g) extremely thinly
   sliced carrots
5 inch (12.5 cm) sprig rosemary
¾ pint (450 ml) pork bone stock,
   or water with bouillon cube
5 fluid oz (150 ml) sweet cider
Seasoned flour
The trimmed white and green of
   3 slim leeks sliced very thinly
Salt
Black pepper

Turn meat pieces to coat thickly in the seasoned flour. Pack into slow-cooking pot. Add vegetables, bury rosemary sprig, blend cider with stock or water mixture, swill over pot contents, cover and switch on at Low. Leave for 8 hours. Taste, correct seasoning with salt and black pepper and stir well. Then serve from the pot with steamed potatoes or rice.

SLOW-COOKING POT ROASTED CHICKEN

1 × 2½–3 lb (1.25–1.50 kg)
   roasting chicken
1 oz (25 g) butter or chicken fat
Salt
Black pepper

Rub chosen fat over entire bird. Season lightly both inside and out with salt and black pepper. Place in pot and affix lid. Set dial at Low. Leave undisturbed for 7–8 hours depending on bird's weight. Lift out onto a chopping board and carve. Pour accumulated juices into a small jug or sauce boat. Return the bird portions to the inner pot. Lift this out, swathe in a napkin and so take to table.

BOILED CHICKEN WITH ONION SAUCE

Ideal for cooking in a slow-cooking pot.

One 2–2½ lb (900 g–1.25 kg)
  boiling fowl
White bone stock to cover
6 oz (175 g) carrots
6 small onions or ideally shallots
4 parsley stalks
Salt
Black pepper

Make sure your butcher removes the bird's head, neck, feet and innards, and then returns you the neck, liver and gizzard. Put the fowl into a slow-cooking pot. Strew the chosen peeled onions around with the parsley stalks, a rounded teaspoon (1 × 5 ml spoon) of black pepper and the scraped carrots sliced extremely thinly. Add stock, replace lid, switch on to Low and leave for 6 hours.

With an ordinary lidded saucepan just raise to boiling, level off at a gentle simmer and maintain for about 2 hours.

You can then just fish it from the pot onto a dish, strain off the liquor into a jug, discard the parsley stalks and strew the vegetables around, thus saving washing up. Alternatively you can divide the bird onto a heated dish, surround with the vegetables and put the strained stock into a saucepan. Simmer down fast to reduce by half. Then follow Onion Sauce recipe (Eggs, p. 202) using the stock to replace given milk but otherwise following right through to the double cream. If liked, a cupful of tinned unsweetened Libby's milk can be used instead of cream.

SLOW-COOKING POT TRIPE AND ONIONS

1½ lb (750 g) double or
   honeycomb tripe
1½ lb (750 g) peeled weight
   onions
Cold water
Salt
Pepper
1 pint (600 ml) milk and 5 fluid
   oz (150 ml) tinned
   unsweetened milk
1 heaped tbsp (1 × 15 ml spoon)
   arrowroot

Cut tripe into slim, chip-sized strips, then halve across. Slice onions thinly. Just cover meanly with water and replace lid. Switch on at Low and leave overnight for 8 hours.

Drain off all liquor very thoroughly into a saucepan and simmer down hard to reduce this over a strong, top-of-cooker burner to a mere 3 fluid oz (90 ml) of syrupy liquor. Make a paste with a little of the milk and arrowroot. Add remaining milk to liquor. When boiling pour into arrowroot mixture and stir until thick. Then turn in the mixed tripe and onions. Turn all back into the slow-cooking pot. Switch to High and cook for 1 hour. Taste and correct seasoning with salt and pepper.

Serve in heated bowls and eat with a spoon with plenty of brown bread and butter or Gold.

SLOW-BAKED TONGUE

2½ lb (1.25 kg) unsalted tongue
Boiling water

Wash tongue. Place in inner, slow-cooking crock pot. Cover with boiling water and lid. Set dial at Low. Leave overnight to cook for 12 hours. Remove tongue, allow to cool down a little, then skin completely and ram tongue into a 6 inch (15 cm) diameter sliding-base cake tin. Cover with a plate and refrigerate, putting heaviest possible weights on top.

Thus the pressed tongue can

be sliced and served fast either hot with parsley, cheese, caper or mushroom sauce or cold with a salad. With an overnight-cooked item like tongue the slow crock can be used during the day for scrubbed, jacket-baked potatoes. Use small ones, scrub and leave moist. Put into pot, cover and set at Low for 11–12 hours.

Note
Pour the liquor into a measuring jug and you will find that it yields around 1½ pints (900 ml) good stock. Use to make French onion soup or for a filling and excellent casserole of oxtail.

PASTA PIE

12 pieces of green lasagne pasta
¾ pint (450 ml) white sauce
6 oz (175 g) coarsely-grated hard
   cheese ends
Salt
Black pepper
1 large tbsp (1 × 15 ml spoon)
   concentrated tomato purée
8 oz (225 g) cooked pork
1 large peeled onion
2 fluid oz (60 ml) stock
1 medium tin spinach purée
2 skinned, thinly-sliced
   tomatoes
Cooking oil

Plunge lasagne pieces into fast boiling, slightly salted water. Cook for just long enough to make them pliable (approx 7 minutes). Drain, rinse in cold water, wipe and cut each piece in halves. Brush slow-cooking pot's base and sides with oil. Lay in four pieces of lasagne.

   Mince pork with onions. Work tomato purée with stock, mix into pork and onion and season with salt and pepper. Spread half of this over the base lasagne, then cover with four more pieces of lasagne. Beat half the grated cheese into white sauce while still very hot. As soon as the cheese is melted and well blended, season and spread one third over the second lasagne layer. Cover with one third of spinach purée, then add a further four lasagne pieces and repeat with remaining ingredients, in sequence as above, ending with sauce. Cover with a lid, switch on to Low and leave for 4 hours. Add layer of tomatoes and sprinkle 1 oz (25 g) cheese on top. Move setting to High, leave 30 minutes and serve from the pot, handing remaining grated cheese separately.

BONED RIB OF BEEF

2½–3 lb (1.25–1.50 kg) piece of boned rib of beef
8 oz (225 g) diced swedes
8 oz (225 g) thinly sliced carrots
8 oz (225 g) thinly sliced onions
1 teacupful of red wine or beef stock
Salt
Pepper
1 bay leaf

Heat an iron frying pan or griddle until very hot. Slap meat down to sear/seal it. Leave for ½ minute, turn to unsealed area and repeat at ½ minute intervals until whole piece is completely sear/sealed. Put into inner crock pot. Strew mixed, prepared vegetables and bay leaf around and on top. Swill with wine or stock, cover and cook at Low for 8 hours without disturbance. Take out the beef and set on heated dish. Remove bay. Rub tender vegetables through an ordinary sieve or pass through liquidiser with liquor until reduced to purée. Serve from separate, heated bowl with each meat serving, being careful to taste first and correct seasoning with salt and pepper.

226

LAMB PAYSANNE

2½ lb (1.25 kg) half leg of lamb or a small whole one of same weight
12 oz (350 g) thinly-sliced onions
2 oz (50 g) dripping
Salt
Pepper
1 lb (450 g) finely shredded tight white cabbage
1 *bouquet garni* (herb bag)
½ pint (300 ml) good strong stock
1 good-sized peeled, crushed clove of garlic
1 oz (25 g) grated hard cheese

Beurre manié
Work together 1 oz (25 g) butter or substitute and 1 oz (25 g) flour with the back of a wooden spoon in a small bowl, or turn both onto a wooden surface and work up with a small table knife. Roll into little balls the size of cherries. Refrigerate to use as required for instant thickening at the last moment.

Melt and heat the dripping in a shallow pan. When piping hot turn in the onions, cover and reduce heat to low. Give an occasional turn and cook very slowly until soft but not browned. Turn with residue dripping into slow-cooking inner pot. Season with salt and pepper. Add *bouquet garni* and work in crushed garlic clove. Spread the prepared cabbage over and pat down a little. Season lightly again. Lay in the meat, swill with the stock, affix lid and cook at Low for 7 hours before testing flesh with a meat thermometer for rare, medium or well done.

For service, lift lamb onto a heated dish and keep warm. Strain mixed onion and cabbage thoroughly. Turn into a bowl, work in the grated hard cheese, taste, correct seasoning with salt and pepper and use as a border to the joint. Turn strained juices into a small pan. Bring to the boil and stir in two or three small balls of *beurre manié* to thicken. Pour into a jug or sauceboat for service.

227

Main Course Dishes: with Poultry

Chicken in a mountain
Fried chicken
Chicken cocotte
Chickens' livers savoury rice bowl
Curried chicken
Devilled chicken portions
The devil itself
French treatment for left-overs

CHICKEN IN A MOUNTAIN

This is so good and so simple that we want you to be familiar with it from this stage onwards.

2½ lb (1.25 kg) roasting chicken, plucked and trussed

3 lb (1.50 kg) sea salt, either Maldon or French *gros sel*

Wrap the parson's nose securely in a scrap of foil. Lay another small piece over the neck end to stop salt falling inside bird. Line a large casserole with turkey width Alcan Foil and leave enough hanging over edges to enclose. It is important not to use too wide a casserole which merely uses far more salt than is necessary. Trundle in chosen salt to make a 2 inch (5 cm) bed. Set bird on this. Trundle in more salt until bird is completely buried. Bring up loose foil and fold over to enclose all like a parcel. Put into oven on as high a shelf as possible and cook at Gas Mark 8 (approx 450°F, 230°C) for 1¼ hours.

Remove from the oven and bang down onto a working surface to break up the crusted salt. Excavate and lift out the bird. Just dip a pastry brush into oil and brush away any salt grains which may be found lurking in fold of leg, thigh or wing. Transfer to heated serving dish and prove by eating just how much flavour has been held in by this method.

Note

Allow salt to become cold, crumble up and store in a tin to use again and again. It will turn beige eventually but this in no way diminishes its saltiness so there is no waste.

FRIED CHICKEN

For a simpler version, see Meat and Poultry, Part 1, p. 62.

Chicken portions
Oil to fry in a deep fryer with frying basket
3 shallow containers half-filled with a) sifted flour, b) raw, beaten, strained egg and c) fine soft brown or white breadcrumbs

Turn each raw (skinned or unskinned) chicken portion in flour and shake off surplus. Pass carefully through raw beaten egg until portions are completely coated. Lift quickly into crumbs and pat well in. Place on crumb-dusted dish and set in mild refrigeration until required for frying.

Slide portions into slightly smoking hot oil and reduce heat slightly. Leave for exactly 1½ minutes. Turn off heat completely and allow to continue frying in the slowly diminishing oil heat for a further 6 minutes. The precise timing applies to portions weighing approximately 5 oz (135 g). Over this weight allow 2 minutes with heat on and 6½ minutes thereafter in slowly diminishing heat. Below the given weight allow only 1 minute with heat on and 5–5½ minutes thereafter.

For service, arrange portions on a napkin-dressed dish and surround with any of the following: corn fritters; centrally halved peeled bananas fried with or without batter; fried croûtons or fried triangles of thinly-rolled puff-pastry; fresh watercress, fried parsley or fresh Batavian endive leaves; fried, batter-dipped slices of pineapple; shallow-fried peeled, cored apple rings and Duchess Potatoes.

231

CHICKEN COCOTTE

1 large spring chicken (*poussin*)
3 tbsps (3 × 15 ml spoons) oil
A walnut of butter or Gold
Salt
Black pepper

Pour oil onto base of a small casserole. Put in the chicken, either whole or divided in two. Heat over a mere thread, then raise heat a little and brown the bird, or its two halves, all over. Season with salt and pepper, rub the butter or Gold over and put on the lid. Cook on middle shelf at Gas Mark 4 (approx 350°F, 180°C) for 35–40 minutes or until a gentle prod with a skewer into the fatty part of the thigh yields a pale juice just faintly touched with pink. This stage of completion is called by the French *à la Française* but when the juice comes out pale beige, rather reluctantly, *à l'Anglaise* – otherwise beige and dry.

CHICKENS' LIVERS SAVOURY RICE BOWL

12 oz (350 g) brown rice
12 oz (350 g) peeled, diced onions
1 optional crushed garlic clove
2 pints (1.20 litres) strong stock or 1¾ pints (1.05 litres) stock and 5 fluid oz (150 ml) white cooking wine
6 oz (175 g) chickens' livers
4 oz (100 g) shelled shrimps
3 oz (75 g) very clean dripping or 1½ fluid oz (45 ml) oil and 1½ oz (40 g) butter or Gold
Salt
Pepper
1 faggot of herbs (*bouquet garni*)
4 oz (100 g) pork sausage-meat
1 dessertsp (1 × 10 ml spoon) flour

Sift flour onto a working surface and roll very small balls of the sausage-meat in it. Heat chosen fat or oil and butter or Gold in a frying pan. Add rice and turn until well impregnated. Add stock, mix with all remaining ingredients, season lightly with salt and pepper and turn into a casserole. Cover and cook one shelf below centre at Gas Mark 4 (approx 350°F, 180°C) until rice is cooked and has absorbed liquor. Taste, correct seasoning and remove herb bag. Wrap a napkin round casserole and so serve.

232

CURRIED CHICKEN

2 lb (900 g) roasting chicken
   chopped into small pieces on
   their bones
1 large diced onion
1 lb (450 g) peeled diced potatoes
1 lb (450 g) peeled, sliced
   Bramley cooking apples
1 oz (25 g) butter
1 fluid oz (30 ml) oil
1 oz (25 g) currants
1–2 dessertsps (1–2 × 10 ml
   spoons) curry powder or
   masala paste
1 large lemon
3 large diced Jerusalem
   artichokes
Salt
1 pinch powdered cardamom
   seed
2 pints (1.20 litres) stock made
   from smashed down chicken
   carcase (or water)
1 heaped tbsp (1 × 15 ml spoon)
   desiccated coconut

Soften butter in a deep pan, add oil and heat. Soft-fry onions, drain and set aside. Add chicken pieces and turn so that these are browned all over on a fairly strong heat. Sprinkle on, or stir in, chosen curry mixture with the stock or water and add all remaining ingredients. Season lightly with salt. Cover securely, reduce heat to maintain a steady simmer for 25 minutes and check at half time to ensure liquor still covers chicken pieces adding more stock, or water, if considered necessary. Excavate artichokes and rub back through a sieve into pan contents. Stir again. Simmer for 5 more minutes by which time the sieved artichokes will have supplied the necessary thickening without using any flour.

Serve inside a Patna rice border with cut lemon handed separately.

DEVILLED CHICKEN PORTIONS

The divided legs, thighs and
   wings from 2 small chickens
Lemon juice
Soy sauce

Note
Use the chicken carcase for stock and the breasts for another dish.

Set chicken pieces in a shallow dish. Sprinkle with soy sauce, then lemon juice and leave to marinade until required. Then take up each portion, paint with remaining fluids from marinade and set on a grill over charcoal. When done on undersides, turn over, repaint and repeat cooking. Serve with rice or jacket-baked potatoes. Hand the Devil separately.

THE DEVIL ITSELF

3 finely minced shallots or very small onions
1 large crushed garlic clove
1 *bouquet garni* (herb faggot)
1 pint (600 ml) stock
12 drops Worcestershire sauce
1 flat teasp (1 × 5 ml spoon) masala curry paste (from any good Oriental emporium)
1 flat dessertsp (1 × 10 ml spoon) concentrated tomato purée
1 dessertsp (1 × 10 ml spoon) Jamaica style hot pepper sauce (bottled)
1 fluid oz (30 ml) oil
1 rounded tbsp (1 × 15 ml spoon) potato flour or arrowroot
Cold water

Work garlic with prepared shallots or onions, Worcestershire sauce and hot pepper sauce. Then work in oil and all remaining ingredients except chosen thickening agent. Raise to boiling in a small pan. Simmer for 10 minutes. Stir thickening agent with water to form a smooth paste. Tip into simmering pan contents. Stir and use remembering to remove *bouquet garni*.

Note
This 'Devil' is excellent for brushing onto chops, sausages or chicken portions before grilling.

FRENCH TREATMENT FOR LEFT-OVERS (FRITOTS)

A few small thin slices of left-overs of chicken, rabbit or any cooked meat
The strained juice of 1 fairly large lemon
1 level teasp (1 × 5 ml spoon) salt
½ teasp (1 × 2.5 ml spoon) black pepper
1 level tbsp (1 × 5 ml spoon) chopped, fresh parsley heads
1 given batch of Vegetable Fritter Batter (Batters and Pastry Pastes, Part 3)
Oil in pan or deep fryer

Put prepared slices of your choice into a shallow dish and mix with lemon juice, salt, pepper and parsley. Leave 20 minutes. Dip them into batter and slide them into oil at 390–400°F, (195–200°C). Fry until puffy and richly browned. Heap on a heated dish, pour over remaining marinade and serve with tomato or cheese sauce.

Main Course Dishes: with Lamb and Beef

Ragout of lamb
Dutch meat balls
Real shepherd's pie
Small stuffed leg of lamb
Country parson
Oven-braised shoulder of lamb
Lamb Florentine
Skewered offal with orange rice
Modest kebabs and rice
Cabbage ball with cheese sauce
Boiled brisket of beef with dumplings
Cuban hash
Beef Parmentier
Liver and onion parcel
Potato crust
Imitation calves' liver and bacon
Ox kidney sauté
Dripping crust
Italian meat loaf
Beef left-overs

RAGOUT OF LAMB

2 lb (900 g) neck or breast of lamb
5 fluid oz (150 ml) boiling stock
   or water and a bouillon cube
2 oz (50 g) dripping
1 oz (25 g) flour
1 medium onion
1 medium carrot
1 faggot of herbs
1 outside celery stick
5 fluid oz (150 ml) spinach purée
   (tinned or fresh)
Strained juice of half a small
   lemon
Salt
Black pepper

Cut meat into 2 inch (5 cm) squares. Place in a pan and cover with cold water and raise slowly to boiling. This disposes of surplus grease and sets the rest. Lift pieces out and plunge into cold salted water for 5 minutes.

Dice the carrot, onion and celery stick and fry slowly over a low heat in the heated dripping. Do not brown. After 10 minutes sprinkle in flour and stir to make a soft ball on base of pan. Add boiling stock or water and bouillon cube, gradually working all down with a wooden spoon until a smooth sauce results. Immerse lamb pieces and herb bag. Cover and simmer with extreme gentleness until all is tender. Strain sauce back into pan. Arrange lamb on a heated plate, discarding herb bag. Stir spinach purée into sauce and add lemon juice. Season to taste with salt and black pepper. Taste to check seasonings, then pour sauce over meat and serve with a border of mashed potatoes.

DUTCH MEAT BALLS

8 oz (225 g) minced cooked lamb,
   game or poultry
1 dessertsp (1 × 10 ml spoon)
   raw onion juice
Salt
Black pepper
1 flat eggsp (1 × 2.5 ml spoon)
   allspice
1 small separated egg yolk

Mix chosen lamb, game or poultry with onion juice, add a pinch of black pepper and two pinches of salt and work to a smooth paste with egg yolk. Shape into small balls no larger than marbles.

Mix flour in a basin with salt, oil and just sufficient water to

Oil to deep-fry
4 oz (100 g) sifted flour
A generous pinch of extra salt
1 tbsp (1 × 15 ml spoon) oil
Water at blood heat
1 No 3 separated egg white

achieve a batter of thick, coating consistency. Rest for a minimum 30 minutes.

When ready to serve have hot oil ready in a smallish pan. Impale each little ball on a wooden cocktail stick. Whip egg white until stiff, then fold into batter and stir/turn until quite smooth. Dip the balls in, drop them into the hot oil and deep fry until puffy and richly golden brown. Serve napkin-wrapped in a small dish around a central pot of French mustard into which balls are then dunked.
Note
Please do not beat this batter or it may not coat properly.

REAL SHEPHERD'S PIE

12 oz (350 g) cold cooked lamb
2 oz (50 g) finely minced lean gammon
1 medium coarsely grated onion
5 fluid oz (150 ml) stock
1 flat coffeesp (1 × 2.5 ml spoon) salt
1 flat eggsp (1 × 2.5 ml spoon) black pepper
1 rounded dessertsp (1 × 10 ml spoon) milled fresh parsley heads
Potato Crust (p. 000)

Mix thin slices of cooked meat with onions, parsley, salt and pepper and turn into a small to medium pie dish. Place minced gammon in a small pan, add boiling stock and stir/simmer for 5 minutes. Pour over pie dish contents and insert pie funnel. When cold cover with potato crust rolled out very thickly on a lightly floured surface. Turn edge underneath to fit neatly into dish and pinch potato all round to flute it. Score the top surface with a hot, wet knife into diamond shapes, brush with a little raw, beaten egg and make a small hole at centre to release steam. Bake at Gas Mark 4 (approx 350°F, 180°C) on centre shelf for 1 hour.

SMALL STUFFED LEG OF LAMB
(Petit Gigot Provençal)

This is a little unusual so read carefully please.

1 very small half leg of lamb
1 crushed garlic clove
2 heads tarragon
1 small handful of very slender
  spring onion thinnings
Salt
Black pepper
2 firm, medium tomatoes sliced
  thinly
1 small egg plant (aubergine)
  sliced thinly and unskinned
2 tbsps (2 × 15 ml spoons)
  Tomato Coulis (Savoury
  Sauces, Part 3)
1 large onion peeled and diced
6 fluid oz (180 ml) coarse red
  'plonk' wine
Bacon rinds

Begin by skinning the little leg right back to the bone tip but on no account remove this skin. Just roll it back like a stocking top. Mix all remaining ingredients except bacon rinds and wine together and spread them over the leg, season with salt and black pepper and gently peel back the skin right over this stuffing.

Set in an ordinary, smallish meat baking tin on a bed of hoarded bacon rinds with the wine. Baste while roasting at Gas Mark 5 (approx 375°F, 190°C) on middle shelf for 40 minutes for underdone, 55–60 minutes for well done. Carve into pan contents, just excavating the bacon rinds. Slide all onto a heated dish and surround with creamed potatoes.

COUNTRY PARSON

Our forebears' way of using up leftovers.

1 oz (25 g) clean dripping or
  rendered down pork fat
Medium onion, chopped finely
1 oz (25 g) flour
1 flat teasp (1 × 5 ml spoon)
  masala paste (from any Indian
  or Pakistani emporium)
1 small raw, coarse-grated,
  peeled cooking apple
7½ fluid oz (225 ml) stock or
  water and meat cube with a
  splash of soy sauce to lift it

Melt and heat chosen fat in a frying pan. Cook onion over a low heat until soft but not browned. Stir in flour, then work in masala paste and grated apple, after which add given stock gradually stirring after each addition until smooth. Mix in the tomato pulp or sauce and if the mixture is too thick for your taste, add a little more stock. Slide in and turn over the

2½ oz (60 g) soft-cooked, skinned tomatoes or substitute bottled tomato sauce

A little extra stock

Sufficient thin slices of leftover lamb (or poultry) for two hungry people

slices of chosen left-overs. As soon as they are hot tip onto a heated dish. Serve piled onto slices of buttered toast.

OVEN-BRAISED SHOULDER OF LAMB

1 small lamb shoulder
1 crushed garlic clove
2 medium onions, sliced thinly
2 medium carrots, diced small
1 herb faggot
2 oz (50 g) dripping
Quarter of a small, tight white cabbage sliced thinly
Salt
Pepper
5 fluid oz (150 ml) strong cleared lamb bone stock or 5 fluid oz (150 ml) water and 1 bouillon cube

Make sure butcher has skinned fat side of shoulder for you. Score the meat with a Stanley knife. Rub in the garlic pulp. Melt and heat dripping in an ordinary meat baking tin over a low heat. Stir in prepared onions and carrot and turn/fry at strong heat for 3 minutes. Leave in the tin. Mix in the prepared cabbage and moisten with the stock or water and bouillon cube. Bake at Gas Mark 5 (approx 375°F, 190°C) for 30 minutes. Remove shoulder, stir vegetables round so that none crisp or brown. Return shoulder to position. Cook until desired red, pink or beige. You can determine this very easily by testing with a small meat thermometer.

When shoulder is ready for you, remove and keep warm. Taste the vegetables to be sure they are sufficiently cooked. Mix them together and make a bed of them in a heated dish. Lay the shoulder on top for service and surround with steamed potatoes.

239

LAMB FLORENTINE

½ pint (300 ml) very thick white
  sauce
4 oz (100 g) grated, stale cheese
  ends
14 oz (400 g) cooked, diced lamb
Half a small tin of spinach purée
  or 4 oz (100 g) cooked, sieved
  fresh spinach
1 lb (450 g) creamed old potatoes
Butter
Black pepper

Rub a scrap of butter over the base of four individual heat-resistant containers such as scallop shells. Pipe a fat potato border around or just inside the edges. Work half the cheese into the plain white sauce, taste and correct the seasoning with salt and black pepper. Tip prepared spinach into a small pan, season liberally with pepper, add half the remaining cheese and an optional tablespoon of top-of-the-milk or single cream. When boiling divide equally between the four containers and spread over their bases. Stir the lamb into the white sauce, pile on top of the spinach, then cover with potato. Scatter the remaining cheese on top, apply an extra dab or two of butter to top surfaces and just heat through when required on middle shelf at Gas Mark 5 (375°F, 190°C) for 14 minutes.

SKEWERED OFFAL WITH ORANGE RICE

2 lambs' kidneys
4 oz (100 g) thinly sliced liver
2 bay leaves
1 medium onion
A little oil
2 de-rinded bacon rashers
A little French mustard
1 very small eating apple

Skin and halve the kidneys. Cut liver into four pieces. Tear bay leaves in two. Boil onion in a little salted water for 5 minutes, then drain and quarter. Divide bacon rashers in halves and roll into little cylinders. Peel, core and quarter the apple. Impale these on two skewers with half bay leaves on both ends of each skewer load. Brush lightly with French mustard and liberally with oil. Lay on a grill rack with its legs in the lower position and put under a grill. Cook for 5 minutes thus, then turn over, re-apply light mustard brushing and more liberal oil brushing and grill until completely cooked, for approx 8 minutes. Divide orange rice into two equal parts. Mound each on a heated plate, lay on a skewer load and if one of you does not know what to do next just push fork prongs through at one end of skewer holding this over rice. Push hard while withdrawing skewer with the other hand so that all pieces fall neatly in line over the rice.

Orange Rice

4 oz (100 g) Patna rice
Finely grated rind of 1 small
  orange and its strained juice
1 dessertsp (1 × 10 ml spoon)
  salt
2 pints (1.20 litres) boiling water
2 oz (50 g) sultanas
½ fluid oz (15 ml) oil

Cover sultanas with orange juice. Toss rice into fast-bubbling salted water. Stir until water returns to boiling. Steady heat to maintain a strong simmer for exactly 11 minutes. Strain immediately. Return to hot (dried) pan. Stir in orange juice, swollen sultanas, oil and grated orange rind.

MODEST KEBABS AND RICE

Like French *Fritots* this method is ideal for using up left-overs of cooked lamb, preferably slightly underdone. It is a very quick 'cheat' dish when you have hot oil in the deep fryer. Cut the lamb into fat cubes and thread onto skewers, alternating them with scraps of torn, dry bay leaf, quarters of small par-cooked onions and small pieces of green or red pimentos which have been de-pipped and pithed beforehand. When your skewers are loaded, you just lower them into the hot oil, lift out, drain and set on a mound of rice.

Allow 3 oz (75 g) rice per head. You will also need a large pan half-filled with bubbling, salted water, 3 peeled, rough-cut garlic cloves and a tiny envelope of saffron. Shoot rice in, stir until water re-bubbles and maintain for 11½ minutes. Strain immediately. Wipe pan carefully, return strained rice and stir in 1 fluid oz (30 ml) oil, 1 oz (25 g) butter or Gold, 1 generous tablespoon (1 × 15 ml spoon) milled or chopped fresh parsley heads and a small handful of sultanas. Shape into a rectangular panel. Lay the kebabs on and hand chutneys to accompany.

CABBAGE BALL WITH CHEESE SAUCE

1 small tight, white cabbage
Boiling water
Cold or iced water
Forcemeat
Cheese sauce

For forcemeat
1 lb (450 g) raw minced beef or
    veal
1 egg
1 tbsp (1 × 15 ml spoon) tomato
    purée
1 raw grated onion
1 crushed garlic clove (optional)
1 level teasp (1 × 5 ml spoon)
    salt
½ eggsp (1 × 2.5 ml spoon)
    milled black pepper
3–4 oz (75–100 g) rice cooked in
    fast boiling water for only 5
    minutes and then drained
    before adding 1 teacupful
    cooked strained peas or
    uncooked thawed frozen peas
    and 1 rounded teasp (1 × 5 ml
    spoon) mixed dried herbs

Place washed, trimmed cabbage in a large bowl and cover completely with boiling water. Leave for 6–8 minutes. Remove cabbage and plunge it into a big bowl of icy water. Peel off leaves singly. Put in ball of forcemeat in the centre of a smallish leaf and wrap up. This will form the centre of your Cabbage Ball. Spread the remaining forcemeat over as many leaves as it will cover (like thickly spread jam). Overlap these over the central ball until you have made a large one. Wrap this in liberally buttered Alcan Foil. Steam until tender (approx 2 hours). Unwrap onto a heated dish. Cover with cheese sauce and serve immediately.

To make forcemeat
Mix all well together and use as explained above.

BOILED BRISKET OF BEEF WITH DUMPLINGS

Brisket, if bought boned and rolled ready for boiling, is a modest joint. Salted silverside costs a great deal more. Both are cooked in the same way.

3 lb (1.5 kg) prepared, salted
  brisket
6 medium onions
4 large carrots
Water
6–8 medium, peeled, old
  potatoes

For dumplings:
2 oz (50 g) suet
4 oz (100 g) flour
Pinch of salt
Cold water

Note
Left-overs can be minced and turned into Corned Beef Hash (With an Oven, Part 1, p. 104).

Rinse the joint and put into a large, lidded stockpot or saucepan with whole onions and halved carrots. Cover with water and the lid, raise to boiling and steady off at a gentle simmer. Maintain for 35 minutes. Check onions and carrots and if firm but almost cooked, fish out into a dish or bowl and set aside. Having simmered meat for a total 1¼ hours, leave in liquor until cold.

Bring potful to the boil again 20 minutes before eating. Drop in prepared potatoes and dumplings and simmer until swollen and feathery, thus heating and finishing meat and vegetables simultaneously. This method ensures the vegetables are not cooked to a sog.

Slice meat, arrange on heated dish, border with vegetables and serve in old-fashioned soup plates. Pour the liquor into a jug. Provide plenty of made English mustard.

To make dumplings
Sift flour with salt and work in suet. Make a centre well and add water very gradually, working up to a firm texture with an ordinary table knife. Shape into small balls (ping pong size) by rolling between palms of the hands. Drop into boiling liquor.

243

CUBAN HASH

1 lb (450 g) minced or scraped
    beef skirt
5 medium tomatoes, skinned
    and diced
1 medium onion, diced
1 small peeled, crushed garlic
    clove
1 green pimento
1 bay leaf
1 teasp (1 × 5 ml spoon) red
    wine vinegar
2 oz (50 g) clean dripping or oil
10 oz (275 g) rice
3 peeled bananas
6 No 2 eggs
Salt
Pepper
8 oz (225 g) grain-separate
    cooked rice
Butter

Tear bay leaf into small pieces. Melt and heat dripping in a frying pan. Fry onion with garlic until almost tender but only faintly browned. Work in chopped tomatoes and de-pipped, de-pithed and chopped pimento. Cook for 5 minutes. Work in bay leaf, then draw in prepared beef and stir/fry for 10 minutes. Add vinegar. Taste and correct seasoning with salt and pepper.

Have a dish base-spread with the cooked rice ready. Turn the meat mixture on top. Keep warm while frying bananas and eggs. Halve bananas, then split and fry in a very little butter until brown tinged and quite soft. Press over meat mixture, then fry eggs slowly in residue and lay on top.

BEEF PARMENTIER

14 oz (400 g) cold, cooked beef
4 oz (100 g) smoked cooked
    gammon
1 oz (25 g) clean dripping
1 tbsp (1 × 15 ml spoon) mixed
    fresh or dried parsley, chervil
    and tarragon
Salt
Black pepper
2 lb (900 g) old potatoes (peeled
    weight)
A little extra butter or Gold
Milk
1 No 3 egg
Grated cheese

Slice, then cube the beef and gammon and mix both together. Melt and heat the dripping in a frying pan. Turn meat in this, over moderate heat, working in the herbs and seasoning to taste with salt and pepper. Remove from heat. Beat the egg, then beat in fast and set meat mixture aside.

Strain and sieve or emulsify the potatoes into a roomy bowl. Work in a knob of chosen fat, a splash of milk and blend very thoroughly. Season with salt and pepper. Divide into eight

244

equal parts. Put one part into the base of four one-portion dishes. Cover completely with a quarter of the meat/egg mixture, spreading it out smoothly over the potato base. Turn one part of the potato mixture over the top of each container. Ridge with a fork, sprinkle very lightly with grated cheese and dot with extra flakes of butter or Gold. Bake at Gas Mark 5 (375°F, 190°C) on middle shelf for 20 minutes.

LIVER AND ONION PARCEL

For each portion:
5 oz (135 g) slice of thinly cut, milk-soaked, then wiped ox liver
1½ oz (40 g) de-rinded bacon pieces
2 oz (50 g) onion
Salt
Pepper
A scant ½ oz (5 g) clean dripping or oil
3 tbsps (3 × 15 ml spoons) coarse red cooking wine or stock
A pinch of thyme, fresh chopped or dried crumbled

Slice onion extremely thinly. Heat chosen fat in a small pan. Add onion and fry until just softened and yellow. Arrange liver on centre of oiled square of foil. Spread soft-fried onions over liver. Cut bacon pieces small and scatter on top. Add thyme, salt and pepper, moisten with wine or stock, fold up foil loosely and bake on middle shelf at Gas Mark 5 (approx 375°F, 190°C) for 15 minutes.

The pre-frying of the onion is necessary to ensure the liver does not become overcooked by the time the onion is edible.

POTATO CRUST

4 large peeled old potatoes
2 rounded tbsps (2 × 15 ml spoons) butter or Gold
8 fluid oz (240 ml) boiling milk
11 oz (300 g) sifted flour
A little raw, beaten egg

Steam potatoes and then mash to a smooth paste with chosen fat. Work in milk and then flour to make a smooth rolling dough consistency.

245

IMITATION CALVES' LIVER AND BACON

½ pint (300 ml) low grade milk
8 oz (225 g) ox liver
4 de-rinded rashers of streaky
  bacon
Oil, dripping or lard to fry

Buy one day in advance of cooking and see that the butcher slices the liver thinly. Slide it into the milk. Leave until the following evening. Drain and wipe. Discard the fluid (unless you have a cat) which will now be the colour of port wine. The pre-milk treatment makes coarse ox liver taste like calves' liver but it costs a great deal less.

Check the bacon rashers for saltiness and soak for 5 minutes in boiling water if suspicious of them. Then lay on a grill rack and cook while frying the liver. Fry in a very little oil, dripping or lard remembering that overcooked liver is not just an abomination but will also be quite purged of all its iron goodness. Just stiffen it, turn over and repeat. Then taste a scrap. If not still bloody but just tender to the teeth, it will be done.

Serve ideally with cold, cooked, left-over potatoes sliced ¼ inch (5 mm) thick and sautéd in an almost dry pan. A superabundance of frying fat or oil makes these soggy. Just keep moving and turning them with a metal spatula.

OX KIDNEY SAUTE

1 lb (450 g) ox kidney in the piece
4 good-sized peeled, very thinly
  sliced onions
1 pint (600 ml) strong stock
Pepper

Divide the piece of ox kidney lengthwise through the white core. Place in a shallow saucepan, cover with the stock, raise to boiling, maintain for 1

Salt
2 oz (50 g) clean dripping
4 fluid oz (120 ml) beer
1 flat teasp (1 × 5 ml spoon)
made English mustard
1 flat teasp (1 × 5 ml spoon) real
curry powder or ideally
masala paste
A large squeeze of lemon juice
1 rounded tbsp (1 × 15 ml
spoon) milled fresh parsley
heads
1 scant eggsp (1 × 2.5 ml spoon)
ground ginger
1 oz (25 g) flour

minute and then leave until the fluid is quite cold. Remove, cut out the white core and slice both halves of kidney into bite-size pieces.

Melt and heat dripping, turn in onions over a gentle heat and fry until soft and golden. Work in flour, ground ginger and chosen curry flavouring with the back of a wooden spoon, stirring and turning for $3\frac{1}{2}$ minutes to expel all taste of flour. Add the beer and stir until smooth. Add $\frac{1}{2}$ pint (300 ml) of the stock in which the kidney was blanched. Do this gradually, beating well each time until all is absorbed. Work in the onions, made mustard and lemon juice. Taste and correct seasoning with salt and black pepper and finally stir in the parsley. Serve with little triangles of toast around as a border or with cooked Patna rice.

DRIPPING CRUST (Economical)

8 oz (225 g) sifted flour
3 oz (75 g) clean dripping
1 raw egg yolk
Cold water to bind
1 flat coffeesp (1 × 2.5 ml spoon)
salt
Generous pinch of black pepper

Sift flour, salt and pepper into a roomy bowl. Rub in dripping until very fine-grained. Make a well in centre, drop egg yolk into this, add a little cold water and work up, adding more water sparingly to achieve a good rolling dough. Put into a polythene bag and chill in ordinary domestic refrigeration for 1 hour before using.

247

ITALIAN MEAT LOAF

12 oz (350 g) lean minced beef
1 finely chopped green pimento
1 small minced onion or shallot
4 oz (100 g) ricotta cheese
2 oz (50 g) grated Parmesan or
    other hard cheese
1 flat teasp (1 × 5 ml spoon) salt
A generous grate of black
    peppercorns ground in a mill
3 No 2 eggs, well beaten and
    strained

Mix all prepared ingredients very thoroughly, binding with the eggs. Shape into a rectangle on an oiled baking sheet. Bake on middle shelf at Gas Mark 3 (approx 325°F, 160°C) for 45–50 minutes. Serve with a cheese sauce.

BEEF LEFT-OVERS

These little French gratins are ideal for people who are out all day. They are quick to assemble, only take 25 minutes in the oven and are very welcome on a cold night.

Slices of cold, cooked beef
4 oz (100 g) small button
    mushrooms
1 level tbsp (1 × 15 ml spoon)
    milled or chopped parsley
3 small onions or shallots
1 small teacupful finest soft
    white or brown breadcrumbs
2 fluid oz (60 ml) dry white wine
    'plonk' or gravy left over from
    first serving of meat
Salt
Black pepper
A walnut of butter or Gold

Rub a Pyrex heat-resistant plate, soup plate or flan dish with chosen fat. Mix together the prepared mushrooms, parsley, onions or shallots and breadcrumbs. Season lightly with salt and pepper. Scatter half over buttered base of chosen container. Cover with the meat slices. Cover with remaining mixture. Moisten gently with chosen fluid, cover with Alcan Foil and cook for 25 minutes one shelf below centre at Gas Mark 4 (approx 350°F, 180°C).

Note
We sometimes cover this with creamed potatoes, remembering to butter the top surface to obtain a good brown during cooking time.
    Pork can be used instead of beef.

Main Course Dishes:
with Pork and Veal

The roasting of pork
Apple sauce
Sage and onion stuffing
Pork and bean casserole
Meat mould
Tomato fondue
Tomato fondue sauce
Gammon slices with pineapple
Baked gammon and cheese
Bacon and pineapple pizza
Crusty gammon bake
Modest veal casserole

THE ROASTING OF PORK

Should a leg or loin of pork come within your catering orbit, there are three points to remember: always roast slowly until thoroughly well cooked, pay no heed to the hilarious instructions which have been written about how to obtain perfect crackling and, for your health's sake, steer clear of it in extremely hot weather.

Begin operations with a Stanley knife, used by decorators to cut linoleum but superb for scoring pork to obtain perfect crackling! Score the raw rind in ¼ inch (5 mm) spaced cuts deep enough to cut fractionally into the underlying fat. Use either real sea salt (Maldon or French *gros sel*), or a coarsely grated block of salt and rub a handful with great vigour into the cuts you have made all over the rind.

Stand the pork in an ordinary meat baking tin with just 3 fluid oz (90 ml) of cold water run over the base of tin. Roast on middle shelf at Gas Mark 4 (approx 350°F, 180°C), allowing 15 minutes for each pound. Remove from the oven. The pork fat will have oozed out by this time and collected in the base of the pan. Baste the top liberally. Return to the oven for 15 minutes *one shelf above centre* this time, raising heat to Gas Mark 8 (approx 450°F, 230°C). Remove, baste again and return to same shelf but turn the joint round so that the reverse side faces front. Ten minutes later that crackling will *fly*. In fact when we made it on TV and gave a piece to our young assistant to eat, it crunched so loudly that we had to remain silent until he had swallowed it, after which transmission was resumed.

Serve with sage and onion stuffing rolled into little balls and baked in a separate container underneath the joint and, if liked, hand apple sauce at table.

APPLE SAUCE

1 large Bramley, or other substitute cooking apple
A fat pinch each of salt, powdered cloves and black pepper
1 fluid oz (30 ml) water

While the joint is roasting, peel and core apple, slice very thinly and mix with remaining ingredients in a small pan. Stir occasionally until light and fluffy. Beat hard or rub through an ordinary sieve.

SAGE AND ONION STUFFING

4 oz (100 g) peeled, sliced and minced or chopped Bramley, or other cooking apple
4 oz (100 g) peeled, minced or

Put all dry ingredients into a roomy bowl, blend well, then add beaten egg and work up to a firm paste with a few drops of

finely-chopped onion or
shallot
4 oz (100 g) fine, soft brown or
white breadcrumbs
2 oz (50 g) suet
1 flat eggsp (1 × 2.5 ml spoon)
grated lemon or orange rind
1 scant flat teasp (1 × 5 ml spoon
salt
½ coffeesp (1 × 2.5 ml spoon)
black pepper
1 beaten No 3 egg to bind
1 heaped teasp (1 × 5 ml spoon)
crumbled dried sage leaves
A few drops of strong stock
(optional)

stock if found absolutely
necessary.

PORK AND BEAN CASSEROLE

2 pints (1.20 litres) pea or Navy
beans
1½ lb (750 g) fatty salt pork
1 rounded teasp (1 × 15 ml
spoon) Whitworths dark
brown molasses sugar
2 oz (50 g) Fowler's black treacle
12 drops of Worcestershire sauce
Boiling stock or water
1 teasp (1 × 5 ml spoon) made
English mustard
1 teacupful soft brown
breadcrumbs (optional)
8 fluid oz (240 ml) boiling water

Wash the beans. Soak overnight,
drain, then cook in water to
cover for 2 hours or until beans
are tender but not broken or
collapsed. Drain and turn into
chosen casserole pot. Cover with
salt pork cut into cubes. Mix
sugar, treacle, Worcestershire
sauce and mustard with boiling
water. Pour over pot contents,
cover and bake one shelf below
centre at Gas Mark 3 (approx
325°F, 160°C) for 7–8 hours. Add
more stock to keep beans just
covered. Remove lid for last 30
minutes.

A teacupful of soft brown
breadcrumbs may be sprinkled
over the exposed top for the last
30 minutes. These absorb some
of the fat in the pork and form a
browned crust.

251

MEAT MOULD

4 oz (100 g) minced veal
4 oz (100 g) minced pork
½ inch (1.25 cm) thick slice of
  crustless bread
A little milk
1 small minced onion
1 small de-seeded and
  de-pipped pimento (red or
  green)
A generous pinch of both salt
  and black pepper
1 small egg
A scrap of dripping to rub inside
  container
2 tbsps (2 × 15 ml spoons)
  tomato fondue

Mix pork, veal, onion, pimento, fondue and seasonings in a bowl. Moisten bread slice to a pap with milk and beat into bowl mixture with the well beaten egg. Blend all thoroughly. Rub base and sides of a 1 lb (450 g) pudding basin with dripping, turn in mixture, press down, cover with a circle of greased or oiled greaseproof paper. Cover with Alcan Foil, secure with a rubber band and steam for 45 minutes.

Uncover and unmould onto a heated dish for service. Either hand Tomato Fondue Sauce separately or pour right over the mould.

TOMATO FONDUE

1 lb (450 g) rough-chopped, very
  ripe tomatoes
3 oz (75 g) butter or Gold
Salt and pepper to season

Soften chosen fat in small thick pan. Turn in tomatoes and set over a low heat. Stir occasionally until all becomes a soft mass. Rub through an ordinary sieve, taste and correct seasoning with salt and pepper.

TOMATO FONDUE SAUCE

The residue tomato fondue after
  removing 2 tbsps (2 × 15 ml
  spoons) for Meat Mould
1 small sprig of finely chopped
  or milled fresh tarragon or 1
  flat teasp (1 × 5 ml spoon)
  powdered dried tarragon
4 fluid oz (120 ml) top-of-the-
  milk or single cream

Heat the sieved tomato fondue through in a small thick pan with prepared tarragon and a pinch of both salt and black pepper. Stir in the cream or top-of-the-milk and allow to simmer for 4 minutes. Stir and serve either hot or cold.
Note
For garlic lovers only, a very small peeled crushed garlic clove may be added from the onset.

GAMMON SLICES WITH PINEAPPLE

Cut cooked gammon into thick slices. Set on a dish with pineapple rings from a tin, allowing one to every gammon slice. Pour the pineapple syrup into a small pan. Heat through with an equal quantity of strong, cleared bacon-bone stock. Thicken with 1 rounded dessertspoon (1 × 10 ml spoon) potato flour or arrowroot stirred to a smooth paste with either water or sherry. Pour straight into pan fluid, stir and mixture will immediately thicken and clear. Add 1 level dessertspoon (1 × 10 ml spoon) fresh, milled parsley and serve with creamed potatoes.

Note

Try using tinned black cherries in syrup instead of pineapple and cooking-type port instead of sherry.

BAKED GAMMON AND CHEESE

8 × ½ inch (1.25 cm) thick slices of crustless white bread cut from a sandwich loaf

Butter or Gold

5 oz (135 g) Mozzarella cheese or substitute Bel Paese

4 oz (100 g) cooked, very thinly sliced gammon

Black pepper

Spread bread slices with chosen fat, halve and overlap over base of a heat-resistant dish which has been rubbed lightly with extra fat. Cut gammon slices into 1 inch (2.5 cm) squares and put over bread. Slice chosen cheese thinly. Lay over gammon squares. Bake on middle shelf at Gas Mark 6 (approx 400°F, 200°C) until cheese bubbles and turns golden brown. Serve immediately.

BACON AND PINEAPPLE PIZZA

½ inch (1.25 cm) thick bread slice cut from base of a cottage loaf

3 grilled rashers of thin-cut streaky bacon

Oil

1 generous tbsp (1 × 15 ml spoon) green tomato chutney

8 stoned halved black olives

12 small segments of tinned or fresh pineapple

½ small teasp (1 × 2.5 ml spoon) oregano or wild thyme

Flick over bread with drops of oil. Scatter on dried oregano or wild thyme. Cover with strips of the grilled bacon interspersed with pineapple segments spread with chutney. Dot with halved black olives and moisten fairly liberally with oil. Bake at Gas Mark 4 (approx 350°F, 180°C) on middle shelf for 10 minutes.

253

CRUSTY GAMMON BAKE

Cook gammon as explained, p. 221. Remove, wipe and place in an ordinary meat baking tin.

4 oz (100 g) soft brown sugar
1 tbsp (1 × 15 ml spoon) Tate & Lyle's black treacle
Grated rind and strained juice of 1 small orange
Fat pinch of cayenne pepper
6 fluid oz (180 ml) cider

Study the shape of your gammon joint after ripping off the rind. Make a small pad of Alcan Foil and use to prop the disclosed fatty surfaces as level as possible in the tin. Make a paste with the sugar, treacle, orange juice, grated rind and cayenne. Spread thickly over the fatty surface. Pour cider around joint and bake for 30–35 minutes one shelf above centre of Gas Mark 6 (approx 400°F, 200°C) or until a crusty top forms from the paste. Lift onto a heated dish, strain pan liquor into a small jug or sauceboat and serve.

MODEST VEAL CASSEROLE

Veal is so costly that we have only included one recipe in this section.

1 lb (450 g) pie veal
1 tbsp (1 × 15 ml spoon) seasoned flour
1 lb (450 g) onions peeled and chopped small
2 oz (50 g) clean dripping
1 scraped diced 3 oz (75 g) carrot
1 *bouquet garni* (herb faggot)
4 fluid oz (120 ml) inexpensive dry white 'plonk' wine and 6 fluid oz (180 ml) veal, pork or chicken bone stock or ½ pint (300 ml) boiling water stirred with 1 chicken meat cube
1 dessertsp (1 × 10 ml spoon) soy sauce

Melt and heat dripping in a medium frying pan. Turn veal pieces in seasoned flour. Fry briskly all over in hot dripping, drain and transfer to a small lidded casserole. Fry onions and carrots in residue pan fat, turning briskly over a fairly strong heat. Add to meat in the casserole. Inset the *bouquet garni*, swill with chosen wine and stock or substitute, cover and cook one shelf below centre at Gas Mark 3 (approx 325°F, 160°C) for 1¼ hours. Serve from the pot.

Vegetables

Steamed old potatoes
Steamed new potatoes
Roast potatoes
Creamed potatoes
Jacket-baked potatoes
Stuffed baked potatoes no 1
Stuffed baked potatoes no 2
Souffléd baked potatoes
Milk and potato bake
Sauté potatoes
Vegetable pie
Steamed cauliflower
Fried cauliflower
Jerusalem artichoke pie
Stuffed tomatoes
Broad beans with parsley butter
Grilled tomatoes
Bubble and squeak
Crispy fried onion rings
Eggplant fritters
A leek gratin
How to cook spinach

Whole spinach
Spinach purée
Ratatouille
Austrian red cabbage

We in Britain grow some of the finest vegetables in the world. Some of them just suffer a bit when they reach our kitchen doors.

There are over five hundred classic ways of cooking Sir Walter Raleigh's great discovery, but the average potato cooking range runs from boiled, creamed and roasted round-the-joint to chips and jacket-baked. If we are to be honest, there are too few who use even these treatments to the top of their potential form, so we shall begin with them and then limit ourselves to sharing some of the simplest, quality recipes which justify the initial preparation and cleaning.

Let us begin with what you and we call 'chips', ignorant caterers call 'French fried', which they are *not*, and what the average fish and chip shop erroneously believes should resemble giant fried fingers. If you have ever enjoyed slim French *pommes frites*, twice-cooked as they should be, crisp and browned outside, and seasoned before coming to table with both real (sea) salt and freshly ground black peppercorns, you will be more than halfway to being persuaded to take the extra little bit of trouble with them which results in their being a pleasure to eat by themselves (Vegetables, Part 1).

You will find no recipes in this book for 'canteen cabbage', marvellous to use as a poultice and allegedly splendid for drawing boils, but absolutely no good for the human tum. Just try our recipe for cabbage (Vegetables, Part 1) and we are confident you will go on using this quicker, easier and far more palatable way.

As you may know already, the vogue for lightly cooked vegetables has come, overspent itself and is now, mercifully, on the way out. Crisp they should be, and almost *al dente* or firm to the teeth, but this does not mean just warmed through and practically raw as some have been serving them. It may be 'smart' still in some circles but then 'smart' is a nasty word anyway and we only want vegetables to be 'enjoyable'.

As for the wicked habit, rife in seaside boarding houses of the worst kind, of cooking green vegetables with a bit of washing soda, it

256

makes us want to campaign for the return of the 'cat'.

You can manage without a proper chip pan by just using a large saucepan, but make sure it is a deep one and never more than one-third filled with oil or real lard. When raw chips are lowered – gently – into slightly smoking hot oil or lard, the stuff *seethes* and, if the pan is over filled, will bubble up and over and catch fire. So please be careful and even if you do not have a deep-fryer, do invest in a long-handled frying basket which fits easily into the chosen pan.

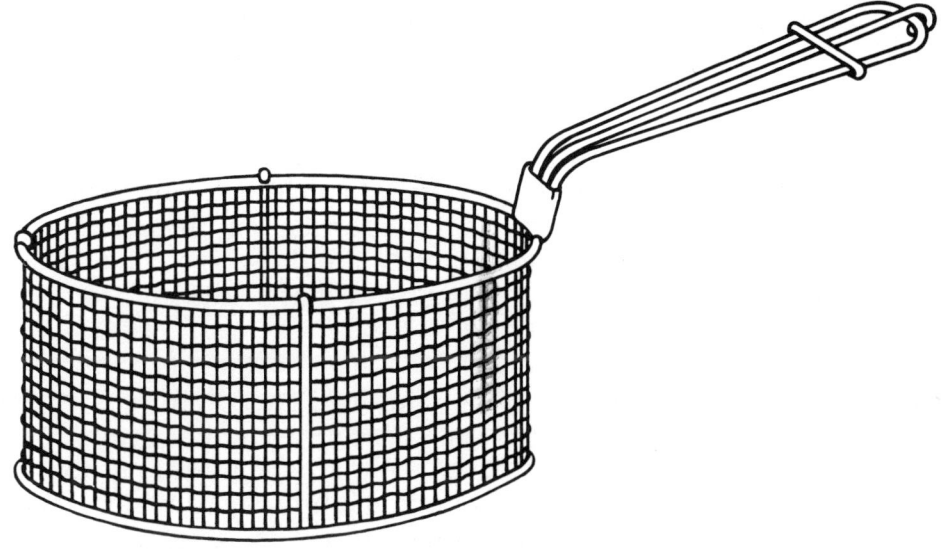

Finally and as we have already said in Part 1, do invest in a proper steamer of at least two tiers. It will save you cooking fuel, diminish the dreaded washing-up and conserve the flavour of vegetables. When boiled these wave goodbye to a great deal of their taste as you sling the water down the kitchen plug hole.

You *should* boil kohlrabi, beetroots, corn on the cob, turnips, globe artichokes and swedes. All the rest should be *steamed*, then given post-cookery touches of enhancement.

STEAMED OLD POTATOES

Just scrub them, before putting in the top of a steamer, under a lid and over a base pan half-filled with water. Raise water to boiling and then simmer to steam until just tender. Remove steamer lid, take out potatoes and let them become sufficiently cool to hold in an oven glove. In less time than we can write this, whip off those paper-thin skins leaving all the goodness that is wasted when you peel potatoes raw. Put back into the steamer top as you rip off the skins. Replace the lid and just heat through again in moments. The counsel for perfection is to give them a dollop of butter or Gold, a sprinkling of milled or chopped parsley heads and finely scissored chives and then put them on the table under a lid for hot 'seconds'.

STEAMED NEW POTATOES

In France everyone eats *pommes vapeur* or steamed new potatoes, *with the skins left on*. They are meticulously scrubbed first, then cooked as already explained and turned into a little lidded pot to come to table. No peeling, no straining after cooking, isn't that just the job?

ROAST POTATOES

In these days of diminishing ability to afford joints of meat, it is just as well that really super roast potatoes *never* go round any joint.

Peel large old potatoes, then cut to even-sized pieces and boil for exactly 7 minutes in already fast-boiling, slightly salted water. Drain thoroughly. Have ready a pie dish or other piece of oven-ware containing at least 2 inches (5 cm) in depth of melted dripping (see Reminders for Beginner Cooks, Part 1 for how to clean dirty dripping). Put this into the heated oven before you start preparing the potatoes. Then it will be really hot when you slide in the potatoes to cook *under* the joint or *over* a casserole as high up as you can get the dish. Allow about 30 minutes, then turn the potatoes over and cook until all round themselves they wear rich brown exteriors which never, ever turn into those unbelievably nasty leather-overcoats.

CREAMED POTATOES

2 lb (900 g) well-scrubbed old
  potatoes
Salt
Pepper
Milk
Butter or Gold
Optionally, some finely chopped

Steam as described, peel and fork down rather roughly. Add a generous splash of milk, a knob of chosen fat and mash away until the mixture is fine enough for you to beat it hard. Taste, add salt and pepper, beat again

258

chives and/or parsley heads

and, for special occasions, beat in your chosen herb.

Of course if you have a potato roller and an ordinary round sieve, and if you have cooked the potatoes sufficiently in the first place, you can just rub them through the sieve, add the seasonings, milk and fat and then bash away with a wooden spoon.

JACKET-BAKED POTATOES

Choose 8–10 oz (225–275 g) old potatoes. Scrub them spotless, then put slap onto the bars of the middle shelf with the heat at Gas Mark 5 (approx 375°F, 190°C) and leave for 1¼ hours, by which time they will be soft inside when squeezed gently.

Post-baking treatment: make a large X at top centre of each one. Fold the four quarters back sufficiently to ram in a large blob of Parsley Butter (Basics, Part 1) or, if you know your companions' tastes, a goodly smear of Garlic Butter (Basics, Part 1) instead.

STUFFED BAKED POTATOES No 1

These are a very good way of assuaging hunger when short of funds but famished.

2 × 10 oz (275 g) old potatoes baked as described above

1 heaped tbsp (1 × 15 ml spoon) simple cheese sauce

3 oz (75 g) fat and lean of bacon from one of Sainsbury's excellent, low-priced bags of bacon pieces

2 No 2 eggs

Black pepper

1 oz (25 g) butter or Gold

Let the oven-baked potatoes cool down sufficiently for you to handle them comfortably. Slice off a small lid and set aside. Scoop as much potato 'flour' as you can from the interiors into a bowl. Mash down and beat in the cheese sauce. Cook the bacon, chop the pieces up small and mix them into the potato mixture. Then taste and add pepper – no salt will be needed. Pack back into the potato skins, dividing the mixture equally between them. Scoop out a hole at centre and hold back the removed potato mixture. Break

259

an egg into each hollow, cover with the potato mixture, lay the potato skin lid on top and bake on middle shelf at Gas Mark 6 (approx 400°F, 200°C) for 14 minutes.

STUFFED BAKED POTATOES No 2

Strictly for use when in funds.

Delete the bacon from previous recipe but otherwise make as before, adding 4 oz (100 g) shelled shrimps and 1 tablespoon (1 × 15 ml spoon) milled, fresh parsley heads and blending well. Taste, correct seasoning with pepper and only a very little salt – if any. Blend in 4 fluid oz (120 ml) plain yoghurt and 2 tablespoons (2 × 15 ml spoons) thick cream, replace potato skin lids and bake as before.

SOUFFLED BAKED POTATOES

2 × 10 oz (275 g) old potatoes
2 No 2 eggs
1 oz (25 g) grated hard cheese, ideally Parmesan
1 dessertsp (1 × 10 ml spoon) milled parsley heads
Salt
Black pepper
Walnut of butter

Scrub and bake as already described. When cool enough to handle, slice 'lids' from the tops lengthwise and scoop out all the 'flour' leaving two hollow cases.

Mash 'flour' of potatoes with salt and pepper. Add a walnut of butter and beat in the egg yolks. When ready to finish, whip up the egg whites very stiffly, fold in the grated cheese and work in the creamed potato and milled parsley heads. Pile into emptied potato cases, dome off tops and bake one shelf above centre at Gas Mark 7 (approx 425°F, 220°C) for 8–10 minutes.

MILK AND POTATO BAKE

This is quick, easy and delicious.

1¼ lb (500 g) old potatoes, peeled weight
4 oz (100 g) raw onion grated to pulp
Salt

Scrub, steam and slice potatoes into ¼ inch (5 mm) thick rounds. Brush interior of chosen dish with oil or dripping. Lay down a layer of potato slices. Cover with

Black pepper
1 oz (50 g) grated hard cheese
   ends
A little oil or dripping
Milk, but not more than ¾ pint
   (450 ml)

a sprinkling of grated onion pulp
and so continue, adding a light
seasoning of both salt and
pepper to each layer and always
finishing with a final layer of
potato. Pour in milk until this
just shows through the last layer
of potatoes, sprinkle with the
grated cheese and bake at Gas
Mark 4 (approx 350°F, 180°C)
under a light covering of oil on
centre shelf for 20 minutes.
Remove foil and finish by
allowing top potatoes and
cheese to become richly
browned.

SAUTE POTATOES (with cooked potatoes)

Strictly speaking these are not real sauté potatoes but they are quick and very acceptable.

¼ inch (5 mm) thick slices of
   cold, cooked old or new
   potatoes
A small amount of cleaned
   dripping

Let the dripping melt in a frying
pan and begin to sizzle. Lay in
the slices to cover pan's base
completely. Cook over a brisk
heat until well browned
underneath. Turn slices over,
allow 3 minutes, then cover pan
with a plate and pour off any
surplus pan dripping. Finish
sautéing in dry pan. When
browned all over, sprinkle with
salt and pepper and serve. If
carefully cooked there should be
no surplus dripping to mop up
on absorbent paper.

VEGETABLE PIE (from left-overs)

This mixture can be used for small individual pies or bigger ones for two or more. We give ingredients for one portion but these can be multiplied at will.

2 oz (50 g) cold, mashed potato
½ oz (10 g) butter or Gold
Salt
Black pepper
½ oz (10 g) grated cheese
1½ oz (40 g) cold, cooked, sliced
  carrots
2 fluid oz (60 ml) simple cheese
  sauce
1 very small, raw grated shallot
  or onion

Rub the inside of a small Pyrex or earthenware dish with half the fat and spread over half the potato. Sprinkle very lightly with salt and pepper and spread over half the cheese sauce. Sprinkle with half the onion pulp, then the carrot and cover with remaining potato. Season again. Sprinkle on cheese, melt and add remaining butter, cover with a scrap of Alcan Foil and bake at Gas Mark 4 (approx 350°F, 180°C) one shelf above centre for 15 minutes.

Now go ahead and work out other vegetable combinations, always beginning and ending with potatoes.

STEAMED CAULIFLOWER

Begin by chopping through the hard base stem, close to the flowering head. Discard and then slice cauliflower from top to base into quarters. Wash and then place in steamer, laying pieces down on their sides. Cover and steam until still firm but not half raw.

This is palatable when seasoned with salt and pepper and served with a little melted butter; nicer if given a light covering of simple cheese sauce and delicious if a mixture of cheese, soft crumbs and melted butter is sprinkled lightly on top over the sauce and the whole then browned lightly under a medium strength grill.

FRIED CAULIFLOWER

1 small cauliflower
2 rounded tbsps (2 × 15 ml
  spoons) flour
1 smallest egg white
Cold tap water
Salt

Remove all green and hard stem from cauliflower and cut flowerets into small sprigs with as much stalk as possible on each piece. Tumble into a steamer over boiling water in

Pepper
Powdered paprika (optional)
Hot oil in pan to fry

base pan. Cover and steam until firm but cooked through – this only needs a few minutes.

Make a smooth thick batter with the flour and a thin trickle of tap water, stirring at first, then beating vigorously. When mixture is as thick as whipped cream, stop please. Cover and rest until the cauliflower sprigs are cold. Whip up the little egg white very stiffly, beat into the batter and twirl each sprig round in it until thickly coated. Drop into slightly smoking hot oil (390–400°F, 195–200°C) allow to puff up and turn a rich golden brown. Drain on absorbent kitchen paper or newspaper. Sprinkle lightly with salt, pepper and maybe paprika.

Do not keep waiting too long or the crispness of texture will be lost.

JERUSALEM ARTICHOKE PIE

1 lb (450 g) peeled weight of artichokes, well washed and dried
½ pint (300 ml) simple cheese sauce (p. 24)
Salt
Pepper
1 oz (50 g) hard grated cheese
Butter

Slice raw, prepared artichokes thickly. Steam for 8 minutes only. Butter a small pie dish. Mix artichoke slices with cheese sauce. Taste and correct sauce's seasoning, turn mixture into pie dish, scatter with the grated cheese and bake for 20 minutes on middle shelf at Gas Mark 6 (approx 400°F, 200°C).
Note
If you hard-boil (8 minutes) and shell 2 No 3 eggs, slice them in too and serve with plenty of hot dripping toast, this pie makes an appetising hot supper dish.

263

STUFFED TOMATOES

4 large tomatoes
2 rounded tbsps (2 × 15 ml
  spoons) roughly crumbled
  white or brown bread
3 wiped anchovy fillets,
  chopped small
2 oz (50 g) cooked diced ham or
  gammon
1 No 3 egg
2 oz (50 g) cooked rice
1 oz (25 g) very finely grated
  shallot or onion
¼ garlic clove, crushed
  (optional)
A little oil

Slice tops of tomatoes meanly. Remove all seed and cut away interior pulp with a small pair of scissors. Mix anchovy fillets, chosen meat, rice and well-beaten egg together in a bowl. Season with salt, pepper, and crushed garlic. Pack back into prepared tomato cases and return their 'lids'. Brush the base of a small heat-resistant dish and tops and sides of tomatoes with oil and set in position. Bake one shelf below centre at Gas Mark 3 (approx 325°F, 160°C) for 20 minutes.

BROAD BEANS WITH PARSLEY BUTTER

1½ lb (750 g) shelled, young
  small broad beans
1 level dessertsp (1 × 10 ml
  spoon) Parsley Butter (Basics,
  Part 1)

Steam beans until each one pops willingly out of its little overcoat. Ideally, the alternative is to cook them gently in stock to cover or in a bouillon cube dissolved in ¾ pint (450 ml) water. Then strain off the liquor and reserve for a soup or sauce. Either way, stir in parsley butter in a serving dish. Let folk add salt at table if they wish.

GRILLED TOMATOES

Firm but ripe tomatoes
Garlic Butter (Basics, Part 1)

Halve the tomatoes around their middles, not from stem to base. Make an X-cut across tops, nicking skins for a scant ¼ inch (5 mm). Spread with garlic butter and cook on a grill rack with its legs in low position under a moderate grill until tender but not collapsed.

BUBBLE AND SQUEAK

8 oz (225 g) rough chopped,
  steamed old potatoes
8 oz (225 g) cooked chopped
  cabbage
1 medium onion, sliced finely
3 oz (75 g) clean dripping
Salt
Black pepper

Fry onion in 1 oz (25 g) of hot dripping over a mere thread of heat so that it becomes soft and golden but not browned or crisp at the edges. Mix with potatoes and cabbage very thoroughly and season to taste with salt and black pepper.

Melt remaining dripping in a medium-sized frying pan. Heat through, then pat the vegetable mixture down on top. Raise heat to medium. Fry until a slice, eased up from underneath, confirms that the base has become crisp and browned. Drive the slice under as far as you can and turn over; repeat with any part which has not been turned, so that unbrowned mixture is now on the base. Pat down again and continue to fry. Repeat this procedure three times in all. It is worth the trouble because at the finish all the dripping has been absorbed and the crusty brown bits are mixed right through. Turn off the heat.

Place a large plate over the pan and swiftly reverse so that Bubble and Squeak falls onto plate like a flat cake. Keep warm while frying 2 eggs apiece. Place these on top and eat with plenty of buttered toast.

CRISPY FRIED ONION RINGS

Contrary to the general conception, these are absurdly simple to make. For onion lovers they are also very 'more-ish' and only those who have served them know just how many the average male will ingest with proper French chips and any form of grilled meat. But they must be right.

The Three Rules:

1   The batter must be thin, like fresh, single cream.
2   The onions must be cut into fine rings. If the knife slips while cutting and breaks the rings do not worry. They fry equally well provided each ring or part of ring is *separated*.
3   The oil in pan or fryer must be very hot indeed, which means 390–400°F, (195–200°C).

Large, round, firm, peeled
  Spanish onions
Flour
Tap water
Salt
Black pepper
Oil for frying

Heat oil over a low burner making sure that it never fills chosen container to more than one-third of its overall depth.

Put 2–3 really heaped tablespoons (2–3 × 15 ml spoons) flour into a large pudding basin and hold under a very thin trickle of tap water. Work with a wooden spoon. Beat flour with water, pulling bowl away from tap as you work to ensure not having too much water and so beat to the consistency – we repeat – of fresh single cream.

Slice onions as already explained and, if not frying them immediately, put into a bowl and cover with cold water. When left exposed, cut onions absorb all the impurities in the air.

When required turn heat under oil to full. Drain onions and dry in a cloth. Turn, a few at a time, into batter and lift out – we use our fingers – shake off the surplus and slide in just enough to keep all separate as they seethe and you turn them in the hot oil, until they are *a rich golden brown*. Pallid, beige ones both look and taste very nasty. Drain the first batch, pile onto a dish and keep warm while you repeat. The whole process is so swift that in 10 minutes you can fry a large dishful. Optionally scatter over a light seasoning of salt and black pepper.

EGGPLANT FRITTERS (Aubergine)

One of the best ways of serving this vegetable.

1 large, hard black egg plant
   with nose and stalk ends
   sliced off
Oil to fry
Flour
Water
Salt

Slice egg plant into ⅙ inch (4 mm) thick rounds. Lay on any working surface. Sprinkle on ground sea salt, cover with a cloth and leave for a minimum 1 hour to draw out bitterness which thus forms small brown drops. Wipe and drop into a batter made of sifted flour and water whipped to the consistency of day-old single cream. Turn in the wiped, sliced egg plant. Heat oil in pan or deep fryer and when this smokes slightly, drop in just sufficient slices of egg plant each time for them to swell and brown separately. Drain on absorbent paper. Pile into a dish and scatter lightly with salt, pepper and paprika powder for service and repeat. Each batch only takes a few moments to puff and brown.

A LEEK GRATIN

8 slim leeks
½ oz (10 g) dripping
Salt
Pepper
1 oz (25 g) Sainsbury's diced
    bacon pieces
½ teacupful fine, soft
    breadcrumbs
1 fluid oz (30 ml) cooking sherry
1 fluid oz (30 ml) stock

Trim and wash leeks very carefully. Lay in a steamer and cook under a lid over boiling water until just soft. Run a little dripping over base and sides of a shallow, heat-resistant dish. Split leeks lengthwise and lay top to tail alternately, using half the total number to make one layer. Scatter over the diced, dry-fried fat and lean of bacon pieces. Sprinkle lightly with salt and strongly with black pepper. Then repeat with second layer of leeks. Swill with the sherry, then with the stock. Scatter on the crumbs, cover with a butter paper or piece of Alcan Foil and bake on middle shelf at Gas Mark 4 (approx 350°F, 180°C) for 15 minutes. Push up heat to Gas Mark 6 (approx 400°F, 200°C), remove paper or foil and allow to brown lightly.

HOW TO COOK SPINACH

Wash and pick over 2–3 lb (900 g–1.50 kg) spinach. Remove thick parts of stalks. Pack into a pan without any additional moisture. Place over a low heat and stir occasionally until the leaves have collapsed, created their own liquor and become a very dark green. This takes 6–8 minutes. When soft, serve either as whole spinach or spinach purée.

WHOLE SPINACH

Chop cooked spinach roughly. Season with salt, pepper and a pinch of nutmeg. Add a nut of butter. Serve plain, or sprinkle with 2 oz (50 g) mixed grated hard cheese (ideally Parmesan) and fine soft breadcrumbs. Moisten these with melted butter and brown under a mild grill or in the oven on top shelf at Gas Mark 6 (approx 400°F, 200°C) for about 10 minutes. Alternatively serve with the cheese stirred in, then mound on a serving dish, indent at centre and spoon in a little cream.

SPINACH PUREE

Drain off the liquor from cooked spinach. Place liquor in a small pan with 2–3 tbsps (2–3 × 15 ml spoons) double cream and (optional) 1 tbsp (1 × 15 ml spoon) Sercial Madeira or dry sherry. Simmer until reduced to about 3 tbsps (3 × 15 ml spoons). Set aside. Rub spinach through a sieve, season with salt and pepper to taste, add a generous pinch of nutmeg and fold into pan liquor. Reheat gently. Fork up into a neat mound on a serving dish and surround with small triangles of hot crustless toast.

For special occasions
Indent a hollow in the top of mounded spinach with the back of a spoon. Pour in 2½ fluid oz (75 ml) hot double cream and serve as explained above.

RATATOUILLE

Very versatile. This makes splendid pizzas and is a supper dish when served with fried eggs on top.

1 lengthwise-split red pimento
1 lengthwise-split green pimento
4 medium-sized ripe, skinned and halved tomatoes with seeds pushed out
1 large, extremely thinly sliced onion
8 oz (225 g) peeled, cored, diced vegetable marrow
1 peeled, crushed garlic clove
4 oz unskinned, scalded, then chopped mushrooms and their stalks
3 fluid oz (90 ml) oil
Salt
Pepper
1 teasp (1 × 5 ml spoon) dried *Herbes de Provence* or just a standard faggot of herbs
1 generous teasp (1 × 5 ml spoon) concentrated tomato purée

Dice the pimentos with onion. Heat 2 fluid oz (60 ml) oil in a small pan and fry pimentos and onion slowly until just soft. Work in herbs and rough-chopped tomato flesh. Meanwhile steam diced marrow flesh until tender. Work mushrooms into pan and fry with garlic clove. Add remaining oil and when all is mixed and soft, remove herb faggot. Taste, correct seasoning with salt and pepper and finally work in tomato purée with the back of a wooden spoon so that mixture is well broken down.

269

AUSTRIAN RED CABBAGE

1 small, tight red cabbage
(approx 2 lb (900 g))
8 fluid oz (240 ml) dry white
cooking wine or dry cider
8 fluid oz (240 ml) cold water
1 level breakfastcupful
Billington's molasses sugar
1 herb faggot
7 fluid oz (210 ml) red wine
vinegar
1 level eggsp (1 × 2.5 ml spoon)
powdered or grated nutmeg
1 fat pinch of powdered ginger
Strained juice and lightly grated
rind of 1 orange
1 level dessertsp (1 × 10 ml
spoon) Groult's potato flour
Cold water

Cut cabbage very thinly into strips. Place in roomy pan. Add both wine and water, raise to boiling and simmer with occasional stirs from a wooden spoon for 30 minutes. Add herbs, sugar, vinegar, nutmeg and ginger. Stir again and simmer, with occasional turns, for 1½ hours. Stir in orange juice and rind. Cook for a further 30 minutes. Stir potato flour in a small container with a little water. Pour over pan contents, stir fast until this clears. Either serve, or keep hot *au bain marie* for later service.

Cheese

Our Welsh rarebit
Hungarian stuffed pimentos with cheese
Cheese fritters
Cheese rissoles
Poor man's fondue
Cheese and tomato pudding
Egg and cheese stuffed tomatoes
Cheese flan
Racket
Potted cheese
Toasted potted cheese
Fried potted cheese
Cheese pizza
Ratatouille and cheese pizza
Pastry pizza

For the professional, as for all really serious home cooks who have the means, there are few cooking cheeses. The two which are considered to be the best are Gruyère and Parmesan. Gruyère is a Swiss melting cheese used for the great cheese fondues, of which Switzerland has one for each Canton. It has a poor relation which does very well on all but the highest culinary levels: Emmenthal, which can be distinguished from its aristocratic relation by its holes. Big holes signify Emmenthal, small ones denote Gruyère. Alas, in Britain today both are costly and the average assistant in a supermarket does not know one from the other.

For Italian cookery the leaders are Parmesan, Mozzarella, Provolone – seen dangling in bunches above Italian delicatessen counters in the shape of little pigs – and Fontina. They too are costly.

On the substitute level within the range of limited housekeeping budgets, there are cottage cheese, which can be used for many pizzas in these days of price escalation, and Cheddar. In fact the majority of cheese cookery depends upon Cheddar today. When making cheese soufflés (Eggs, p. 191) which are among the least costly of dishes by any comparisons with meat or fish, the type of Cheddar is important. Where you would use 2–3 oz (50–75 g) of Parmesan, you need 3–3½ oz (75–85 g) of grated Cheddar, making sure that the type you buy is 'Mature', which has a far greater strength than 'Farmhouse'.

Bel Paese is the soft Italian cheese we can substitute for Mozzarella. Ricotta can be replaced with home-made cream cheese or even sieved cottage cheese. These are examples of the substitutions we shall make in this Part 2. Later on you will find the classic recipes employing the classic cheeses, so the choice, as it always should be, is yours.

The cheese which is regarded by many *fines bouches* or gastronomes as the greatest is Roquefort, from which – thereby creating an exception – M Roger Vergé, whose superb restaurant Le Moulin des Mougins has the coveted 3 stars of the *Guide Michelin*, has created a *Soufflé de Fromage au Roquefort* which is unforgettable.

THE CARE OF CHEESE

On the very highest level in professional catering it is accepted that more money is lost proportionately over maintaining a good cheese board than over almost any other foodstuff. Cheeses have a very short life at perfection level. Refrigeration is their enemy.

One of the other heinous tricks is practised with such cheeses as Camembert and Brie. When these are at their best, they are almost ready to take off – gooey, oozy and bulging out of their chalky overcoats. So what happens when they are, in fact, firm and solid? They are wrapped in towels which have been wrung out in boiling water, left for 20 minutes, then enclosed in cloths wrung out in iced water, left for a further 20 minutes and the process is then repeated. A short while later the cheeses begin to *gallop*, but this treatment is immensely deleterious to their flavour.

Oddly enough Cheddars respond best to refrigeration. Wrap them very tightly in Alcan Foil and they will last much longer. You can reckon on a minimum of 2 weeks in refrigeration after so treating.

When we have a goodly assembly of cheeses we put them on a wicker tray, cover them with a cloth and suspend the tray from hooks in a draughty storage area.

Grated cheese always has a shorter life than a block or piece. The top layers dry out while the base mildews with infuriating celerity.

It is also worth remembering that the best cheeses – cut into small cubes – for wine tasting are Gruyère, Emmenthal and Cheddar, while the best of table marriages are between fine red wines and cheeses which develop and stimulate the wines by their effect upon the palate.

273

OUR WELSH RAREBIT

This was laid on at the Paris restaurant, which was, some years ago, the unofficial HQ of the Paris Rugger Club, and was consumed there in enormous quantities. It should be served in old fashioned, heat-resistant soup plates which, if they are Pyrex, can be slipped under the grill.

For the toast:
Cut two thick slices from a sandwich loaf. Set some butter or Gold to melt in a shallow container. As soon as each slice is toasted, slap it down in the melted, chosen fat for a moment and keep buttered slices warm.

The rarebit:

2 oz (50 g) butter or Gold
2 oz (50 g) flour
5 fluid oz (150 ml) beer
½ pint (300 ml) milk
5 oz (135 g) grated Cheddar
1 level teasp (1 × 5 ml spoon)
　dry mustard
1 tbsp (1 × 15 ml spoon) wine
　vinegar
Salt
Pepper
1 teasp (1 × 5 ml spoon) Lea and
　Perrins Worcestershire Sauce

Soften chosen fat, work in flour and mustard, then thin down gradually with beer. Add vinegar, a light seasoning of salt and pepper and the cheese. Thin down to a loose, but well-holding goo with the milk. Place each piece of prepared toast in a separate heat-resistant container, pour over half the mixture and brown under a brisk grill – never a slow one. This mixture serves two hungry people.

HUNGARIAN STUFFED PIMENTOS WITH CHEESE

4 small-to-medium red or green
　pimentos
1 rounded tbsp (1 × 15 ml
　spoon) finely chopped onion
2 oz (50 g) butter or Gold
6 oz (175 g) home-made or
　bought cream cheese
1 rounded tbsp (1 × 15 ml
　spoon) finely scissored chives
½ oz (10 g) powdered paprika
1 flat teasp (1 × 5 ml spoon)
　cumin seed
A light seasoning of salt and
　black pepper

Slice the tops off the pimentos. Excavate and discard all pips and pith from interiors. Cook prepared onion in chosen fat until tender. Cool and then work in the cheese, chives, paprika and cumin. Taste, correct seasoning with salt and pepper. Divide equally between the four prepared pimentos, replace lids and serve with any chosen green salad.

274

CHEESE FRITTERS

When wanting a hot snack on returning home after an evening out, you can make these in a few moments and serve them with tomato or onion sauce.

Butter or Gold
White or brown bread
Thin slices of fresh, soft Cheddar
Oil to fry
Made English mustard (for
   Cheddar only)
4 oz (100 g) flour
1 flat teasp (1 × 5 ml spoon) salt
1 tbsp (1 × 15 ml spoon) oil
Lukewarm water
1 No 2 egg white

Spread an even number of bread slices with chosen fat. Lay thin slices of the cheese over half the slices and spread mustard lightly over the remainder. Press firmly together, remove crusts and cut each slice into four small squares. (This can be done before you go out, if convenient.)

Sift flour with salt into a bowl, make a central well, add the oil and work up with water to a thick fritter batter. Cover and leave, or use at once. At this stage heat oil in a smallish saucepan until a faint haze can be seen on top. This equals 390–400°F (195–200°C). Meanwhile whip egg white and whip into batter mixture. Tow each little 'sandwich' through this batter and slide into hot oil. Allow to puff and turn brown underneath. Turn over with a slice and repeat on reverse side. Drain on absorbent kitchen tissue and eat at once.

Note
This can also be done with any left-overs of sweet or savoury sandwiches.

275

CHEESE RISSOLES (Fondues Frites)

This is a comparatively inexpensive luxury which makes an ideal hot hors d'oeuvre or delicate supper dish. There are a few salient points to remember. The potato mixture must be really dry and thick. The cheese must be Gruyère or Emmenthal. The flouring, egg-washing and breadcrumbing must be done carefully and thoroughly to form the infinitesimal wall which prevents the inner cheese mixture from oozing out during frying time. The prepared fondues must be well-chilled before frying. Finally, the crumbs must be very fine indeed as well as very soft, or the finished fondues will be unsightly and of a disagreeable outer-taste and texture.

1 lb (450 g) cold, firm Duchess potato mixture without adding butter and egg yolk
8 oz (225 g) finely grated Gruyère or Emmenthal cheese
1 level teasp (1 × 5 ml spoon) salt
1½ level eggsp (1 × 2.5 ml spoon) pepper
2 No 2 egg yolks
Shallow dishes containing:
  a) raw beaten, strained egg
  b) sifted flour c) fine soft crumbs
Oil for frying
Parsley or watercress to garnish

Place prepared potato mixture in a bowl and add cheese, salt and pepper. Work in egg yolks and continue working until mixture is thoroughly blended. Sift flour over a small working surface area. Take 3–4 oz (75–100 g) pieces of mixture and drop onto floured surface. Roll into neat sausages, reflouring when necessary, and dip ends carefully into flour. Pass these rolls through raw beaten egg, lift, drain and drop (singly) onto the fine crumbs. Roll and pat thickly and thoroughly; then set on a flat dish, well dusted with remaining crumbs. Place in refrigeration and leave there (minimum 1 hour).

When oil in deep fryer is beginning to throw a faint haze of smoke, put two or three 'fondues' at a time into a frying basket making sure they do not touch each other. Plunge basket into hot oil and *turn off heat*. These should fry to a rich golden brown in slightly diminishing heat as this minimises the danger of bursting. Arrange on a paper napkin-covered dish and garnish with sprigs of parsley or watercress. Serve immediately. The inside will be soft and creamy, the outside crisp and fine.

POOR MAN'S FONDUE

An uncut sandwich loaf
5 fluid oz (150 ml) beer
8 oz (225 g) Cheddar cheese
1 dessertsp (1 × 10 ml spoon) arrowroot

Shred cheese finely or grate on coarsest side of a grater. Put into a thick pan. Stir arrowroot to a thin paste with just a spoonful or two of the beer. Pour the rest of the beer over the cheese. Set the pan over a heat diffuser mat which has been set over the lowest heat possible. Leave until cheese melts and settles in a goo on the base of the pan. Stir up the arrowroot paste, pour on and stir with a wooden spoon until mixture thickens. Set pan over a small portable hot plate on a table in the sitting-room. Cut about half the bread crust and all the crumb into 1 inch (2.5 cm) cubes, crust and all.

Each person impales a cube on a fork, swirls it around in the cheese fondue and transfers it speedily to the mouth. Serve beer to accompany this friendly dish.

CHEESE AND TOMATO PUDDING

8 medium, very ripe tomatoes
2 No 3 eggs
1 small teacupful stale, grated
    Cheddar cheese
3 small teacupfuls fine, soft
    breadcrumbs
1 rounded teasp (1 × 5 ml
    spoon) milled fresh parsley
    heads (or used dried)
Salt
Black pepper
4 fluid oz (120 ml) milk or stock
1 oz (25 g) very clean dripping

Cover tomatoes with boiling water. Leave 4 minutes. Remove skins and break down thoroughly with a fork. Work in three-quarters of the cheese, the crumbs, parsley and a light seasoning of salt and pepper. Beat up eggs and milk or stock with a fork. Work into dry mixture. Rub half the dripping over base and sides of a medium pie dish. Turn in mixture, level off, sprinkle with remaining grated cheese and dot with flakes of remaining dripping. Bake at Gas Mark 4 (approx 350°F, 180°C) on middle shelf for 35–40 minutes. Serve piping hot.

EGG AND CHEESE STUFFED TOMATOES

4 large tomatoes
A little butter or Gold
2 No 4 eggs
A generous pinch of cayenne
    pepper and salt
2 oz (50 g) grated Cheddar
    cheese

Halve the tomatoes and scoop out interiors into a small bowl. Add a flake of chosen fat to each hollowed tomato. Set on a heat-resistant dish, cover with a butter paper and bake at Gas Mark 4 (approx 350°F, 180°C) on middle shelf for 12–15 minutes. Remove from oven. Beat eggs with well-crushed tomato pulp and a pinch of salt and pepper. Fill hot tomato cups, sprinkle cheese equally over these and return to oven until just set and the cheese has collapsed into a lightly browned top.

278

CHEESE FLAN

3 No 3 eggs
4½ fluid oz (135 ml) milk
5 oz (135 g) grated Emmenthal or
  Gruyère cheese
1 heaped tbsp (1 × 15 ml spoon)
  flour
1 rounded tbsp (1 × 15 ml
  spoon) butter or Gold
Salt
Black pepper
3 oz (75 g) unskinned, blanched
  and chopped mushrooms

Heat milk. Mix cheese and flour with a generous pinch of salt. Make a roux with the chosen fat and flour. Dilute with boiling milk, beating well after each addition until all is absorbed. Beat in the chopped mushrooms, season to taste with salt and pepper and finally beat in the cheese. Turn into a well greased flan dish. Bake one shelf above centre, at Gas Mark 6 (approx 400°F, 200°C) until well risen and browned on top, but do not bake to cake consistency. The flan should be moist at centre when served.

RACKET (La Raclette-Swiss)

Only for those who have open fires in their sitting-rooms.

A piece of Wensleydale cheese
  set on a large, heat-resistant
  dish or platter before a roaring
  fire
Plain boiled potatoes
'Soldiers' of buttered toast

Set the chosen large or small piece of Wensleydale with its cut face to the heat of a hot fire. Let it begin to soften and slide down in rivulets onto the platter. When a sufficient accumulation of hot melted cheese has formed, bring in the plain, boiled potatoes. Put a good-sized one on each plate, then scoop up the goo over it and eat with fingers of buttered toast.

A glass of Mulled Ale as an accompaniment does not come amiss (Drinks, Part 1).

279

POTTED CHEESE

1 lb (450 g) either Cheshire or
    Cheddar cheese
3 oz (75 g) butter or Gold
1 generous pinch each
    powdered mace, cayenne
    pepper and powdered bay
1 flat teasp (1 × 5 ml spoon) dry
    English mustard
1 tbsp (1 × 15 ml spoon) sharp
    cider or white cooking wine

De-rind chosen cheese, grate coarsely and add softened chosen fat. Work up, ideally with a hand electric mixer. Add remaining ingredients, and when whipped down to a smooth paste, taste and season with salt, mace and black pepper.

Either put into little pots, cover each with a disc of waxed paper and refrigerate; or pack into a large jar and do likewise.

TOASTED POTTED CHEESE

Spread two ½ inch (1.25 cm) thick slices of toasted white or brown bread with dripping, butter or Gold. Spread thickly with Potted Cheese. Bubble and brown under a moderate grill and optionally sprinkle powdered paprika over the tops.

FRIED POTTED CHEESE

Gather up any bought or home-made puff paste trimmings and roll out very thinly. Cut into 3 inch (7.5 cm) squares. Wet edges with cold water. Shape Potted Cheese into walnut-sized pieces and set in centre of paste squares. Lift up all four corners and overlap them, one above the other, at centre. Press down firmly and, when required, drop into slightly smoking hot oil to puff up and turn a rich golden brown. Turn off heat after first minute and turn to reverse side to brown all over. Drain and serve with a little extra melted butter.

PIZZAS

These are generally made with ordinary bread dough when making bread at home. As a substitute, use a pack of Jus-rol puff paste, or just ½ inch (1.25 cm) thick slices of bread or 6, 7 or 8 inch (15, 18 or 20 cm) rounds cut from the base of a cottage loaf. Trim off the crusts.

CHEESE PIZZA

1 × 8 inch (20 cm) round of
    bread or raw Jus-rol puff paste
    rolled out ¼ inch (5 mm) thick
1 large ripe tomato

Brush surface of bread or puff paste with oil. Slice tomato thinly. Lay on top interspersed with small pieces of cheese,

2 wiped, chopped anchovy
  fillets
2 oz (50 g) Mozzarella cheese
6 stoned black olives
Oil
Salt
Black pepper
1 flat eggsp (1 × 2.5 ml spoon)
  dried oregano or wild thyme
Concentrated tomato purée

chopped anchovy and olives.
Dot with a few tiny blobs of
tomato purée, sprinkle with
chosen herb, season with salt
and pepper lightly, and give a
generous top-brushing of oil
with a pastry or sterilized ½ inch
(1.25 cm) paint brush. Lift onto a
flat metal baking sheet and bake
pastry pizza one shelf above
centre at Gas Mark 7 (approx
425°F, 220°C) for 8 minutes, then
reduce heat to Gas Mark 4
(approx 350°F, 180°C) and bake
until risen, well-browned and
bubbling slightly. Bake bread
pizza on middle shelf at Gas
Mark 6 (approx 400°F, 200°C) for
15 minutes.

RATATOUILLE AND CHEESE PIZZA

6 oz (175 g) ratatouille
  (Vegetables, p. 255)
Oil
Salt
Black pepper
2 oz (50 g) grated hard cheese
1 6–7 inch (15–18 cm) bread
  round, or raw Jus-rol puff
  paste

Roll puff paste to ¼ inch (5 mm)
thickness and cut a round of 6–7
inch (15–18 cm) diameter or use
bread (brushing sides with oil).
Spread ratatouille over thickly.
Season lightly with salt and
black pepper. Moisten liberally
with oil and scatter cheese on
top. Bake bread pizza on middle
shelf at Gas Mark 6 (approx
400°F, 200°C) for 15 minutes.
Bake pastry pizza one shelf
above centre at Gas Mark 7
(approx 425°F, 220°C) for 8
minutes, then reduce heat to
Gas Mark 4 (approx 350°F,
180°C) and bake until
well-browned and bubbling.

PASTRY PIZZA

Pastry paste:
6 oz (175 g) sifted flour
1 No 2 egg
2 oz (50 g) lard
1 flat teasp (1 × 5 ml spoon)
   baking powder
Cold water

Filling:
1 oz (25 g) butter or Gold
2 flat tbsps (2 × 15 ml spoons)
   flour
1 pint (600 ml) milk
2 separated No 2 egg yolks
3 oz (75 g) diced Bel Paese
3 oz (75 g) cream cheese
3 oz (75 g) grated hard Cheddar
6 oz (175 g) of any diced, cooked
   meats such as salami, garlic
   sausage or mortadella
2 rough chopped, hard-boiled
   No 3 eggs
3 oz (75 g) sultanas
Salt
White pepper
A generous pinch of nutmeg
2 stiffly whipped No 2 egg
   whites

Make the paste first. Sift flour with baking powder and then rub fat in until very fine-grained. Drop in egg and a mere splash of water. Work up with a table knife, adding more water as needed to produce a soft paste of good rolling consistency. Roll out thinly. Line any deep, round, heat-resistant dish, like a soufflé or charlotte mould.

Put chosen fat into a saucepan, soften over low heat. Work in flour and stir for 3 minutes to expel flour taste. Boil milk in a separate pan and add this very gradually, beating between each addition. Remove from heat when smooth. Beat in all remaining ingredients, except egg whites. Taste and correct seasonings with salt, pepper and nutmeg. Leave mixture until cold and beat in stiffly whipped egg whites. Turn into paste-lined dish, level off and remove any pastry paste which comes above the level of filling with a sharp knife. Wet trimmed paste edges with cold water. Gather up paste trimmings and roll out to form a lid. Place on top of wetted edges, press down lightly and bake on middle shelf at Gas Mark 6 (approx 400°F, 200°C) for 25–30 minutes. Optionally brush paste top with milk before baking.

Puddings

Victoria pudding
Hot chocolate and banana pudding
Egg custard
German custard
Creamy rice pudding
Caribbean baked bananas
Sweet banana and cream cheese pizza
Baked batter pudding with golden syrup
Sweet orange pizza
Baked custard
Meringue and apple bake
Apple turnovers
Black cap pudding
An excellent semolina pudding
To cook hard little pears
Baked jam roll
Stuffed baked apples
Brown Betty
Crumble pie
Very easy Spanish breadcrumb pudding
Jam sauce
Our hot chocolate sauce

Pears in chocolate sauce
Spiced tangerine sections
A proper fruit salad
Special winter compôte
Our apple and sultana mixture
Golden syrup flan
Apples in cider
Apricot whip
Dried apricots in China tea
Apricot junket
Milk jelly
Summer pudding
Fruit fools
Sauce to serve with cream ices
Easy orange meringue pie
Little chocolate pots

VICTORIA PUDDING

2 No 3 eggs
1 rounded tbsp (1 × 15 ml
    spoon) caster sugar
4 oz (100 g) seeded raisins
17½ fluid oz (525 ml) milk
1 pkt vanilla-flavoured sugar
4 rectangular shop sponge cakes
Oil
Flour
Butter

Melt a scrap of butter and mix with 2 oz (50 g) of given raisins; arrange these over the oiled and floured base of a 2 lb (900 g) pudding basin. Crumble the sponge cakes with the caster and vanilla sugars into a bowl. Add the remaining half of the rough-chopped raisins. Beat eggs, add to milk, stir well and then pour gently down one side into the prepared basin. Cover with Alcan Foil and secure with a rubber band. Stand in a steamer with an Alcan Foil strip (Improvise and Make Do, Part 1) and steam for 1½ hours. Unmould onto heated dish. Serve with custard or cream.

Note
Water in base of steamer should just simmer steadily.

HOT CHOCOLATE AND BANANA PUDDING

6 oz (175 g) sifted flour
3 oz (75 g) butter or Gold
3 medium bananas
4 oz (100 g) cane caster sugar
1½ oz (40 g) Cadbury's
    powdered drinking chocolate
1 rounded teasp (1 × 5 ml
    spoon) baking powder
1 No 3 egg
A little milk

Sift flour with baking powder into a roomy bowl. Rub in chosen fat until very finely grained. Sieve in sugar and chocolate powder. Blend through well-scrubbed fingers. Add beaten egg and a splash of milk and beat to bind smoothly. Beat in the well-mashed bananas. Turn into a greased, medium pie dish and bake at Gas Mark 5 (approx 375°F, 190°C) on middle shelf for approx 45 minutes or until set at centre. Serve with hot egg custard.

EGG CUSTARD

½ pint (300 ml) milk
3 oz (75 g) sugar
1 No 3 egg
1 rounded dessertsp (1 × 10 ml
   spoon) cornflour

Heat milk. Whip egg with cornflour and sugar until a paste results. When milk boils pour over this paste and stir well. Pour back into pan and repeat twice more, pouring from bowl to pan and back again. Set over moderate heat and stir until the mixture thickens and when tasted, leaves no cornfloury flavour. Add more sugar to taste.

If wishing to ensure no crust forms on top, pass the bowl of a heated tablespoon over some butter and then pass it over the custard's top. For short periods this is totally effective. If wishing to refrigerate for next day's service, cover the top with a circle of greaseproof which you have first run under a cold tap.

GERMAN CUSTARD

This is plain custard made with egg yolks only. When completed the stiffly whipped whites of the eggs are folded in and blended thus making a very light and rather fluffy mixture.

CREAMY RICE PUDDING

Made in a slow-cooking pot.
3 oz (75 g) Patna rice
1 split vanilla pod
3 oz (75 g) caster sugar (or vanilla
   sugar mixed with caster sugar
   or just caster sugar stored in a
   tin with old vanilla pods)
1½ pints (900 ml) milk
5 fluid oz (150 ml) single or
   coffee cream (or use 1¾ pints
   [1.05 litres] milk)

Bring milk to boiling point in a saucepan and then pour into a slow-cooking pot's inner container. Stir in rice and sugar. Add vanilla pod. Cover, switch to Low and cook for 5 hours. Stir in cream and cook for a further 30 minutes. When using milk only, just cook undisturbed for 5½ hours.

CARIBBEAN BAKED BANANAS

4 bananas
Strained juice of 1 lemon
½ oz (10 g) butter or Gold
Brown Barbados sugar
1 breakfastcupful grated fresh
   coconut or the same of
   desiccated, moistened to a
   thick pap with a few drops of
   milk
1 miniature bottle white rum
2 tbsps (2 × 15 ml spoons)
   granulated sugar
2 tbsps (2 × 15 ml spoons) cold
   water

Peel the bananas and halve lengthwise. Rub chosen fat over base and sides of a small pie dish. Lay in banana halves. Pour lemon juice over the fruit, then sprinkle thickly with the Barbados brown sugar. Cover with the chosen coconut and moisten with the granulated sugar and water melted together to form a syrup in a small pan. Bake at Gas Mark 4 (approx 350°F, 180°C) on middle shelf for 20–25 minutes.

SWEET BANANA AND CREAM CHEESE PIZZA

1 large banana
Half a small lemon
7 inch (18 cm) diameter circle of
   ⅛ inch (3 mm) thick bought
   Jus-rol or home-made puff
   paste
1½ oz (40 g) cream or cottage
   cheese
Lemon curd
1 flat dessertsp (1 × 10 ml spoon)
   caster sugar
A little sifted icing sugar

Pinch the edges of the chosen paste circle between finger and thumb to flute all round. Lay on a flat baking sheet. Slice peeled banana thinly and lengthwise and lay over paste to cover completely. Sprinkle on caster sugar. Bake in oven on middle shelf at Gas Mark 6 (approx 400°F, 200°C) for 25 minutes. Then brush all over with slightly warmed lemon curd and dust with sifted icing sugar before serving.

BAKED BATTER PUDDING WITH GOLDEN SYRUP

Fattening and delicious, particularly when served with Cornish clotted cream.

6 oz (175 g) sifted flour
1 pinch salt
1 No 3 egg
1 extra separated egg yolk
9 fluid oz (270 ml) milk
6 oz (175 g) golden syrup
2 fluid oz (60 ml) water

Sift salt with flour into a basin, make a central well and tip in egg and extra yolk with a splash of milk. Beat with a wooden spoon, or for speed and ease use a hand electric beater. Switch on to medium speed, adding trickles of milk until all is absorbed. Whip at full speed for 1 minute. Pour into a medium, buttered pie dish, put on middle shelf at Gas Mark 3 (approx 325°F, 160°C) and leave until batter begins to rise. Heat syrup and water together until runny, then quickly open oven door and swill over pudding, close door fast and leave until completely cooked, by which time the batter will have absorbed syrup and risen above it.

SWEET ORANGE PIZZA

This can be made with ordinary bread dough, but it can also be made without any dough that needs proving. Use a flute *or stick of Fresh Mill long-lasting French bread. Remove the thick transparent pack, split the bread lengthwise and thus make two pizzas or two different kinds simultaneously.*

Chosen bread base
4 oz (100 g) bought or
   home-made cream cheese
3 small, very thin-skinned
   oranges
1 oz (25 g) flaked almonds
1 oz (25 g) caster sugar
A little sifted icing sugar
2 oz (50 g) apricot jam
1 tbsp (1 × 15 ml spoon) wine or
   water

Note
For sweet pineapple pizza, replace orange slices with pineapple slices but otherwise follow the instructions for Sweet Orange Pizza.

Spread one surface of the bread completely with chosen cream cheese. Cut peel and inner pith from oranges with a very sharp knife, thus removing both simultaneously. Slice oranges a mean ¼ inch (5 mm) thick. Remove all pips and tiny centres of pith. Overlap right over cream cheese. Sprinkle with caster sugar. Bake at Gas Mark 8 (approx 450°F, 230°C) for 9–10 minutes. Remove and, while hot, spread all over with mixed warmed jam and water, or wine. Scatter on flaked almonds, brown fast under a grill and finish with a light dusting of sifted icing sugar.

288

BAKED CUSTARD

This can be cooked in the oven or on top of the cooker.

1 pint (600 ml) best possible milk
1 vanilla pod
2 No 3 eggs and 2 extra egg yolks
3 oz (75 g) caster sugar

Raise milk very slowly to boiling in order to give vanilla pod time to infuse. Remove, wipe and store to use again. Whip eggs and extra yolks with sugar. Then pour on hot milk and pour back and forth three times from pan to bowl and back again.

Pour into little custard cups or a heat-resistant dish. Stand the former in a wide, shallow pan (or meat baking tin). Set over a low heat on the cooker, having poured boiling water around to come two-thirds up the sides of the custard cups. Settle the heat at a temperature which will cause the water to shiver but not bubble up. Cover each custard cup with a scrap of Alcan Foil. Cover container with a lid or flat baking sheet and thus steam until creamily set – approx 35 minutes. For oven cooking, stand chosen large container in a meat baking tin. Pour boiling water around covered container and bake at Gas Mark 2 (approx 300°F, 150°C) for 45–50 minutes one shelf below centre.

MERINGUE AND APPLE BAKE

1 teacupful fine, soft
  breadcrumbs
8 oz (225 g) apple and sultana
  mixture (p. 298)
1 No 2 egg
1½ oz (40 g) caster sugar
A scrap of butter or Gold

Rub the insides of two individual, heat-resistant bowls with chosen fat. Mix apple and sultana mixture with crumbs and separated egg yolk to a stiff paste and fill evenly into containers. Whip egg white until very stiff and fold in caster sugar. Spread this over apple mixture, then rough up into small peaks with a fork. Bake on highest shelf at Gas Mark 1 (approx 275°F, 140°C) until the little fork-peaks are lightly browned and meringue has had time to become crisp (approx 30 minutes).

Note
Never add salt when whipping separated egg whites.

APPLE TURNOVERS

1 large Bramley apple
Soft brown sugar
Cold water
A little raw egg white
10 oz (275 g) sweet short paste
Half a lemon
Caster sugar

Roll out pastry paste to ⅛ inch (3 mm) thickness. Cut into 5 inch (12.5 cm) squares.

  Peel, core and cut apple into quarters. Slice each quarter thinly into separate little piles. Turn each one thickly in brown sugar, reassemble the sugared slices into quarters and place one such in the centre of each paste square. Sprinkle on a light, extra sugar-dusting, moisten with a generous squeeze of lemon juice and brush all exposed paste area with cold water. Bring the four corners up to overlap at centre, press down lightly and pinch the four corners together between finger and thumb. Brush completed turnover with raw egg white and scatter caster sugar on top.

Bake at Gas Mark 5 (approx 375°F, 190°C) on middle shelf for 15 minutes, then turn heat down to Gas Mark 3 (approx 325°F, 160°C) to give apple slices time to cook through while pastry is turning a good golden brown on top.

BLACK CAP PUDDING

3–4 oz (75–100 g) blackcurrants
Grated rind of 1 medium lemon
3 No 3 eggs
4 oz (100 g) sifted flour
4 oz (100 g) caster sugar
1 oz (25 g) softened butter or substitute

Butter a 2 lb (900 g) pudding basin carefully. Press blackcurrants down firmly over base. Whip eggs, sugar and lemon rind in a medium-sized bowl, standing in a large outer bowl filled with boiling water just as you begin whipping. When the mixture becomes thick, pale and very foamy, remove bowl to a work surface and fold in flour gently but thoroughly. Finally, fold in softened butter. Turn into prepared pudding basin, cover first with butter papers, then Alcan Foil. Fold the foil into a pleat at centre before so doing to ensure the pudding has ample room to rise. Put into a slow-cooking pot with foil strap in position and cook at High for 3½ hours.

291

AN EXCELLENT SEMOLINA PUDDING (Beignets de Semoule)

This is quickly made and very appealing to children. Serve with jam or jelly sauce.

1 pint (600 ml) milk
3 oz (75 g) semolina
3 oz (75 g) caster sugar
1 oz (25 g) butter
2 separated No 3 egg yolks

Boil milk. Stir in sugar and sprinkle semolina on gradually while stirring with a wooden spoon. Continue stirring until really thick and absolutely smooth; then stir in butter. Remove from heat. Beat in yolks.

Brush a cold working surface with oil. Spread out semolina mixture to a thickness of ¾ inch (1.75 cm). Stamp into 1½ inch (3.75 cm) rounds with a plain cutter or just a glass. When cold, fry the little rounds in hot melted butter in a shallow pan until golden brown on each side. Keep warm on a serving dish in the oven.

For the sauce
Slide into pan residue 4 generous tablespoons (4 × 15 ml spoons) of jam or jelly. Work down with the back of the wooden spoon adding a splash or two of water. Pour over the *beignets* and serve.

TO COOK HARD LITTLE PEARS

When small, brown-skinned pears stubbornly refuse to ripen, just peel without removing stems and pack down carefully into a stone jar or slow-cooking pot. Have ready 1 pint (600 ml) water and 6 oz (175 g) red currant jelly. Melt jelly and water in a small pan, pour over pears, cover jar with a piece of Alcan Foil and stand on your oven floor at Gas Mark ½ (approx 250°F, 120°C). If using a slow-cooking pot, just replace the lid, switch on to Low before going to bed and leave. The pears will have become soft and bright pink by morning. Sometimes small ones are ready around 8 a.m. Larger, more stubborn pears may need 2–3 hours longer by this method.

BAKED JAM ROLL

12 oz (350 g) sweet short paste
Raspberry jam
A little milk

Roll paste to ⅛ inch (3 mm) thickness and trim edges to form a 12 inch (30 cm) square. Spread jam to within a generous 1 inch (2.5 cm) of edges on all four sides. Fold over the two edges at left and right and roll up. Brush top, sides and ends with milk and bake on middle shelf at Gas Mark 6 (approx 400°F, 200°C) for 15 minutes. Reduce heat to Gas Mark 4 (approx 350°F, 180°C) and continue baking for a further 10 minutes.

STUFFED BAKED APPLES

Prepare Bramley apples as explained (With an Oven, Part 1 p. 95). Before baking fill the central cavities, made by removing the cores, with any of the following mixtures:

Thick honey mixed with any chosen nuts
or
Lemon curd mixed with chopped dates
or
Sultanas packed in with lemon juice squeezed over
or
Thick honey mixed with cream cheese and any chosen chopped nuts
or
A mixture of chopped glacé cherries, angelica and currants into thick honey.

BROWN BETTY

5 oz (135 g) suet
10 oz (275 g) flour
1 rounded dessertsp (1 × 10 ml
   spoon) baking powder
Cold water to bind
4 oz (100 g) soft brown sugar
2 tbsps (2 × 15 ml spoons) Tate
   & Lyle's golden syrup
Strained juice and grated rind of
   1 lemon
As much crumbled stale Madeira
   or light fruit cake as mixture
   will absorb

Sift flour with baking powder. Blend in suet with well-scrubbed fingers and bind to a stiff paste with gradual additions of cold water. Flour a working surface. Roll out the dough to a generous ¼ inch (5 mm) thickness and use to line out a well-oiled 2 lb (900 g) pudding basin. Trim off the edges with the rolling pin by just rolling this across the rim of the basin. Gather up remaining dough trimmings, re-roll with a further light dusting of flour to yield two ¼ inch (5 mm) thick discs, one the diameter of the top of the basin and the other 1 inch (2.5 cm) smaller.

Put the sugar, golden syrup, lemon juice and lemon rind into a small saucepan. Allow syrup and sugar to melt and blend. Then work in as much crumbled cake as the mixture will take to become thick but just floppy when dropped from a raised wooden spoon. Divide this in two. Put one half into the dough-lined basin, lay the smaller dough disc on top, add the remaining filling and use the larger dough disc to form the 'lid'. Wet and press down at edges. Cover with Alcan Foil, giving the piece a fat pleat over the centre to allow for expansion while the pudding is steaming. Cook for 2½ hours. Serve with custard or cream.

CRUMBLE PIE

1 lb (450 g) of any fresh fruit, notably fairly ripe gooseberries, raspberries, strawberries, loganberries, cultivated blackberries and any of the stone fruits, provided these are first skinned and stoned, then sliced

3 oz (75 g) butter or Gold

5 oz (135 g) soft brown sugar (never use demerara)

6 oz (175 g) sifted flour

Place prepared chosen fruit in a medium pie dish. Scatter over 1 oz (25 g) of given sugar. Place flour in a basin with chosen fat. Rub in until extremely fine-grained. Blend in remaining sugar. Pile over fruit, level off and press down firmly. Bake on middle shelf at Gas Mark 4 (approx 350°F, 180°C) for 45 minutes or until well-browned and crisp on top.

Note
If desired polythene bags of the actual 'crumble' (ie, the finely blended mixture of butter, sugar and flour) may be stored in either a freezer or the freezing compartment of a refrigerator.

VERY EASY SPANISH BREADCRUMB PUDDING (Chufletes)

1 lb (450 g) soft white or brown breadcrumbs

1 rounded tbsp (1 × 15 ml spoon) caster sugar

5 fluid oz (150 ml) 'plonk' white wine

2 separated No 3 eggs

Oil

Put crumbs into a bowl and mix in sugar. Beat egg yolks into wine, pour over crumbs and leave for 30 minutes after mixing well. Then give the crumb mixture a jolly good stir. Whip egg whites very stiffly and fold into main mixture. Heat oil in a fryer or saucepan as for deep-frying and drop in dessertspoonfuls of the mixture when the oil is at 390°–400°F (195°–200°C). Let them fry to a rich golden brown, lift out, drain well and pile onto a dish. Dust with sifted icing sugar for special occasions. Otherwise serve with a hot jam sauce, which is also very swiftly and simply made.

JAM SAUCE

3–4 huge tbsps (3–4 × 15 ml spoons) jam

2 tbsps (2 × 15 ml spoons) wine or water

Rub jam through an ordinary sieve into a small saucepan. If using jelly, this can go straight into the pan. Stir over a low heat for a few minutes, adding wine or water. Hand in a small jug.

OUR HOT CHOCOLATE SAUCE

It never hardens and can be re-heated as required.

5 oz (125 g) chocolate chips or *couverture* (cooking chocolate)

2 level tbsps (2 × 15 ml spoons) dark, soft brown sugar

2 tbsps (2 × 15 ml spoons) cold water

2 oz (50 g) unsalted butter

2 dessertsps (2 × 10 ml spoons) rum

Put chosen chocolate into a small pan, add sugar and water and stir over a low heat until smooth and melted. Beat in the butter gradually in small flakes. Finally beat in rum. You can then re-heat any surplus over hot water to use again.

Note
Excellent for serving over bought or home-made ices, choux buns, large gâteaux or unorthodox trifles.

PEARS IN CHOCOLATE SAUCE

When serving tinned pears, drain the fruit and set each pear half over a scoop or fat spoonful of bought or home-made ice cream – vanilla is best for this treatment. Hand our hot chocolate sauce in a small jug and let each person pour it over their pear and ice cream.

SPICED TANGERINE SECTIONS

1 small tin tangerine or mandarin segments

2½ fluid oz (75 ml) water

2½ oz (60 g) Whitworths soft brown sugar

The extremely thinly cut peel from 1 tangerine and its juices

1–2 inch (2.5–5 cm) stick of cinnamon

Put tangerine juice into a small pan, withhold the fruit but add all other ingredients. Simmer gently for 15 minutes. Remove tangerine peel and cinnamon stick. Turn in the tangerine or mandarin sections. Divide between two small glass bowls. Serve icily chilled with the *petits fours*.

A PROPER FRUIT SALAD

This salad requires a straight-sided jar or glass vase normally used for flowers.

Prepared fresh fruit
Sifted icing sugar

For summer mixtures:
Use all or any combination of
    raspberries, strawberries,
    loganberries, blueberries,
    black and white cherries,
    peaches, blackcurrants,
    nectarines, Victoria or
    Monarch plums, red currants,
    white currants and grapes

For winter mixtures:
Use all or any combination of
    bananas, pears, oranges,
    tangerines, sweet apples,
    chopped pineapple flesh and
    stoned chopped dates

Essential reminder:
Any fruits which discolour
    easily, like peeled banana,
    apple or pear, must be soaked
    before using in equal parts of
    lemon juice and water for 15
    minutes

First hull strawberries, raspberries, loganberries currants and blueberries; stone and halve cherries; stone, skin and slice peaches, nectarines, Victoria and Monarch plums; skin and de-pip grapes; peel and core apples and pears; and check the rest for stalks.

Pack chosen, prepared fruits in 1 inch (2.5 cm) layers with liberal dustings of icing sugar sifted through a small sieve between each layer and finally over top. Refrigerate overnight. In the morning the sugar will have drawn some of the natural juices from the chosen fruits, thus dispensing with the need to use any *tap water*. Just stir and serve icily chilled.

Note
The sole variation on the above is to add, when you stir the refrigerated mixture just prior to service, a miniature bottle of brandy and/or any chosen liqueur or *eau-de-vie* which you decide will suit the assembly.

You *can* serve cream too but we submit that this is superfluous.

SPECIAL WINTER COMPOTE

8 oz (225 g) chestnuts
2 medium oranges
¾ pint (450 ml) water
3 oz (75 g) Tate & Lyle's pure
    cane granulated sugar

Cover chestnuts with cold water, raise to boiling, remove from heat and peel off both outer and inner skins. Return to pan any whose inner skins do not come away easily and heat again.

Put sugar and water into small pan, boil and maintain for 5 minutes. Add chestnuts and simmer with extreme gentleness until these are semi-transparent and syrup is fairly thick. Meanwhile cut away rind and inner skin, together, from the orange and remove segments without skins. Stir any escaped orange juice into chestnut syrup. Stir to blend and when cold, fold in the orange segments and divide between two small bowls.

OUR APPLE AND SULTANA MIXTURE

To every 1 lb (450 g) of peeled,
    cored, thinly sliced apples use:
3 oz (75 g) soft brown sugar
Thinly peeled rind of half a
    medium lemon
3 oz (75 g) sultanas
3 fluid oz (90 ml) cold water

Place water, then sultanas, then apple slices intermingled with lemon peel and finally the sugar in a lidded casserole, cover and cook low down in the oven at Gas Mark 2 (approx 300°F, 150°C) until the apple begins to turn light brown. Stir well and turn into a dish to serve with egg custard or whipped whipping cream.

Note
We do this in bulk when windfalls are plentiful. The mixture is then frozen in waxed cartons and either thawed and reheated or served cold.

298

GOLDEN SYRUP FLAN

This has become the star feature on week-end menus at golf clubs. We offer you two versions: the traditional and our own.

Tate & Lyle's golden syrup
Bought or home-made short
  paste
Fine soft white or brown
  breadcrumbs
Top-of-the-milk

Half fill a small saucepan with water and remove lid from syrup tin. Stand tin in water over low heat and leave until really runny.

Roll out paste to ½ inch (1.25 cm) thickness. Roll up on a handleless (proper) rolling pin. Hold over an 8 inch (20 cm) diameter Victoria sponge tin or Pyrex heat-resistant glass flan dish. Unroll off pin and push into the sides of tin or flan dish with closed knuckles. Tip up rolling pin and roll right over rim to remove surplus pastry paste, thus avoiding those dreaded doorsteps of pastry to chew through before reaching the filling.

Fill to two-thirds the container's depth with chosen crumbs. Hold tin of hot runny syrup firmly round its middle in a folded cloth and doodle over the crumbs until all are completely covered to a depth of a generous ¼ inch (5 mm). Gather up trimmings, re-roll thinly and cut into ¾ inch (1.75 cm) wide strips. Twist these by turning the ends opposite ways. Lay on top of the syrupy crumbs in a criss-cross pattern. Brush over with a little top-of-the-milk. Bake on middle shelf at Gas Mark 5 (approx 375°F, 190°C) for 30 minutes.

Our own version
Use finely crumbed stale Madeira cake instead of breadcrumbs. Mix with a small handful of sultanas. Half fill paste-lined container with cake crumbs. Moisten with drops of the strained juice of 1 medium lemon. Doodle on golden syrup as explained above and bake as before too.

APPLES IN CIDER

½ pint (300 ml) sweet cider
5 fluid oz (150 ml) water
5 oz (135 g) red currant jelly
10–12 smallish cooking apples,
   ideally cider apples

Heat water, stir in jelly until completely melted and add cider. Peel apples whole, optionally removing cores, and place side by side in a shallow pan. Pour on the fluid mixture and, if this does not cover the fruit to just over half way, add a little more water. Set over a lowish heat so that liquid comes to the boil slowly and then just simmer extremely gently. Leave until the apples are semi-transparent, then turn over carefully and repeat. Remember that if the water bubbles strongly, the apples will collapse – then the whole exercise becomes pointless. Lift apples carefully onto a dish. Boil the liquor as hard as you like, because you now follow the precept of all the finest sauces: simmering down lightly-flavoured thin fluid to strongly-flavoured syrupy fluid. Pour over apples, chill and serve.

APRICOT WHIP

1 pint (600 ml) apricot syrup
   from cooked fruit (see
   following recipe)
1 pkt lime jelly
2 stiffly whipped No 2 egg
   whites
5 fluid oz (150 ml) double or
   whipping cream
6 apricots cooked in China tea

Chop the apricots roughly. Melt the jelly in the apricot syrup, pour into a bowl and allow to cool down to blood heat. Stand in an outer bowl of crushed ice. Whip in the chosen cream very gradually, beating well between each addition. Whip in the egg whites. Finally fold in the chopped apricots and pile into a glass dish. Serve well chilled.

DRIED APRICOTS IN CHINA TEA

8 oz (225 g) apricots
Strained China tea
Soft brown sugar
Small 'leaf' of lemon peel
1 vanilla pod

Soak apricots in the tea with the vanilla pod. Turn into a small casserole with plenty of soft brown sugar and a small 'leaf' of lemon peel. Cook, under a lid, in this soaking agent on lowest shelf at Gas Mark 2 (approx 310° F, 150°C) until the apricots are swollen and tender. See how much better the puffy, soft apricots taste than when just cooked in tap water.

Note
This treatment applies equally to dried prunes and pears.

APRICOT JUNKET

1 small tin apricots
1 pint (600 ml) milk
1 rounded dessertsp (1 × 10 ml spoon) Tate & Lyle's cane caster sugar
1 large teasp (1 × 5 ml spoon) rennet
1 little pkt vanilla sugar

Strain apricots. Melt sugar and vanilla sugar in milk over a low heat. When only lukewarm stir in rennet and pour into a glass dish. Leave until set. Then arrange apricots, cut-side downwards, over top surface. Put drained syrup into a small pan, reduce to half quantity by simmering. When cold pour over apricots.

Note
Rennet is rare in some districts. Ask at your local Boots. Head Office has given us an official ruling that they *will* supply on application. Be firm with local assistants who simply may not know this.

MILK JELLY

1 standard pkt orange jelly
8 fluid oz (240 ml) cold water
2 fluid oz (60 ml) bottled, packet
  or fresh orange juice
A scant ½ pint (300 ml) milk

Melt jelly in water, stir in chosen orange juice and leave until cold but do not allow to set. Then stir in milk and pour into wetted pudding basin or ornamental mould. When set unmould for service.

SUMMER PUDDING

This can be made with any small soft fruits.
Bread
1 lb (450 g) chosen soft fruit
4 oz (100 g) Whitworths soft light
  brown sugar

Cut ¼ inch (5 mm) thick slices of white or brown bread and remove all crusts. Press one slice down over the base of an un-buttered 1 lb (450 g) basin. Then press more slices round the sides and fill in the gaps thus made with small pieces until the entire basin is completely lined out.

Choose between hulled fruit, like raspberries, or mixed raspberries and red currants; stoned black or white, or mixed cherries; topped and tailed ripe gooseberries; strung blackcurrants; well-washed hedgerow blackberries or cultivated ones; and stoned, peeled, sliced apricots, plums or greengages. Mix chosen fruit with sugar and pack into prepared basin. Cover with more bread. Cover with a butter paper and put heavy weights on top from your scales (or use your heaviest tin). Refrigerate.

The next day remove the weights and papers. Ease a table knife gently around the sides, just at the edges. Invert onto a serving dish, give a vigorous shake and the pudding will fall out, disclosing that the juices have soaked the bread wall completely. Serve with extra sugar and custard.

FRUIT FOOLS

This treatment applies to all soft fruits.

Any soft fruits
Sifted icing sugar
Confectioners' custard and
  cream or just cream

Pack fruit down without any water into a stone jar, cover with a scrap of Alcan Foil and place on the floor of your oven, when this is in use. Leave undisturbed until the fruit has collapsed completely. Remove, rub through an ordinary sieve, weigh and use in the proportions 1 lb (450 g) fruit purée, sugar to taste and either ¾ pint (450 ml) confectioners' custard (Puddings, Part 3) and 5 fluid oz (150 ml) double or whipping cream or 1 pint (600 ml) whipping or double cream whipped to only a loose peak first. Add chosen custard and cream or just cream and whip and whip and whip . . .

SAUCE TO SERVE WITH CREAM ICES

4 oz (100 g) Whitworths soft,
  pale brown sugar
2 tbsps (2 × 15 ml spoons) Tate
  & Lyle's golden syrup
1½ oz (40 g) butter or Gold
2½ fluid oz (75 ml) Libby's
  tinned unsweetened milk, or
  single cream

Put sugar, syrup and chosen fat into a small pan. Set over a low heat and allow all to melt. Stir to blend. Set pan in an outer one of boiling water, add unsweetened milk or cream and stir until sauce thickens to a smooth cream. Pour hot over individual servings of chosen cream ices.

303

EASY ORANGE MERINGUE PIE

1 teacupful each of Del Monte packet orange juice and of pineapple juice
A little water
1 hugely heaped tbsp (1 × 15 ml spoon) cornflour
2 separated No 3 egg whites
4 oz (100 g) caster sugar
Cooked pastry pie base

Heat orange and pineapple juice together in a small pan. Mix cornflour with just enough cold water to make a smooth runny paste. When the fruit juices boil, pour over cornflour paste and stir. Return all to pan and continue stirring until the mixture is very thick and begins to bubble and blow in pan. Turn over cooked pastry pie base and allow to become completely cold and set.

Whip egg whites to a loose peak. Whip in 1 oz (25 g) of given sugar and whip for 2 minutes. Stop whipping and fold in remaining sugar very lightly. Spread and smooth over cold filled pie base. Bake at Gas Mark 1 (approx 275°F, 140°C), one shelf above centre for 15 minutes. Serve only when cold.

LITTLE CHOCOLATE POTS
(Petits Pots de Chocolat)

4 oz (100 g) chocolate chips or couverture (cooking chocolate)
2 tbsps (2 × 15 ml spoons) single cream
3 No 3 eggs

Note
Add 1 rounded dessertspoon (1 × 10 ml spoon) of Brooke Bond Brazilian Instant Coffee Powder, before adding cream, for Little Mocha Pots.

Use a double or porage saucepan. Put chosen chocolate into the top pan over the base pan half-filled with boiling water. Set over a moderate heat. Add the cream and stir until smooth and creamy. Remove from the heat. Beat in the egg yolks, then beat in the stiffly whipped egg whites gradually. Fill into little custard glasses or small wine glasses; when set, cover tops with a scrap of foil.

Serve with spirals of whipped cream.

Brunches
and Sandwiches

How to make a toast box
How to make a hot roll box
How to make egg cosies
Easy baking powder doughnuts
Mrs Hudson's hot breakfast cakes
Hot citrus fruit winter drink
Tuna fish spread
Devilled ham or gammon spread
Liver sausage spread
Vegetarian spread
Sardine spread
Salad spreads
Other savoury spreads
Toasted sandwiches under an ordinary grill
Croque M'sieu 2
Croque William
Giant croques
The special tomato sauce
Croque Papa
The devil no 2
Croque de la fermière
Sweet croque Mademoiselle
Sweet toasted sandwiches for small fry
Deep-fried croques

BRUNCHES

There are basically two different kinds of brunches: breakfast ones, served around 11 a.m. and designed to do away with the necessity for luncheons, and Sunday brunches which presuppose that everyone has had the equivalent to a continental breakfast some hours beforehand. The latter are generally served around 2 p.m.

Breakfast brunches can be very elaborate and luxurious, beginning with Buck's Fizz, (which is champagne shaken over crushed ice with fresh orange juice) and continuing with freshly made, piping hot coffee and hot milk throughout the meal. Baskets of home-made croissants and brioches should be tucked into napkins and served with either salted or unsalted French butter, black cherry jam, quince jelly and orange and lemon marmalades. Either arrange in small quantities down a large table or put with coffee, milk and sugar on a small side table with side plates, cups and saucers, and jugs of plain fruit juices. Everyone helps themselves.

The breakfast dishes are similarly laid out under covers and over hot plates. These include kedgeree, grilled kippers, oven-baked sausages, grilled kidneys and bacon, scrambled eggs with mush-rooms, boiled eggs in egg cups with egg cosies over them and toast in toast boxes, never – on any culinary level – in toast racks, which Fanny's mother defined so accurately as 'draughts with wires round'.

On the most modest level serve hot, napkin-wrapped, white and brown Fresh Mill rolls bought in packs, split open and set on dry baking sheets. Bake one shelf above centre at Gas Mark 8 (approx 450°F, 230°C) for exactly 9 minutes. Each pack is dated and they have an extremely long storage life on an ordinary dry goods shelf. You can keep them coming throughout the meal provided you possess a pinger enabling you to sit down with your guests until this buzzes and thus avoid burned rolls. We use Fresh Mill rolls frequently now and have a special box for keeping them piping hot, while sliced bread is served toasted in the toast box.

For the least demanding breakfast-brunch restrict your main courses to a kedgeree, a dish of grilled bacon and bangers and Grandfather's Special (Fish, page 207).

It goes without saying that breakfast cereals, milk and Whitworths light or dark soft brown sugar and glasses of Del Monte's pure orange juice, mixed pineapple and orange juice or grapefruit and orange juice served well-iced, or our Hot Citrus Fruit Winter Drink, (p. 309) replace the Buck's Fizz at the onset. You will find the method for making proper coffee on p. 76. This can be made in an ordinary enamel jug without benefit of a modern coffee percolator.

HOW TO MAKE A TOAST BOX

Assemble 1 Tupperware plastic lidded box measuring 8 inch (20 cm) × 6 inch (15 cm) × 4 inch (10 cm), UHU adhesive, 8 inch (20 cm) strip of metre-wide black or green felt, the same of any chosen material for covering the exterior of the box, and 28½ inch (142 cm) of narrow braid or galon for edging.

Cut a strip of felt 20 inch (50 cm) long and 8 inch (20 cm) wide and paste with UHU to an inside, lengthwise edge of the box. Paste this right down one side, over the base and up the opposing side, thus leaving a flap 6 inch (15 cm) long, so that when the toast slices are halved diagonally and thus stood upright inside the box, the flap covers them and keeps them warm. Paste two pieces measuring 6 inch × 4 inch (5 × 10 cm) to the inside ends of the box. Cover the lid and the exterior with chosen fabric (we used turquoise velvet to match our dining-room curtains). Trim off raw edges neatly when stuck down firmly with UHU. Use the galon all round lid and box rim to conceal raw edges.

HOW TO MAKE A HOT ROLL BOX

Use a 13 inch (32.5 cm) × 8 inch (20 cm) × 2¾ inch (6.75 cm) standard Tupperware rectangular plastic box (this holds 12 Fresh Mill rolls). Line out with felt and cover with appropriate fabric and galon or braid exactly as described in previous instructions for how to make a toast box.

HOW TO MAKE EGG COSIES

Trace the diagram onto a piece of greaseproof paper. For each egg cosy, cut out two shapes in fabric matching your toast and hot roll boxes and stitch together from A to B. Cut two shapes in felt and stitch them together from A to B. Turn out fabric shape and slip over the felt one with the raw edges inside. Slip-stitch the bases together tucking the raw edges inside. Edge with very narrow matching cord.

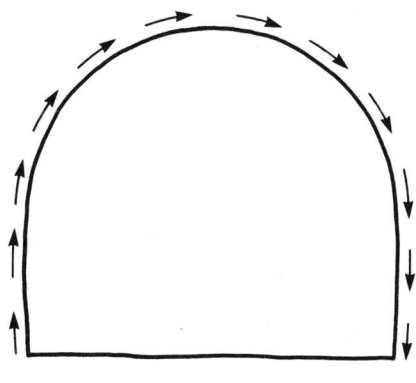

EASY BAKING POWDER DOUGHNUTS

Very popular when served with hot coffee at 'brunch' parties.

10 oz (275 g) sifted flour
1½ oz (40 g) butter
1½ oz (40 g) granulated sugar
¼ oz (5 g) baking powder
1 No 3 egg
Milk
A little extra flour
Raspberry jam
Cold water
4 oz (100 g) caster sugar
Optional powdered cinnamon

Note
Add 1 teaspoon (1 × 5 ml spoon) powdered cinnamon to the caster sugar if liked.

Sift baking powder with flour into a roomy bowl. Make a hole in the middle, break in the egg and work up with a table knife and little splashes of milk to make a dough of the consistency of pastry paste.

Roll out on a floured board until only ¼ inch (5 mm) thick. Stamp into rounds with a plain 2 inch (5 cm) diameter pastry cutter or any inverted glass of matching size. Brush all tops with cold water. Place a small blob of jam at centre on half the rounds. Lay on the other half and pinch the edges together carefully to offset any danger of jam oozing out during frying. Rest with a cloth over them for 20 minutes to swell a little. Slide into a deep-fryer with oil at 385°F (193°C) or just a little below the slightly-hazed-with-heat stage.

Test the first doughnut after frying to a rich brown on both sides. If test doughnut is slightly undercooked at the centre, adjust the heat under the fryer accordingly. Then fry away, draining each doughnut on absorbent kitchen paper and burying them immediately in extra sugar.

Get all the initial work done, leave the raw doughnuts ready under the cloth and fry them just before serving. They are so much more 'moreish' when served hot.

MRS HUDSON'S HOT BREAKFAST CAKES

1 lb (450 g) flour
1 generous pinch salt
4 oz (100 g) butter, gold or
   rendered-down chicken fat
A little buttermilk to bind

Sift flour with salt into a roomy bowl. Rub in chosen fat until very fine-grained. Bind to a smooth rolling dough with buttermilk. Turn onto a floured working surface. Press out lightly with a rolling pin to ¼ inch (5 mm) thickness. Stamp into rounds with a tumbler, or a plain 2 inch (5 cm) diameter pastry cutter. Grease ordinary baking sheets with butter or chicken fat. Lay down the little cakes. Bake at Gas Mark 4 (approx 350°F, 180°C) one shelf above centre for 8–10 minutes. Spread each with butter or Gold. Clap together in pairs and send to table inside a toast or roll box.

HOT CITRUS FRUIT WINTER DRINK

1 fluid oz (30 ml) each of lemon,
   grapefruit and orange juice
½ oz (10 g) butter
Boiling water
1 flat dessertsp (1 × 10 ml spoon)
   thin honey

Put juices, honey and butter into a napkin-wrapped tumbler with a long spoon. Top up with boiling water, stir and drink at breakfast or bedtime instead of shocking your cold, empty tum in winter with chilled juices.

SANDWICHES

Packed luncheons save money. Therefore it pays those who go out to work to make a five-day week's supply of sandwiches in one batch, pack them inside layers of waxed paper in compact square or rectangular boxes and tuck them into the freezer compartment of any small refrigerator. Then you can snatch a day's supply as you race for the train or bus, secure in the knowledge that they will be thawed, soft and wholly edible by the time you break for luncheon.

The word 'sandwich' has come a long way since Lord Sandwich clapped slices of underdone beef between wedges of bread during protracted gaming sessions. Some of the Swiss pastrycooks in towns like Zurich, Lausanne, Basle and Berne excel in producing exquisite

309

mouthfuls which they sell at the very reverse of 'flumpence' for bridge and committee teas and drinks parties. The French, who in the main care little for them, content themselves with stuffing slices of ham between lengths of French bread. At least they justify the comment to the originator, 'What's that you're eating, my dear fellow – *a tram*?' The Viennese, who are the only people to eat seven meals a day, make tremendous play with their elaborations. The Scandinavians serve over five hundred as open sandwiches. Somewhere in between come the English, with their pinwheel, five-tiered, rolled (like miniature Swiss Rolls), three-decker and other elaborate ones.

We concern ourselves here with delicious fillings, new breads, and softened butter or Gold for making everyday sandwiches to take to work. Many of these freeze well – which is indeed the treatment meted out by bulk sandwich sellers in all but the shops where they are made in front of you to your choice.

Use alternate slices of white and brown bread, or, if you can run to it, black bread or pumpernickel, or just new white or brown bread. Turn back to Kitchen Guidance for the Inexperienced, Part 1 for the gen on cutting new bread easily.

Choose from any of the following sandwich fillings.

TUNA FISH SPREAD

3 oz (75 g) tinned tuna fish, drained, flaked and blended with 1 tablespoon (1 × 15 ml spoon) strained lemon juice, 1 teaspoon (1 × 5 ml spoon) grated onion and 1 chopped hard-boiled egg, with a little mayonnaise to bind.

DEVILLED HAM OR GAMMON SPREAD

4 oz (100 g) chopped ham or gammon mixed with 1 oz (25 g) grated hard cheese, 1 chopped hard-boiled egg, 1 heaped teaspoon (1 × 5 ml spoon) horseradish sauce and 1 teaspoon (1 × 5 ml spoon) chutney.

LIVER SAUSAGE SPREAD

4 oz (100 g) liver sausage, mashed with 1 teaspoon (1 × 5 ml spoon) lemon juice, ½ teaspoon (1 × 2.5 ml spoon) Worcestershire sauce, 1 eggspoon (1 × 2.5 ml spoon) paprika powder, a moistening of top-of-the-milk and 1 tablespoon (1 × 15 ml spoon) fine chopped white of celery.

VEGETARIAN SPREAD

Mix 2 oz (50 g) chopped dates with 1 oz (25 g) chopped nuts, 2 oz (50 g) grated hard cheese and 1 eggspoon (1 × 2.5 ml spoon) paprika powder. Bind with yoghurt.

SARDINE SPREAD

Drain the oil from a small tin of Marie Elisabeth sardines. Sieve 1 hard-boiled egg. Remove spine bones and tails from sardines, mash with sieved egg and bind with 1 heaped tablespoon (1 × 15 ml spoon) mayonnaise.

SALAD SPREADS

Here sprouting seeds come into their own. Wash, chop and press onto chosen buttered bread, with sliced tomato, unskinned cucumber, salt and pepper with a thick layer of mayonnaise on top.

Put salad sprouts on buttered black bread with chopped scallions and ideally home-made green tomato and apple chutney.

Put fenugreek sprouting seeds over watercress on buttered brown bread with sliced hard-boiled egg and mayonnaise.

Put mixed sprouting seeds over paper-thin slices of raw, peeled Jerusalem artichokes which taste like Brazil nuts when so treated. Top with a spread of ideally home-made apple chutney.

OTHER SAVOURY SPREADS

1 Slices of Cheddar covered with tomato slices.
2 Spreads of cream or cottage cheese covered with thin spreads of preferably home-made chutney.
3 Thinly sliced tongue, ham, salami, mortadella, garlic sausage or pork lunchoen meat. Add, to choice, sliced tomato, chopped gherkins, or chopped hard-boiled egg, all mixed to a paste with a little real mayonnaise.
4 Cream cheese and onion spread comprising 1½ oz (40 g) cream cheese mixed with 1 tablespoon (1 × 15 ml spoon) grated onion, lightly seasoned with salt and pepper.

TOASTED SANDWICHES UNDER AN ORDINARY GRILL

Just slip assembled sandwiches into an Alcan Roastabag. These bags are sold very inexpensively in packs. Before using for these sandwiches make a 2 inch (5 cm) slit on either side of centre on both sides of bag. Slip in up to 6 sandwiches, set on the base of an ordinary grill pan and tuck in the open ends. Use grill at medium strength, thus allowing contents to heat through and melt, while bread toasts. Then reverse to repeat on opposite side.

CROQUE M'SIEU 2

2 crustless ½ inch (1.25 cm) thick slices from a sandwich loaf
Butter
½ inch (1.25 cm) thick matching slice of Gruyère, Emmenthal or any other melting-type of cheese

Spread both bread slices with butter. Press the chosen cheese onto one and press on the other. Put into hot Saindoux-brushed (With an Oven, Part 1) croque iron. Press down lid very firmly and when a peek confirms base half is well browned, reverse the iron until brown on the other side.

Alternatively, slip into an Alcan Roastabag and grill as already explained, or deep fry (Eggs and Cheese, Part 1, p. 58).

CROQUE WILLIAM

2 thin, crustless slices of either milk or brioche bread
Butter
1 ripe, peeled pear, sliced fairly thinly
Either cream or cottage cheese
1 dessertsp (1 × 10 ml spoon) any chopped nuts

Butter chosen bread slices, spread on chosen cheese thickly, scatter with nuts, press these in with a knife and then cover surface with pear slices. Cover with second buttered bread slice and cook by either of our given methods.

GIANT CROQUES

Make four to justify bread treatment.
1 fresh sandwich loaf
8 oz (225 g) corned beef hash (With an Oven, Part 1)
4 oz (100 g) onions, soft fried in ½ oz (10 g) dripping
Salt
Black pepper
Special tomato sauce
A jug of boiling water
Garlic butter (Basics, Part 1 p. 24) or butter

With a very sharp knife cut off all crusts from the loaf and divide the crumb into eight even lengthwise-cut slices. Spread all on one side with either butter or garlic butter. Lay four out on working surface. Divide slightly mashed corned beef hash equally between them and smooth off evenly. Then spread a quarter of the sliced, soft-fried and drained onions over each. Season lightly with salt and black pepper. Finally spread

312

with the tomato sauce. Press the four remaining slices firmly on top to complete the four long sandwiches. Slide into prepared Alcan Roastabag in pairs, turn in the ends and toast under the grill on both sides.

THE SPECIAL TOMATO SAUCE

This puts bottled tomato sauces' noses well out of joint.

12 oz (350 g) very ripe tomatoes
1 medium onion
1 small garlic clove
1 sprig of fresh or
   dried thyme   } all
1 bay leaf   } tied
1 inner stick of celery | together
4 parsley stalks
½ coffeesp (1 × 2.5 ml spoon) sugar
2 flat dessertsps (2 × 10 ml spoons) butter
Salt
Black pepper
10 tbsps (150 ml) cold water

Slice peeled onion finely and turn into a very small pan. Add 2 tbsps (2 × 15 ml spoons) of the water and the butter. Stir occasionally over a low heat until onion is soft but not browned, approx 6 minutes. Skin the tomatoes, halve and press out all seeds. Add tomato flesh to onion with garlic, herb faggot, sugar and a generous pinch of salt. Still over a low heat, stir/cook for 10 minutes, adding remaining water. Remove herbs. Emulsify or sieve the rest. Alternatively pass through an all-purpose blender switching on/off for two short bursts of 10 seconds with a matching pause between.

Note
If liked, 2 basil leaves may be added to herb faggot and 2 scant tablespoons (2 × 15 ml spoons) oil but this is optional.

313

CROQUE PAPA

2 × ½ inch (1.25 cm) thick slices of crustless brown or white bread
A little chicken or other poultry fat instead of butter
Salt
Pepper
Thin slices of cooked lamb or pork
The Devil

Spread both bread slices with chosen fat, cover with chosen meat and season lightly with salt and pepper. Then spread fairly thickly with the Devil mixture. Cover with second bread slice and cook.

French Papas expect these Croques to be served with a little pot of Devil on the side for use at table.

THE DEVIL No 2

4 small peeled shallots
1 small, peeled garlic clove
8 drops Worcestershire Sauce
1 faggot of herbs (*bouquet garni*)
2½ fluid oz (75 ml) red wine
1 tbsp (1 × 15 ml spoon) red wine vinegar
1 rounded teasp (1 × 5 ml spoon) dry English mustard
1 scant oz (25 g) flour
2½ fluid oz (75 ml) water
1 scant oz (25 g) dripping
1 eggsp (1 × 5 ml spoon) salt
1 eggsp (1 × 5 ml spoon) black pepper

Mince or chop shallots and garlic finely. Melt dripping and stir flour to form a roux. Cook for 3 minutes to expel all taste of flour. Add all remaining ingredients, stirring until all is well blended. Then cook over a low heat for 12 minutes, remove herbs and rub through a sieve or emulsify and put into a small screw-topped jar for storage.

CROQUE DE LA FERMIERE

Half a chopped hard-boiled No 3 egg
1 flat teasp (1 × 5 ml spoon) milled parsley heads
Quarter of a small peeled, fine diced sweet apple
1 de-rinded and diced bacon rasher
Salt
Pepper
A little extra bacon fat from

Frizzle the bacon gently in a dry pan. Drain and set aside while frizzle-frying bacon rinds. Blend egg, parsley and apple, with a light seasoning of salt and pepper. Spread mixture over first bread slice. Press on the diced bacon, cover with the chicken, season again and drip the bacon fat over one side of remaining bread slice. Then lay

314

frizzled bacon rinds
Paper-thin slices of cooked
   chicken
2 × ½ inch (1.25 cm) thick
   de-crusted slices of brown or
   white bread

over and press down firmly for
cooking in either of given ways.

SWEET CROQUE MADEMOISELLE

2 thin slices plain Madeira cake
Raspberry jam
Flaked almonds
Melted butter
Very thick custard
Sifted icing sugar

Spread both cake slices with
jam, cover one with custard and
lay over second cake slice. Toast
by either given method. Remove
and set on rack of grill pan. Dust
lightly with icing sugar, sprinkle
over flaked almonds, repeat
dusting with sugar, then
moisten with drops of melted
butter and brown under a very
strong heat for moments only.

SWEET TOASTED SANDWICHES FOR SMALL FRY

2 × ½ inch (1.25 cm) thick slices
   from a currant loaf
Butter
Apricot jam
Peeled, lengthwise-sliced
   banana trimmed to fit
1 dessertsp (1 × 10 ml spoon)
   grated milk chocolate

Butter bread slices. Cover one
with apricot jam, lay on banana
slices, scatter with chocolate and
press on the second bread slice.
Cook as explained, either way.

315

DEEP-FRIED CROQUES

These Croques *or toasted sandwiches can also be deep-fried. The assembly is different but this old-fashioned method is excellent for* Croques M'sieu, Croques Madames *and any others made with melting-type cheeses.*

2 crustless slices of ½ inch (1.25 cm) thick buttered new bread

1 matching slice of *any melting cheese* like Gruyère, Emmenthal or English Cheshire (one of the best is the French Comté)

Shallow containers of:
  beaten, strained egg
  fine soft crumbs

Oil

Place chosen cheese on buttered bread. Cover with remaining slice. Press well together. Halve and draw slowly through beaten egg to impregnate all over without making them soggy. Drain and set on crumbs. Pat these all over very carefully. Slide into slightly-hazed-with-smoke oil. Turn off bottom heat and allow to cook in the slowly diminishing heat until a rich golden brown with the cheese melted and gooey inside.

For Sunday and Holiday Teas

Soda bread
Bun loaf
Simple sultana scones
Simple teacakes
Sweet cinnamon butter
Flapjacks
Victorian puffett
Hermits
Coconut pyramids
Henry VIII's shoe buckles
Old-fashioned raspberry buns
A really successful butter sponge
Gingerbread
Old-fashioned parkin
Date fingers

SODA BREAD

4 oz (100 g) flour
1 level eggsp (1 × 2.5 ml spoon)
   cream of tartar
5 fluid oz (150 ml) soured milk
1 level eggsp (1 × 2.5 ml spoon)
   soda bicarbonate
Pinch of salt

Sift flour with soda bicarbonate and cream of tartar into a roomy bowl. Make a well at centre and drop in the soured milk. Work up to a sturdy dough with a table knife. Turn dough onto a floured working surface dusted with extra sifted flour.

Roll dough out in panels measuring 4 inch (10 cm) × 10 inch (25 cm) × 1¼ inch (3 cm) in depth. Brush with a little extra milk and bake at Gas Mark 6–7 (approx 400–425°F, 200–220°C) for 30–35 minutes.

Alternatively for scones, roll out to ½ inch (1.25 cm) thickness and divide into 2½ inch (6.25 cm)–3 inch (7.50 cm) squares with a very sharp knife. Heat iron frying pan or griddle over a low heat, then rub with a piece of raw, unsalted pork fat on the rind. Lay on the scones. Raise heat very slightly and cook for around 7 minutes. Turn over and repeat for a further 8 minutes. Cool on a rack. Split and spread with butter or Gold before serving in a covered dish.

BUN LOAF

We used to make this in the shortage times of the Second World War. We ate it frequently in each other's houses but never tired of it. Leave for 24 hours after making and keep wrapped in a tea towel in a tin.

8 heaped tbsps (8 × 15 ml
   spoons) flour
2 tbsps (2 × 15 ml spoons)
   golden syrup
1 tbsp (1 × 15 ml spoon) black
   treacle

Sift flour into a roomy bowl. Make a centre well and drop in all remaining dry ingredients. Work up to a light dough with gradual additions of milk or cold tea. Turn into a 9 inch (22.50 cm)

1 heaped tbsp (1 × 15 ml spoon) marmalade
2 heaped tbsps (2 × 15 ml spoons) sultanas
1 heaped tbsp (1 × 15 ml spoon) mixed diced peel
Milk or strong, strained tea to bind

× 4 inch (10 cm) × 2½ inch (6.25 cm) deep rectangular bun tin, which has been well rubbed with oil. Bake at Gas Mark 4 (approx 350°F, 180°C) for exactly 1¼ hours. Serve in thin buttered slices.

SIMPLE SULTANA SCONES

Serve hot or cold on day of baking. Thereafter split, toast, spread with butter or Gold and serve while piping hot.

8 oz (225 g) sifted flour
1 rounded tbsp (1 × 15 ml spoon) baking powder
2 oz (50 g) lard
2 oz (50 g) butter or Gold
2 rounded tbsps (2 × 15 ml spoons) soft brown or white sugar
Milk to bind
3 oz (75 g) sultanas

Sift flour with baking powder into a roomy bowl. Rub in given fats until extremely fine-grained. Mix in the sultanas and sugar, then work up with milk to a light dough. This should be of the consistency of good pastry paste. Turn onto a lightly floured surface. Press out gently with a rolling pin to a ¾ inch (1.75 cm) thickness. Stamp into 2½ inch (6.25 cm) rounds with a plain cutter or a 2½ inch (6.25 cm) diameter emptied tin. Set on a lightly floured baking sheet.

Gather up the trimmings, work gently together, press out as before and thus use up every scrap. Add to the scones on the baking sheet. Brush the tops with milk and bake one shelf above centre at Gas Mark 5 (approx 375°F, 190°C) until well-risen and lightly browned on top (16–20 minutes).

SIMPLE TEACAKES

8 oz (225 g) sifted flour
1 smallest egg
1 heaped tbsp (1 × 15 ml spoon)
  baking powder
A pinch of salt
1 flat teasp (1 × 15 ml spoon)
  caster sugar
A little milk

Sift flour with baking powder, sugar and salt into a roomy bowl. Beat egg with 2 fluid oz (60 ml) milk. Turn into a central well in the flour mixture and work up, adding more milk sparingly until a soft dough is achieved. Press into a 6 inch (15 cm) diameter lard-greased and then flour-dusted cake tin. Press out, doming very slightly at centre. Score a ¼ inch (5 mm) deep X across the top. Bake at Gas Mark 5 (approx 375°F, 190°C) one shelf above centre for approx 45 minutes or until springy to a light touch at centre. Split into quarters after cooling on a rack, or serve whole and hot with butter or Sweet Cinnamon Butter.

SWEET CINNAMON BUTTER

4 oz (100 g) soft butter or Gold
2 rounded tbsps (2 × 15 ml
  spoons) sifted icing sugar
1 rounded dessertsp (1 × 10 ml
  spoon) powdered cinnamon

Cream chosen fat, then work in remaining ingredients. Press into a small, lidded china pot and take to table.

FLAPJACKS

These can be made without sugar and sultanas if intended for use with savoury items. Flapjacks keep best in an earthenware crock. When taken from the griddle to a cooling rack, they should be sloped, one slightly over the other rather than laid flat.

12 oz (350 g) sifted flour
13 fluid oz (390 ml) milk
2 No 3 eggs
1 rounded dessertsp (1 × 10 ml
  spoon) caster or granulated
  sugar
1 level teasp (1 × 5 ml spoon)

Sift flour into a roomy bowl. Beat eggs into milk. Stir in sugar and stir into flour, working with a wooden spoon until a smooth thick batter is achieved. Sprinkle the cream of tartar over the top and cut in with the side of the

cream of tartar
Saindoux (With an Oven, Part 1
    p. 118) or a small piece of raw,
    unsalted pork fat on the rind

spoon with a turn/fold movement. Let mixture settle, then leave for 3 or 4 minutes before using until bubbles break out over the surface.

Set either a griddle or a thick iron frying pan over a low heat and leave for a few moments. The pork fat or Saindoux should make a slight swearing sound when applied. Polish the pan with the pork fat piece or brush the Saindoux over. Drop large dessertspoonfuls of the mixture on the griddle or pan, spacing them widely. Wait until they rise and again show breaking bubbles on top. Lift up on a spatula and smack them back on reverse side. This helps them to rise still more. When golden brown on both sides cool and store as explained.

Note
2 oz (50 g) sultanas can be folded in when beating in the egg/milk mixture.

VICTORIAN PUFFETT

Ideal for Sunday tea on a cold winter afternoon.

1 level teacupful granulated
    sugar
½ teacupful butter or Gold
1 teacupful flour
2 No 2 eggs
2 rounded teasps (2 × 5 ml
    spoons) baking powder

Cream butter until light and creamy. Beat in sugar and whip to creamy consistency. Sift flour with baking powder. Whip eggs and add alternately with flour to butter mixture, whipping continuously. Our forebears did all this by hand; we merely use a Moulinex food processor. Turn mixture into a round shallow tin which has been both buttered and floured. Bake at Gas Mark 5 (approx 375°F, 190°C) for 30 minutes or until well risen and springy to a light touch.
Serve hot.

HERMITS

In Victorian times warm-hearted cooks in prosperous establishments would make these for little blue-nosed errand boys who came to the back door with the daily deliveries. The rule was, 'One for the pocket to warm your hands while you eat the other.'

6 oz (175 g) seeded raisins
6 oz (175 g) granulated sugar
2 oz (50 g) butter or Gold
1 scant flat teasp (1 × 5 ml
    spoon) soda bicarbonate
A pinch or two of grated nutmeg
1 lb (450 g) flour
A pinch of cinnamon
Milk
2 No 3 eggs

Rub chosen fat into flour and spices until very fine grained. Sift in raisins and sugar through very clean fingers. Blend bicarbonate into 3 tablespoons (3 × 15 ml spoons) milk and add the well-beaten eggs. Bind with this mixture, working it into the other ingredients with an ordinary table knife and adding more milk if found necessary to achieve a firm rolling dough. Roll out on a floured surface to a mean ½ inch (1.25 cm) thickness. Stamp into 3 inch (7.5 cm) rounds. Lay well-spaced on a floured baking sheet and bake at Gas Mark 6 (approx 400°F, 200°C) on centre shelf until just set like any scones.

Split and spread very liberally with butter or Gold the moment you take them from the oven and send to table in a toast box.

COCONUT PYRAMIDS

8 oz (225 g) desiccated coconut
2 No 3 egg whites
4 oz (100 g) caster sugar

Beat up the egg whites to a soft foam. Work in the sugar and coconut. Shape into little cones or pyramids. Set on a flat baking sheet lightly brushed with oil and bake on centre shelf of oven at Gas Mark 2 (approx 300°F, 150°C) for 35–40 minutes or until a light golden brown.

322

HENRY VIII'S SHOE BUCKLES

These are large, sugary buns which can be made with Jus-rol frozen puff paste. They are very easy to make.

8 oz (225 g) Jus-rol frozen puff
   paste
Apricot jam
Water
4 oz (100 g) sifted icing sugar

Roll out the thawed paste fairly thinly on a floured working surface and cut into 4 inch (10 cm) squares. Then make the corner cuts as shown in the diagram by the four dotted lines and having done so, put a heated teaspoon of apricot or other jam in the centre. Wet the paste edges on all four sides, then lift up and overlap every alternate corner over jam. Press all these four corners down lightly and set on a flat baking sheet which has been held under the cold tap and the surplus drops shaken off. Bake at Gas Mark 6 (approx 400°F, 200°C) until puffed and golden brown.

While they are still piping hot, mix the icing sugar with a very few drops of water until it just flops from the lifted spoon. Doodle this over the tops of the shoe buckles with a small fork. It will set in the time the buckles take to become cold.

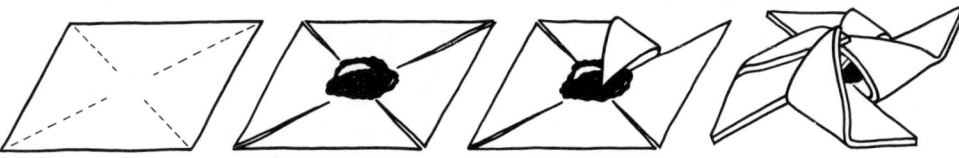

OLD-FASHIONED RASPBERRY BUNS

8 oz (225 g) sweet short paste
Raspberry jam
A little sifted icing sugar
A little top-of-the-milk

Roll out paste to a ⅜ inch (1 cm) thickness. Divide into 4 inch (10 cm) squares. Put a generous teaspoonful of firm raspberry jam on each at centre. Wet edges all round with a little brush dipped in cold water. Bring paste corners up and over jam to overlap each other over centre. Turn upside down on a floured baking sheet leaving a space between each. Brush over with top-of-the-milk, then dust with sifted icing sugar. Bake at Gas Mark 4 (approx 350°F, 180°C) for 25 minutes on middle shelf. Cool on a rack.

Store in a Tupperware 'burper' box for air-tight keeping.

A REALLY SUCCESSFUL BUTTER SPONGE

2 No 3 eggs
2 oz (50 g) preferably unsalted, butter or Gold
2 oz (50 g) caster sugar
6 oz (175 g) sifted flour
A little milk or strained fresh or Del Monte orange juice

Note
When wanting a very close textured mixture use only 4 oz (100 g) flour and sift with 2 oz (50 g) cornflour

Cut a circle of greaseproof to fit the base of an 8 inch (20 cm) diameter cake tin. Butter and flour the paper and then insert.

Whip softened butter until loose and creamy. Add the sugar and repeat the thorough whipping. Add a little of given flour or our flour mix. Then break in one egg with a little more flour, adding a very small splash of milk to keep all of feathery texture. Repeat, add any remaining flour and beat with a final mean splash of milk. The finished texture should spread like whipped cream over the prepared tin. Bake at Gas Mark 4 (approx 350°F, 180°C) for 15–20 minutes or until sponge is just springy to a light central pressure. Never bake beyond this point or the sponge will be dry. Turn onto a cooling rack.

When cold either serve plain with only a top dusting of sifted icing sugar or split centrally and spread with jam and whipped cream, then reassemble and again top-dust with sifted icing sugar. Alternatively use lemon or orange curd and cream as the filling.

GINGERBREAD

This keeps for a long time if left in the tin in which it is baked with just a close covering of Alcan Foil.

5 oz (135 g) lard

5 fat tbsps (5 × 15 ml spoons) Tate & Lyle's black treacle

7 oz (200 g) sifted flour

2 rounded teasps (2 × 5 ml spoons) powdered ginger

An optional 2 oz (50 g) sultanas or 2 oz (50 g) finely-diced, crystallised ginger

1 No 3 egg

2½ oz (60 g) soft brown sugar

2 tbsps (2 × 15 ml spoons) milk

1 rounded saltsp of soda bicarbonate

Line the base of an ordinary meat baking tin with a fitting piece of oiled greaseproof. Dust with flour, brush oil around the tin's sides, dust these with flour too.

Put lard and treacle in a pan over a low heat until completely melted. Sift flour with powdered ginger into a mixing bowl. Make a centre well and pour in the melted mixture. Stir with a wooden spoon until thoroughly blended. Beat the egg and sugar together and beat in next. Stir soda bicarbonate into milk and work in until all is smoothly blended. Turn mixture into prepared tin, level off and bake on middle shelf at Gas Mark 4 (approx 350°F, 180°C) for 27–30 minutes.

OLD-FASHIONED PARKIN

4 oz (100 g) Tate & Lyle's golden syrup
12 oz (350 g) coarse porage oats
4 oz (100 g) butter or Gold
A little oil

Melt chosen fat and syrup together in a small pan. Then gradually work in the oats until a thick dough results. Brush a shallow tin with oil. Press in the mixture and, if possible, smooth off the top surface with a cut lemon. Bake on middle shelf at Gas Mark 4 (approx 350°F, 180°C) for 30–35 minutes.

Remove from oven and mark off with a table knife into small squares, rectangles or fingers without cutting right through. When quite cold break up into the marked sections and store in a tin. This is a splendid 'keeper'.

DATE FINGERS

4 oz (100 g) chopped dates
The strained juice of 1 small lemon
1 oz (25 g) any chopped nuts
1 lb (450 g) sweet short paste
4 oz (100 g) sifted icing sugar
A very little raw, unbeaten egg white

Mix prepared dates and nuts and bind to a rough paste with lemon juice. Roll out pastry paste to ¼ inch (5 mm) thickness. Cut into two matching strips, about 4 inch (10 cm) wide. Spread one thickly with date mixture. Clap second strip over and flatten a little with rolling pin. Lift onto lightly floured baking sheet, using two metal slices. Cut into 1½ inch (3.75 cm) wide fingers. Mix icing sugar with just sufficient unbeaten raw egg white to make a spreading paste. Dip a small knife into boiling water and use to spread paste over date fingers. Bake on middle shelf Gas Mark 5 (approx 375°F, 190°C) for approx 13–15 minutes or until fingers are beige on top.

326

Beginning a Very Modest Wine Cellar

by
Johnnie Cradock

Spice mixture for mulled wines
Wine posset
Cider cup
Churchwarden
Johnnie's simplest mulled wine
Martini No 1
Martini No 2
American dry martini
Bronx
Adonis
Clover club
Negroni

The great problem nowadays is that flats and most modern houses have no cellarage, so you must compromise to obtain the best possible conditions in these circumstances. Choose the coolest and darkest room, cupboard or corner to store your wines and keep a minimum amount to draw on, replenishing from time to time. The classic ruling is to have a cool, darkish, dry cellar where an even temperature of between 50°F(10°C) and 55°F(13°C) can be maintained. You *must* avoid violent changes in temperature which will spoil your wines, and you need a certain amount of draught too.

Many houses have an empty space under the stairs and this can be utilized to very good purpose. One bachelor I know stored 150 bottles in such a space. You can either buy suitable racks from any good wine merchant or, if you are a home carpenter, you can easily make your own.

Use any 1 inch (2.5 cm) × 1 inch (2.5 cm) timber and cut it to fit the relevant space, allowing a 4 inch (10 cm) × 4 inch (10 cm) space for each bottle with a 9 inch (22.5 cm) length from back to front. Thus all table wines will be stored in the *horizontal* position ensuring the corks remain moist and airtight. The reverse is the case for all spirits. These must be kept *upright* or the high alcohol content will gradually destroy the corks.

It is essential to have ventilation, so fit an air-vent into the upper part of the door and bore extra holes in an inconspicuous position in one of the bottom stair treads.

Of course this type of make-do storage is not intended to store wines for very long periods. You should reckon to drink any which are so stored within six to nine months of purchase.

However modestly you start, you will want to know to some extent what wines you would *like* to have, as opposed to what you can afford at the onset. The following list will in the broadest possible terms provide you with something acceptable to all average palates and for all average occasions.

Aperitifs: dry Fino sherry, a medium Amontillado sherry, Sercial or Verdelho Madeira, dry white port, both dry and sweet vermouths.
Table wines: dry white Burgundy, dry white Bordeaux, sweet Sauternes or Barsac, dry light Moselle, dry white Rhône wine, dry white Italian wine, Champagne or sparkling white wine, red Burgundy, red Bordeaux (claret), red Italian wine, tawny or late bottled vintage port, sweet Bual or Malmsey Madeira.
With coffee: Cognac or Armagnac; Marc de Bourgogne, de Champagne or de Provence; or liqueurs or *eaux-de-vie*.

WHICH WINE WITH WHICH DISH

It is generally accepted that a dry white wine goes best with fish dishes and white meats and red wines with red meat and game; but a light claret is equally successful with white meat and, of course, a sweet white wine with puddings. The wines that will go with anything throughout a meal are Champagne and *vin rosé*.

If whatever I say about wines and their manifold usages and abuses is ever illogical, degenerating into merely 'because I say so', just ignore it. There is far too much nonsense written about wines and I flatly refuse to subscribe to any of it. If you have a palate, you will soon discover for yourselves that certain kinds of wine do go better with different dishes than others, but in the first instance I say insist that *the wine you like is a good wine for you.*

It is better to drink the wrong wine with a dish than to deny yourself the pleasure of drinking wine at all. When I was a very young man, I was sent to live in Paris and started my wine drinking with a half bottle of Barsac because it was nice and sweet and akin to ginger beer which had previously been my favourite tipple. But living with a wine-loving Frenchman, I soon developed a palate which enabled me to differentiate.

If you do acquire a real interest in this most fascinating study and perhaps later on have the means to indulge yourself further, please turn to Volume Three where I elaborate considerably on wines and also deal with the subject of glasses. Here I merely place on record that *the greatest wines in the world can be served confidently to the greatest connoisseurs, from one 6⅔ fluid oz (200 ml) plain, uncut and uncoloured, tulip-shaped wine glass.* Unless you are a consistent breaker, a dozen of these should last you a considerable time.

You may very well ask, 'Why that specific glass?' The answer is that a 'tulip' wine glass is by its shape one whose bowl is wider in the centre than at the base or rim. You must remember that there are three distinct pleasures in drinking a good wine: first comes the 'nose' or fragrant aroma, then the colour and lastly the impact on your taste buds.

The 'nose' or 'bouquet' is helped considerably by a 'tulip' shaped glass because it holds that 'nose' for long enough for you to sniff and appreciate it. The glass should be plain because if it is cut or coloured, the colour of the wine – which should be absolutely clear – is denied you because the cut and/or colour distort it completely. When it comes to the taste, you hold the stem of the glass, cupping your hand round a red wine to use the warmth of your hand to develop both nose and taste; but in the case of a white wine, which is always served slightly chilled, you steadfastly *avoid* letting your hand come into contact with the bowl of the glass by holding the stem only. In fact clasping a warm hand round the bowl of a wine glass containing a white wine is certain evidence of knowing *nothing*.

Lastly you should never fill a wine glass more than two-thirds full at the most. The reason being that if you want to sniff the 'bouquet', you will enhance it by twirling the wine round gently in the glass. If this is filled, you will make a nasty mess on the table and be most unpopular.

ADDITIONAL WINE STORAGE

I would suggest very strongly that you seek the advice of a reputable wine merchant. He will not only give you good counsel as to the best wines to choose from the types I have indicated, but will regulate his choice for you within whatever price limits you set. Additionally, in almost every instance he will provide storage assistance.

This applies, of course, to those of you wanting to lay down a case or cases for future drinking and who have not the necessary space and conditions in your first home.

SPICE MIXTURE FOR MULLED WINES

1 oz (25 g) powdered cinnamon
1 oz (25 g) powdered or grated
 nutmeg
1 oz (25 g) powdered cloves
½ oz (10 g) ground ginger
1 inch (2.5 cm) cut from a dry
 vanilla pod and ground to
 powder

Sift all together through a fine sieve. Store in an air-tight container on a dry goods shelf.

WINE POSSET

1 pint (600 ml) fresh milk
5 fluid oz (150 ml) dry white
 wine
1 generous pinch each of
 powdered cinnamon, bay and
 lavender
The finely grated rind of half a
 medium lemon
Soft brown sugar to taste

Put milk and wine in a thick pan and heat until milk curdles. Strain off the whey into a second pan and melt sugar in it over a low heat, stir in spices and set aside. Rub curds through a fine sieve or tamis. Whip vigorously into whey and serve in small cups immediately.

CIDER CUP

1 slice of toast
Half a nutmeg
1 eggsp (1 × 2.5 ml spoon)
    ground ginger
The rind of half a medium lemon
    peeled very thinly
8 pieces loaf sugar
5 fluid oz (150 ml) dry sherry
3 pints (1.80 litres) cider
1 miniature bottle brandy
10 ice cubes
1 small bottle Schweppes soda
    water
Whenever possible, 2 sprigs of
    borage in flower

Mix all together, except ice cubes, soda water and borage. Refrigerate until 30 minutes before service. Add soda water and ice. Immerse borage sprigs and pour into ordinary wine glasses from a jug.

CHURCHWARDEN

1 large lemon
1 bottle Roussillon
1 pint (600 ml) strained weak
    Indian tea
4 oz (100 g) loaf sugar

Roast the lemon in the oven at Gas Mark 4 (approx 350°F, 180°C) for 30 minutes. Place in a bowl, pour heated wine over it, stir in the tea and sugar and serve piping hot in napkin-wrapped glasses, with a teaspoon slipped into each before pouring.

JOHNNIE'S SIMPLEST MULLED WINE

Nose-tingling and tum-warming on a cold night.

1 bottle red 'plonk' wine
14 lumps sugar
1 thin-skinned orange stuck with
    6 cloves
1 flat eggsp (1 × 2.5 ml spoon)
    each of powdered cinnamon
    and of powdered ginger
1 torn bay leaf
Strained juice of half a lemon
    and the other half very thinly
    sliced

Place all ingredients in a thick pan over a low heat and raise slowly to just below boiling point. On no account allow the mixture to boil. Stir well and pour into warmed, napkin-wrapped glasses, remembering to immerse a spoon into each.

331

COCKTAILS

Once again the ubiquitous 'cocktail' has become immensely popular. Out from the attic the shakers re-emerge and it is anyone's guess what iced mixture may be thrust upon them in 'cocktail' glasses at drinks parties or before supping or dining.

For those of limited income cocktails can prove hugely expensive as the majority of them require one or more liqueurs in their blending. Several of them can also sublimate appetite and stun the taste buds very effectively. The sourness of these observations confirms my definition of the cocktail, i.e., a number of excellent ingredients ruined by being mixed together. However, demand creates supply and I dutifully give a few of the least costly cocktails.

THE MIXING OF COCKTAILS

Mostly the ingredients are put into a cocktail shaker with ice, shaken and then strained into glasses. These can be garnished with a cherry on a stick, a slice of lemon or orange, etc. Alternatively the ingredients are just put into a tall glass with ice, stirred until cold and then strained into the glasses.

MARTINI No 1
Equal parts gin and Italian vermouth.

MARTINI No 2
Equal parts of gin and French vermouth.

AMERICAN DRY MARTINI
Gin with a mere dash of French vermouth.

BRONX
Half gin with quarter each of French and Italian vermouth.

ADONIS
Two-thirds dry sherry with one-third Italian vermouth and a dash of orange bitters.

CLOVER CLUB
In the past called 'The Flapper's Joy'.

Two-thirds dry gin with one-third grenadine syrup, the juice of half a lemon or 1 small lime, the separated lightly whipped white of 1 small egg.

NEGRONI
Created by Count Negroni and very popular still in Italy.

One-third gin with one-third Italian vermouth and one-third Campari. Serve with a twist of thinly sliced, unpeeled orange.

Index

Adonis, 332
Ale, mulled, 79
Anchovy butter, 167
Anchovy and egg snacks, 38
Apple, charlotte, baked, 114
Apple turnovers, 290
Apple and sultana mixture, our, 298
Apples, baked, 113; stuffed, 293
Apples in cider, 300
Apricot junket, 300
Apricot whip, 301
Apricots, dried, in China tea, 301
Apricots and prunes, dried, 114
Artichoke pie, Jerusalem, 263
Artichoke salad, Jerusalem, 164

Bacon and pineapple pizza, 253
Bacon and watercress salad, 27
Banana and cream cheese pizza, sweet, 287
Bananas, baked, 113; Caribbean, 287
Bananas, fried, 83
Barley broth, Scots, 140
Batter, crisp, for fish frying, 173
Batter pudding, baked, with golden syrup, 287
Bean soup, haricot, 140
Bean and apple salad, kidney, 162
Beans, to string, 69

Beans with parsley butter, broad, 264
Beef, boiled brisket of, with dumplings, 243
Beef, boned rib of, 226
Beef left-overs, 248
Beef Parmentier, 244
Beef and mushroom pudding, slow-cooking pot, 220
Beer soup, iced, 152
Beetroot salad, 157
Beetroot soup, 34; iced, 150
Biscuit cake, Viennese, 82
Black cap pudding, 291
Blackcurrant cordial, hot, 77
Bread, Mum's yeastless, 117
Bread, pulled, 154
Bread fritters, 73
Breadcrumb pudding, very easy, 295
Breakfast cakes, Mrs Hudson's hot, 309
Bronx, 332
Brown Betty, 294
Bubble and squeak, 265
Buffins, 62
Bun loaf, 318
Bun pudding, 118
Buns, Gran's hot, with sugar glaze, 116
Buns, old-fashioned raspberry, 324

Cabbage, Austrian red, 270
Cabbage, delicious, 68
Cabbage salad, raw, 157
Cabbage ball with cheese sauce, 242
Cabbage soup, Portuguese white, 146
Calves' liver and bacon, imitation, 246
Cauliflower, fried, 262
Cauliflower, steamed, 262
Cauliflower salad, 161
Celery soup, emergency, 137
Celery sticks, stuffed, 166
Cheese, potted, 280; fried, 280; toasted, 280
Cheese croissant bake, 100
Cheese flan, 279
Cheese fritters, 57; 275
Cheese gnocchi, 218
Cheese puffs, 99
Cheese rissoles, 276
Cheese and potato salad, 161
Cheese and tomato pudding, 278
Chervil soup from two packets, 137
Chestnut soup, simple, 143
Chicken, boiled with onion sauce, 223
Chicken, curried, 233
Chicken, fried, 231

Chicken cocotte, 232
Chicken in a mountain, 230
Chicken, slow-cooking pot roasted, 222
Chicken portions, devilled, 233
Chicken portions, fried, 62
Chickens' livers savoury rice bowl, 232
Chips, crisp, 66
Chocolate, simple hot, 78
Chocolate pots, little, 304
Chocolate and banana pudding, hot, 285
Churchwarden, 331
Cider cup, 331
Cinnamon butter, sweet, 320
Cinnamon toast, 32
Citrus fruit winter drink, hot, 309
Claret cup, simple (hot), 80
Clover club, 332
Coconut butter, 198
Coconut pyramids, 322
Coffee, iced, 77
Coffee, making perfect, 76
Cole slaw dressing, quick, 157
Conger steak parcels, 174
Consommé, 'cheat', en gelée, 152
Corn fritters, 69
Corn on the cob, 92
Corn soup, simple, 137
Corned beef hash, 104
Corned beef salad, 29
Cornish cutlets, 60
Country parson, 238
Courgette fritters, 67
Courgette soup, 147
Courgettes, stuffed, 107
Croque de la fermière, 314
Croque, deep-fried, 316
Croque, giant, 312
Croque Madame, 58
Croque Mademoiselle, 315
Croque M'sieu, 58, 312
Croque Papa, 314
Croque William, 312
Crostini, Italian, 112
Croûte Landaise, 93
Croûtons, herb-flavoured, 154
Croûtons, soup, 73
Crumble pie, 295
Cucumber salad, simple, 157
Cucumber soup, iced, No 1, No 2, 148
Curate's eye, 44
Custard, baked, 289
Custard, egg, 286
Custard, German, 286
Custard tartlets, savoury, 200

Dandelion salad, 163
Date fingers, 326
Devil, the, itself, 234
Devil, the, No 2, 314
Devilled ham or gammon spread, 310
Doughnuts, easy baking powder, 308
Dripping crust (economical), 247

Egg bake, 206
Egg cosies, how to make, 307
Egg dish, Tunisian, 55
Egg nog, 56
Egg salad, 160
Egg sausages, 51
Egg soup, 143
Egg and bacon pasty-pie, 203
Egg and cheese fritters, 57
Egg and herring salad, 160
Egg and sardine pâté, 205
Egg and spinach cocottes, 198
Egg and sweet corn flan, 203
Eggplant fritters, 267
Eggs: to boil, 42; to fry, 42; to poach, 42; to scramble, 43
Eggs, Belgian, 50
Eggs, Emmeline's, 197
Eggs, Florentine, 200
Eggs, Highland, 201
Eggs, Kramer, 43
Eggs, poached, with onion sauce, 202
Eggs, Scotch, 50
Eggs, Spanish, 204
Eggs, stuffed, 165
Eggs on rice with corn, 199

Fish, fried, 39
Fish cakes, 190
Fish fingers, 189
Fish pie, poor man's Russian, 185
Fish pudding, steamed, 188
Fish puffs, 186
Fisherman's platter, 39
Flapjacks, 320
Fondue, poor man's, 277
Fonduta, Italian, 216
Frankfurter kebabs, 92
French dressing, 22
Fruit fools, 303
Fruit juice rice pudding, 115
Fruit salad, a proper, 297

Gammon bake, crusty, 254
Gammon, baked, and cheese, 253
Gammon cooked in a slow-cooking pot, 221

Gammon slices with pineapple, 253
Garlic bread, 153
Garlic butter, 24
Gazpacho, Spanish, 151
Gingerbread, 325
Gnocchi, Genoese, 68
Golden syrup flan, 299
Grandfather's special, 207
Grape harvest soup, German, 146
Grapefruit, hot baked, 167
Grapefruit and cream cheese salad, 28
Grill successfully, how to, 88

Haddock, smoked, with spinach purée, 179
Haddock Mornay, 180
Haddock and mushroom pie, 178
Hake steaks, baked, 184
Ham and cheese bake, 104
Hamburgers and beans, 64
Hash, Cuban, 244
Health soup, iced, 149
Henry VIII's shoe buckles, 323
Herby bread, 153
Herby breads, 117
Hermits, 322
Herring bake, Swedish, 181
Herring roes in puff pastry, 182
Herring roes on fried bread, 38
Herring and egg cake, Bornholmer, 180
Honey and lemon, hot, for colds, 78
Honeymoon soup, 146
Hot pot, North country, 220
Hot roll box, how to make a, 307
Hunter's pot, a miniature, 97

Jam roll, baked, 293
Jellabys, 83
Jelly cream, 82

Kebabs and rice, modest, 241
Kedgeree, 177
Kidneys in the manner of French butchers, 102
Kipper crusts, 183
Kipper pâté, 182

Lamb, oven-braised shoulder of, 239
Lamb, ragout of, 236
Lamb, small stuffed leg of, 238
Lamb Florentine, 240
Lamb paysanne, 227
Leek gratin, a, 268

Left-overs, French treatment for, 234
Lemonade, home-made, 78
Lettuce soup, iced, 150
Liver sausage spread, 310
Liver and onion parcel, 245

Mackerel, grilled, with gooseberry sauce, 178
Mackerel parcels, 175
Mackerel and mussel pie, 176
Mrs Marshall's remarkable quick soup, 144
Martini: No 1, 332; No 2, 332; American dry, 332
Mayonnaise, real basic, 22
Mayonnaise, simple cream cheese, 164
Meal-in-itself soup, a, 139
Measuring box, 16
Meat balls, Dutch, 236
Meat loaf, Italian, 248
Meat mould, 252
Meat patties, Danish, 64
Melon boats, 166
Meringue and apple bake, 290
Milk jelly, 302
Milk and potato bake, 260
Monkfish cream, 190
Mushroom salad, raw, 159
Mushroom soup, lightning, 34
Mushroom soup, a pkt of dehydrated, 34
Mushrooms, milk-poached, 91
Mushrooms, stuffed, 107
Mussels, skewered, with saffron rice, 186

Negroni, 332
Noodles and cheese, 73

Oeufs à la Bruxelloise, 208
Oeufs sur le plat, 56
Offal, skewered, with orange rice, 240
Omelette, Belgian soufflé, 49
Omelette, Viennese baked, 115
Omelette fillings, savoury, 47
Omelette fillings, sweet, 47
Omelettes: bread, 46; classic French, 44; filling savoury, 48; flat peasant, 48; herb, 46; onion and croûton, 196; potato, 47; Spanish tomato and croûton, 196
Onion rings, crispy-fried, 266
Onion soup, meal-in-itself, 90
Orange meringue pie, easy, 304
Orange pizza, sweet, 288
Orange and cream cheese starters, 167

Oranges, caramelised, 93
Ox kidney sauté, 246

Pain perdu, French, 86
Parcel cooking of one-portion foods, 100
Parkin, old-fashioned, 326
Parkin, Yorkshire, 116
Pasta pie, 225
Pastry paste, dripping, 186
Pâté maison, a very simple, 170
Pea soup, fresh, 36
Pea and pork soup, 142
Pears, to cook hard little, 292
Pears in chocolate sauce, 296
Pimentoes, Hungarian stuffed, with cheese, 274
Pish-pash, 103
Pitt-y-panna, 61
Pizza, cheese, 280
Pizza, pastry, 282
Pizza, ratatouille and cheese, 281
Pizzas, cheat, 111
Plaice with cheese and tomato, baked, 184
Polenta, maize flour, 214
Polenta, substitute, with semolina and processed cheese, 215
Poor knights, 86
Pork, roasting of, 250
Pork pâté, a simple, 168
Pork and bean casserole, 251
Pork and rabbit casserole, slow-cooking pot, 222
Potato bake with shrimps, 109
Potato crust, 245
Potato eggs, No 1, 109; No 2, 110
Potato Macaire, 110
Potato salad, 28
Potato salad, real, 158
Potato soup, 142
Potato and bacon salad, 28
Potatoes: creamed, 258; jacket-baked, 109, 259; mashed, 66; perfect, 66; roast, 258; sauté, 261; steamed new, 258; steamed old, 258
Potatoes, sauté of, with onions, 108
Potatoes, souffléd baked, 260
Potatoes, stuffed baked, No 1, 259; No 2, 260
Puffet, Victorian, 321

Queenie pie, 189
Quick soup, French, 144

Rabbit pâté, a simple, 169
Racket (la Raclette), 279

Ratatouille, 269
Rice, Adriatic, 112
Rice, orange, 241
Rice pudding, creamy, 286
Rock salmon pie, 98

Sage and onion stuffing, 250
Saindoux, 118
Salad, Italian, 164
Salad, Japanese, 29
Salad, New England, 29
Salad, Russian, 162
Salad suggestions, more, 30
Salad Niçoise, No 1, 160; No 2, 161
Sandwich, American club, 31
Sandwich, giant, 30
Sandwiches: Jewish salt beef, 31; meat or poultry, 92; Mum's sweet fried, 85; orange, nut and cream cheese, open, 32; savoury fried, 63; toasted, 90, 311; toasted sweet, 315
Sangria, 79
Sardine rolls, 99
Sardine spread, 311
Sauces: apple, 250; cheese, simple, 24; chocolate, our hot, 296; herb, 197; jam, 296; onion, 202; to serve with cream ices, 303; tomato, special, 313; tomato fondue, 252; white, simple, 24
Sausage rolls, 105
Sausageburgers, 60
Sausages which never burst, 102
Scones, simple sultana, 319
Semolina pudding, an excellent, 292
Shepherd's pie, real, 237
Shrimp and watercress cream soup, cold, 152
Shrimps, hot, cooked in sea water, 173
Slimmers' soup, our, 139
Soda bread, 318
Soufflé, the egg white, 193
Soufflé, the three-egg, 194
Soufflé mixture, basic economical (savoury), 195
Soufflé mixture, basic economical (sweet), 195
Sour cream dressing, 30
Spaghetti pie, 216
Spaghetti, Sicilian, 212
Spaghetti, vegetable, 212
Spaghetti with chickens' livers, 212
Spaghetti with cooked meat and egg, 72
Spaghetti with Italian sauce, 211

Spaghetti with tomatoes and cheese, 72
Spice mixture for mulled wines, 330
Spinach, how to cook, 268; whole, 268
Spinach purée, 269
Spinach and cheese noodles, 111
Spinach and egg cocotte, 199
Spinach and yoghurt soup, iced, 150
Sponge, a really successful butter, 324
Sprats, how to cook, 97
Spreads, other savoury, 311
Spreads, salad, 311
Stock, slow-cooking pot, 222
Stockpot, 141
Summer puddings, little, 302
Swedish birds' nests, 26

Tangerine sections, spiced, 296
Tea, iced, 76
Tea in a jug, 76
Teacake, simple, 320

Toast box, how to make, 307
Toast Melba, 154
Tomato fondue, 252
Tomato juice cocktails, 80
Tomato salad, 159
Toma soup, iced, 149
Tomatoes, grilled, 264
Tomatoes, stuffed, 106, 264; egg, 199; egg and cheese, 278; onion, 165
Tongue, slow-baked, 224
Torrijas, 84
Torrijas, savoury Spanish, 204
Tortellini with cream, 217
Tripe and onions, slow-cooking pot, 224
Trout *pâté*, 91
Tuna fish spread, 310
Tunisian *brics*, 54

Veal casserole, modest, 254
Vegetable pie, 108, 262
Vegetable salad, raw, 159
Vegetable soup, all-the-year round, 138

Vegetable soup, a mini, 35
Vegetable soup, mixed, 138
Vegetable soup from a tin, 34
Vegetables to eat raw, 26
Vegetarian spread, 310
Vermicelli kedgeree, 217
Victoria pudding, 285

Waffle fillings or spreads, 197
Waffles, 52; sweet, 85
Watercress soup, 145
Watercress and mushroom salad, 163
Watercress and spring onion soup, 145
Welsh rarebit, our, 274
Whitebait, 174
Whiting, fried fillets of, 173
Whiting, stuffed baked, 183
Whiting and tomato pie, 98
Wine, Johnnie's simplest mulled, 331
Wine cup, simple (cold), 80
Wine posset, 330
Winter compôte, special, 298